Financial Fitness For Newlyweds

Elizabeth S. Lewin, CFP

Financial Fitness For Newlyweds

Facts On File Publications
New York, New York • Bicester, England

FINANCIAL FITNESS FOR NEWLYWEDS
ELIZABETH S. LEWIN

Copyright ©1984 by Elizabeth Lewin

All rights reserved. No part of this book may
be reproduced or utilized in any form or by any
means, electronic or mechanical, including
photocopying, recording or by any information
storage and retrieval systems, without permission
in writing from the Publisher.

Library of Congress Cataloging in Publication Data
Lewin, Elizabeth.
   Financial fitness for newlyweds.
   Includes index.
   1. Finance, Personal.   2. Married people—Finance,
   Personal.   I. Title.
HG179.L478   1984   332.024'0655   83-14139
ISBN 0-87196-265-9

Printed in United States of America
10 9 8 7 6 5 4 3 2 1

"Thinking about money is an activity which can send one into a state that borders on anything from slight uneasiness to terror."

from *Bread Upon the Waters*
IRWIN SHAW
DELACORTE PRESS

ACKNOWLEDGMENTS

My special appreciation to Bernard Ryan, Jr., whose help made all this possible, and to Sue L. Hudson, whose insights into the psychological aspects of the subject were invaluable.

I also wish to thank Myron I. Dworken, C.P.A., Laventhol & Horwath; Elena Keaveney, C.F.P., Smith, Barney, Harris Upham & Co.; Francine Krentzman, William Raveis Real Estate; Rosemary Manchester, Guidelines, Union Trust Co.; Mildred Schiller, M.S.W.; and Anita Greenhut.

To all newlyweds but especially to those who shared
their goals, dreams, and finances with me:

my daughter and son-in-law, Valerie and James;
Janis and Matt; Cathy and Pat; and Pam and Chris.

CONTENTS

1	WHY I WROTE THIS BOOK	1
2	WHY MANAGE MONEY?	6
	Worksheet I: Individual Goals	9
	Worksheet II: Individual Goals	10
	Worksheet III: Saving for a Specific Goal	12
3	WHO'S GOING TO MANAGE THE MONEY?	14
4	HOW TO MANAGE THE MONEY: YOUR BUDGET	16
	Worksheet IV: Sources of Income	17
	Worksheet V: Expense Sheets	22
5	YOU AND THE LAW: WHO OWNS WHAT?	39
6	THE BAROMETER OF FINANCIAL FITNESS: YOUR NET WORTH	43
	Worksheet VI: Net Worth Statement	45
7	BANKS, BANKERS, AND BANKING	52
	Exhibit 1: Bank Statement	55
	Exhibit 2: Reconciling Your Checking Account	56
	Exhibit 3: Compound Interest Chart	58
	Exhibit 4: Checkbook Register	59
	Exhibit 5: Check Encoding Mistake	60
8	DEBT: HOW TO GET INTO IT, AND OUT AGAIN—WITHOUT GETTING HURT	61
	Exhibit 6: Credit Application	65
	Exhibit 7: Credit Rejection	67
	Exhibit 8: Updated Credit Profile	69

	Worksheet VII: Lists of Debts	73
	Worksheet VIII: Personal Debt Ratio	74
9	YOUR JOB AND YOUR FRINGE BENEFITS	80
10	INSURANCE: HOW MUCH DO YOU NEED? WHAT KIND SHOULD YOU GET?	83
	Worksheet IX: How Much Life Insurance?	86
	Worksheet X: How Much Disability Insurance?	97
	Exhibit 9: Guide to Homeowners Policies	99
11	A PRIMER ON TAXES	104
	Exhibit 10: 1983 Federal Income Tax Brackets	106
	Exhibit 11: Form 1040	108
	Exhibit 12: Schedule C	110
	Exhibit 13: Deductions for Married Couple	111
12	A ROOF OVER YOUR HEAD	113
	Worksheet XI: Your Home as an Investment	117
	Exhibit 14: Binder of Sale (Contract)	119
	Exhibit 15: Residential Loan Application	122
	Exhibit 16: Statement of Sale	126
13	INVESTING	133
14	WHAT PRICE CHILDREN?	142
15	THE LIVE-TOGETHERS	146
	Worksheet XII: Live-Together Budgeting	148
16	RECORD KEEPING, ETC.	154
	Worksheet XIII: Personal Information	162
	Worksheet XIV: Personal Contacts	163
	Worksheet XV: Record Keeping	164
	Worksheet XVI: Location of Other Important Papers	166
17	YOUR OWN BALANCE SHEET	172
	INDEX	175

Financial Fitness For Newlyweds

WHY I WROTE THIS BOOK

This is a book for new couples. It is for any two people who have recently begun to operate one household with probably—at least for the time being—two incomes. Its purpose is to help you gain and maintain Personal Financial Fitness together.

I wrote this book because I believe that you, who have come of age in the 1980's, have special needs and problems, and countless unanswered questions about your personal finances. You may be wondering how to divide financial responsibilities, worrying about how to set up a budget, trying to figure out how to establish a credit rating, asking how much insurance you need, debating when to have children and how many, wishing you could own a home of your own. The aim of this book is to help you find practical, workable answers to such questions.

I also wrote this book because I am convinced that your generation does not want to be deprived of the knowledge of how to manage money as my generation was deprived—and as so many generations before us were deprived.

Why doesn't anybody tell children about money? Why don't parents teach money management? Why don't schools? Why do we deprive our children of the knowledge of money, yet ask them to assume adult responsibility for it?

Most parents send their offspring out into the world totally unprepared to handle their personal finances. Somehow they—the parents—think they shouldn't burden their children with· "financial problems." They think children will feel secure if they don't have to "worry" about money. In most households, good practical talk about money is heard about as often as good practical talk about sex—almost never. Thus, most young people have to learn about money management by trial and error—like learning about sex. On the other hand, while today sex has become an open topic of conversation between increasing numbers of parents and children, money still is not openly discussed.

Why don't parents and children talk about money?

People shun frank and open discussions about money for many reasons. Some parents don't talk about it just because their parents didn't. Some worry that their children will find out they don't make as much as their neighbors or the parents of peers in school. (Only rarely, however, do parents or children who are keeping up with the Joneses really have an accurate idea of the Joneses' annual income; when you're keeping up with the Joneses, it could be the Joneses who are keeping up with *you*.) Some parents fight about money so frequently it frightens their children and they become convinced it is a subject to shy away from.

Why couples fight over money

It's generally accepted that money is the most common cause of disagreements (read, "fights") between couples. But often it isn't money itself that's the problem. Frequently a fight over money is a manifestation of some other problem. In the traditional family situation, the husband's value was based on what he earned. The wife, who was not a breadwinner but a homemaker (read, "housewife" in the more familiar stereotype), sought some recognition of her own. She felt entitled to something, wanted to participate somehow or share in the process of managing the household. So—almost as you've seen it in TV sit-coms—she might spend at the wrong moment in the budget schedule, or more than the budget allowed, as a way of showing her entitlement. And a battle royal would ensue. Very likely she would at some point use the words, "I'm entitled to buy. . . ."

You two are setting up a new financial partnership. Chances are you have received no real training in managing money from your parents (almost certainly you've had none from your schools), and you may find that any strong discussion of money follows lines of emotion rather than reason. It's really very hard to have a financial discussion that doesn't become emotional. Remember, a reasonable discussion never becomes a fight. An emotional discussion usually does become a fight, if not a pitched battle. One of my main purposes in writing this book is to help you avoid not only the battles but the lesser fights, too.

What is money?

Good question. Compound answer: Money is a symbol that has many emotional and psychological meanings. It is . . .

- *Success.* Money is the standard measure.
- *Security.* If only you can get enough money, you'll have no problems. Nice thought. Things aren't all that simple, however.
- *Power.* Money can enable you to buy, manipulate, control—not only things but people. Sometimes.
- *Love.* Money provides a way to show affection. It's a measure of caring. It's birthday and Christmas checks from Gramps and Grannie.
- *Anger.* Sometimes even hate. Money withheld is punishment, an inducement toward changed behavior.
- *Freedom.* Money gives independence from the control of another.

A medium of exchange

Forget all the symbolic meanings of money. Look at it for what it really is: *a medium of exchange for the goods and services we need and desire.* Think of it as a useful tool. Like a power mower, maybe. You can learn how to run it to trim and control your ever-growing environment, when to let it sit idle, how to keep it from getting out of control. But remember: If you don't learn how to handle it, it can cut off your toes.

The key word is *awareness.* You need to be aware of why you handle money the way you do, and of what changes in behavior you may need to make to put you in control of your money—so that you don't find it in control of you.

By managing your money soundly, you will cut down on anxiety and frustration. You will find yourself living within your income, taking care of your own financial needs, reaching your financial goals.

This book shows you practical ways of getting the most value out of money as a medium of exchange, to help give you the kind of life you want. I'll try not to preach. I've concentrated on demonstrating how the money you make can be managed to provide the home and lifestyle, the travel and other leisure-time activities, the education of your children, the protection against possible setbacks—all the things you are likely to desire and need throughout your life.

INTRODUCING THREE VERY SPECIAL YOUNG COUPLES...

Say hello to three couples in their twenties: the Nicholses, the McQuarters, and the Bucks. Each is a typical young couple starting out their lives together. They will turn up here and there throughout these pages to illustrate how to apply some of the principles and advice in this book to your own situation.

Valerie and James Nichols

Married just over a year, Valerie and James are struggling young musicians. They live in Texas, a state they moved to after figuring out that, in their profession, they could probably make a better living there than anywhere else. But it is tough. One month they feel rich, the next poor. "We hadn't realized our income would be going up and down like a yo-yo," says Valerie. "We've really had to work out a tight budget and stick to it."

James admits he was spoiled when he was growing up. Looking back, as the youngest of four (the other three are sisters), he realizes that his parents were always sacrificing to give to him. From the time he was 10 years old he never had to account to his parents for the way he spent his allowance, but he did get into the habit of saving money. In his early teens he worked in his father's hardware store as a helper, until his father died suddenly when James was 16. His dad had just bought him a car and had promised to help pay for its upkeep and gas. James mowed lawns and worked as a busboy in restaurants while finishing high school, then went to a local junior college for two years.

Throughout his youth, James's parents recognized his talent for music, bought him instruments, and paid for music lessons. After his father died, his mother's Social Security payments helped keep the music going. Finally, after junior college, he sold his car to pay part of his tuition at a music school.

His mother's Social Security payments stopped when he, her youngest child, turned 22.

Valerie grew up in rather affluent suburbs in the East. Her allowance started when she was very young. She was made responsible for buying her own clothes—but could always get extra money from her parents if she ran short. "I grew up in an area where everybody had plenty of money," she remembers. "Then I went away to camp and found out that not everybody had as much as I had." This small dose of financial reality became big medicine when her parents were divorced. Her family lifestyle changed and she realized "the free ride was over."

In college and music school, Valerie's parents paid for her tuition and room and board. She added to her allowance by working in a beach resort restaurant each summer and picking up odd jobs as a musician whenever she could.

When Valerie and James were married, she owned a beat-up car that was not long for this world. It died soon after they moved to Texas, and they used wedding gift money (luckily they had saved it) for the down payment on a new car. The bank refused to lend them the balance without a cosigner because their income was not "steady." They also ate into their gift money during their first few months in order simply to survive.

Valerie receives a small yearly income from an inheritance, which gives them a little sense of security. In fact, because they have this income—and because they live in an area where housing is affordable for young people and developments offer "starter" homes with small down payment requirements and attractive financing plans—they are seriously considering buying a house. "That's an investment," says James, "and it will be *ours*." Adds Valerie, "It will give us a garden, so we can grow things."

Cathy and Patrick McQuarter

Cathy and Patrick have been married for five years. She is 27; he is 25. Both grew up in the Midwest, she in Des Moines, he in St. Louis.

Cathy's father is a lawyer. "He spoiled me rotten," she says with a smile. "When I went to college, he paid for everything. He even gave me his credit card." Yet she knows that her parents did not live beyond their means; finances at home seemed to be under control. In fact, she says the best education she got in terms of money management was the example her mother and father set at home.

That education was reinforced when she came home from college and started teaching school. Living at home, she found she was nevertheless responsible for her own expenses. Her father asked her to pay rent. "What a lesson!" she exclaims. "He sat me down and made me work out a budget. It was all Greek to me at first, but did I learn!" As she figured out how to juggle payments and watch prices, she realized that her parents had carefully saved for everything they had bought over the years.

After a year of living at home and teaching in Des Moines, Cathy moved to St. Louis at the urging of her college roommate, who was teaching there, and she helped Cathy get a job. In St. Louis Cathy met Patrick.

Pat's father is a business executive who had been relocated by his company almost every other year while Pat was a boy. Finally, when Pat was 12, they settled permanently in St. Louis. At 12, he fibbed about his age and got a job as a busboy in a downtown delicatessen. Next he became a dishwasher in a popular Italian restaurant. At 17, having tinkered with electronics and cameras for several years, he got a job operating a camera at a local TV station.

Patrick worked at the TV station while he went to a St. Louis community college—but he loved the work more than college and never finished his formal education. Living at home, he had no rent to pay. His income covered all his expenses. When the TV station sent him to Chicago to intern for nine months, he worked odd jobs while he was there and lived with a roommate, with whom he split expenses. "I was raised with a strong work ethic," he says. "I believe that if I work hard, there will be a big payoff."

Cathy and Pat had met before he went to Chicago. After he had been there for six months, they were married and she went to live with him in Chicago. The last three months there they lived in a rented room with an ice chest and a camp stove—and she worked in a local department store. During this time they tried to borrow at a bank so they could buy a small refrigerator, but were refused a loan because they had no credit rating. The store then gave them credit, and they now owned a refrigerator—just in time to move it to St. Louis.

"After living that way in Chicago," says Patrick, "we decided that saving for a house was our primary goal." When they moved back to St. Louis, Cathy started teaching, and Patrick returned to the TV station. He became the producer of a major local program. They found a reasonably priced apartment and moved in with furniture Cathy's grandmother had left them.

Then came the big debate. Cathy, working with children every day in the classroom, was beginning to want children of her own. Patrick, remembering those dismal days with the ice chest and camp stove in that rented room in Chicago, was determined they would have a home of their own before they started having a family. Their goals were basically the same—the building of the nest—but they saw different ways to approach them. "Babies can live in apartments," Cathy said more than once. "They manage to do it all the time. I've seen them."

"Not mine," said Patrick. "First we get a home that we know is ours—and theirs."

Looking back now, Cathy recalls: "We compromised and worked it out by being determined to save as much as we could as fast as we could. We put away $200 a month, and more than that when we got raises. We brown bagged it to work, but we did go out to dinner quite a bit—never any place expensive, though, just nearby diners and pizza palaces. And we budgeted for movies and for the theater, because we love it."

At the time they were married, Pat was earning $12,000 a year, Cathy $11,000. Five years later, he is earning $20,000 and she is making $15,000. Now they are buying a house. And saving just as hard—for their family.

Jane and Chris Buck

The Bucks have been married three years. He is an accountant and is now taking his exams to become a CPA. She works for an advertising agency. Each is 26 years old.

Chris's parents were born in Italy. When Chris was born, the youngest of five, his father was 60 and his mother 46. When Chris was 21, his father died. A landscape gardener, he had taken care of all the family finances in a very conservative way—paying for everything with cash, never borrowing, never lending. After he died, Chris introduced his mother to the idea of a checking account and began writing the checks for her—which he still does.

Chris started working when he was 14, doing odd

jobs and helping his father in the landscaping business. One summer during high school he worked for a construction company and earned enough to buy a car just before he entered college. During college (he commuted from home to a state college) he worked nights at a gas station. His mother paid his tuition, but he paid all his other expenses, including his clothes, and contributed to her grocery money.

Chris studied accounting in college and then went to work for an accounting firm at $12,000 a year. He lived at home, continuing to contribute to the grocery budget and paying for all his own expenses—but his mother wouldn't let him pay rent. During the two years before he was married, he piled up some real savings, working and living at home. He has stayed with the same firm, and is now earning $24,000.

Jane's father was a court reporter. Her mother stayed at home to raise the family. Jane recalls the unselfishness of her parents: They gave material things to their three daughters but wanted little for themselves. Each girl had her own stereo and was dressed well and went to summer camp. "Whatever they bought," she remembers, "they paid cash. I almost never saw a credit card put to use. If they did charge something, it was for convenience's sake, because they always had the money set aside before they bought anything."

Jane grew up in a New Jersey suburb of New York City, where her parents had bought a house more than 20 years ago with a $2,000 down payment. Though she was well provided for, she was aware that many of her schoolmates had more than she had. At college the difference was even more noticeable, and she found herself trying to keep up with girls from much more affluent families.

After college, Jane lived at home. She got a job as a receptionist, making $11,500. With no rent to pay and no responsibilities for helping to contribute to the household, she spent her entire take-home pay on bus fare to and from work, lunches, and her wardrobe. She saved nothing.

Jane has changed jobs a couple of times. She now works for an advertising agency, earning $18,000. With Chris's $24,000, they have a combined income of $42,000.

When they got married, Jane and Chris talked a little about what they wanted to do with any spare money above and beyond the basics for everyday living. He had been on the verge of buying a daysailer just before they were married. "Nothing doing," said Jane. "Not until we get the apartment furnished just the way we want it. Our home has got to come first."

Chris set his sailboat dream aside and they began decorating the apartment. "But it took more than we thought it would," Jane remembers. They used the money Chris had saved, plus money received as wedding gifts. When they had spent $10,000—and another $2,000 taken from Chris's savings had gone into the down payment on a new car—they charged still more on credit cards. Even then, the place wasn't quite complete, and they knew they would want to put more into it within a year or so. They also used their credit cards extensively to buy clothing and pay for entertainment.

Looking at their monthly statements, they realize how much they have spent and how little they have in the bank for an emergency. "We've really been living hand to mouth," says Chris. "Now we're trying to cut down on expenses. But it's hard when you've been spending more every time you get a raise. We've just been buying things on credit for too long." He sighs, then adds, "And still no sailboat."

WHY MANAGE MONEY?

2

We fall in love.

We know the color of our loved one's eyes.

We know his or her favorite book . . . favorite song . . . favorite meal.

But we never know how much is in the bank account. And we never know how much the one we love knows about finances.

Why manage money? Why set financial goals?

Because it will cut down on anxiety and frustration. Because it puts you both in charge. Because you can actually make it fun to handle money—part of the total fun of your marriage. Because, among other things, *marriage is a financial partnership*.

Let me take you back to about the time you were born. In the early to mid-1960's, the silver lining looked permanent. We came out of the 1950's living fairly high on the hog. The typical middle-class American family had a suburban home with a two-car garage and probably two cars in it. Incomes rose steadily. Inflation had not yet reared its head. Spendable income was abundant, and there was plenty to spend it on.

In the early 1970's, inflation hit and the bubble burst. The energy crisis shot gasoline prices from 30 cents a gallon to over a dollar, then higher. Prices escalated faster than personal incomes. Interest rates soared. Parents went around the house screaming: "Turn off the lights." "Why do you have to use that hair drier twice in one day?" "What do you mean, you've got to make another trip downtown?"

By the 1980's many young people were making three times as much as their parents had ever dreamed of making, yet were not living as well as their parents had once lived. But they had a range of financial options that had not been available to their parents:

- New financial products: half a dozen types of savings accounts at every savings bank and the "money market" or "liquid assets" funds that compete with savings bank accounts.
- Variable-rate mortgage loans: Home buyers could now take their chances on inflation coming down in three years, and the interest rate dropping with it. (Or, both can rise.)

FINANCIAL FITNESS FOR NEWLYWEDS

- Revolving charge accounts: "cash reserve" banking, which allows you to overdraw your checking account with every check you write, and catch up with every deposit—so long as you keep making more deposits and paying the finance charges. And VISA, MasterCard and American Express invite you to keep charging, paying up, charging again.
- Deregulation of fixed-term savings certificates: banks paying whatever interest rates they choose on fixed-term accounts running more than 31 days. With some certificates, investors may set their own maturity dates; penalties on early withdrawals have been relaxed.

This changing economy and the new financial options are important to the change you two are making in your lives. From your previous "singles" outlook, which generally dictated that your number one priority was "I" and "me," each of you is now adopting a "we" and "us" outlook. You are ready to work together, in your financial partnership, to buy into the American dream. If the need to manage money is not recognized and discussed, you could also buy into trouble.

A million choices

You have immediate choices and long-term choices to make. Should you buy furniture? A car? Rent an apartment? Buy a condominium? A house? Start a family? Spend on vacations and travel during your first two or three years of marriage and then have children? Get more education so you can qualify for better jobs? Take on a second job, to add income?

The result of all these possibilities is bewilderment that your parents may never have had to cope with at the same age.

Don't think you won't make mistakes. And don't be afraid to make some. Everybody does, at one time or another. Until two marital financial partners live together, neither knows how the other handles money. Neither knows what the other's dreams and desires, in relation to money, are—until they both begin to communicate them. Good financial habits—*mutually agreeable* financial habits—have to grow out of communication. If they start to grow at the same time your marriage starts, you will find it a lot easier than if you wait until some crisis forces you into trying to set up some good financial habits.

The key thing to communicate is goals.

Everybody needs financial goals

True. Everybody needs financial goals. But you are the only two people who know what your particular goals are. And only you two—together—can put your goals on paper so you can set up a sensible framework for reaching them. Writing them down on paper will enable you to:

- View money as more than something to have and use here and now. Most people have very little concept of money for the future, for the expensive trip next year or the year after, for the car to replace this car, for the major anniversary. They'll think about that next year—or the year after. But then it will be too late.
- Establish a way of gaining financial security. This means having a steady source of income and seeing that it increases each year to keep up with inflation and with your needs and desires; having money set aside for emergencies small (getting a broken appliance fixed) or large (an unexpected medical expense); having protection in case of disability or death.
- Utilize your income to best advantage. This means planning for your home, vacations, family.
- Accept the reality of your particular situation. This means spending against your plan, rather than against a dream.

In addition to writing them down, you and your spouse must talk freely, openly, at length about your goals. You must communicate your individual financial objectives to each other and reach a good understanding about them.

How do you establish your goals?

The first question is, What's important to us? Your goals reflect two value systems: the attitudes each of you were raised with. They may be almost the same. They may have some variances you didn't even know existed until you started talking about them. So it's important for you to figure out where each of you is "coming from." And where you want to go.

For most people, values are based on what is desirable and worthy. And the value systems of most people are usually fairly inflexible. They are passed down from grandparents and parents. All the more reason for lots of open talk, because values produce attitudes.

Values are tied closely to ego fulfillment. And ego fulfillment is tied closely to money. Money, in turn, is a major measure of success. And success brings the circle around again to ego fulfillment.

The fulfillment of one's ego, and one's involvement in his or her success, may often leave little room for recognition of what's going on with a mate's success—or lack of it. The result is the stuff of which TV situation comedies have been made for many years: wives who don't understand how hard a husband is working ("Another business trip? Another three-day vacation in Chicago?") . . . husbands who don't appreciate how successfully a wife is managing household finances . . . spending to "get even" (yes, corny as it sounds, it does happen). And there are husbands who don't understand the ego fulfillment—measured by earnings—that a working wife is getting from a full-time job.

Often, success and ego fulfillment are communicated through material signs. A Mercedes-Benz automobile, Gucci shoes, a Louis Vuitton bag, a Hermes scarf, an Izod Lacoste shirt—these tell the world that the owner belongs to the right group. They are used to demonstrate that one is successful in our society, for one can afford its trappings. Although their owners may not talk about such signs very much, values are expressed by them.

Values also dictate habits. And habits set priorities. Suppose you've been raised with a value system that says home ownership is a must. That may dictate saving $150 a month for a down payment. But maybe your habits conflict with reaching that goal. You decide you cannot save $150 a month. Or you put another goal first—maybe traveling before you start a family, or owning a boat, or buying a sports car. Your habits are then showing you that the home-owning goal is a lower priority than your value system said it was.

Tip: When values clash, talk it out.

Goals have priorities

Put each of your goals into one of the following categories:

- *Short-term goals.* What you need for next year. Paying for some furniture. Planning Christmas shopping. Buying a vacation in advance, so you have the money in hand on the day you set out.
- *Middle-term goals.* Three to five years away. Buying a house. Or the sports car. Having your first child; at today's projected costs of $225,000 per child from age 1 to 22 a child can definitely be a long-range goal.
- *Long-term goals.* Education for the children. A second home for weekends. Retirement.

The "blind worksheets" on goals

At this point, why don't each of you take one of the two "blind worksheets" on individual goals (Worksheets I and II) and list your most important three or four short-term and long-term goals. Do this separately and without comparing notes until you have the worksheets all filled in, then see how close you come to having the same goals. Remember that almost any goal is money-related. For example, if your goal is to play racquetball twice a week, obviously you will have to budget for the court time, and maybe for a couple of beers afterward. (Two beers a budget item? Yes, if they are consumed twice a week times 50 or 52 weeks a year.)

WHEN THE NICHOLSES JOTTED DOWN THEIR GOALS . . .

. . . they found that Valerie's first short-term goal was to get a new guitar, while James's was to replace their dilapidated car. "No point in the new guitar," he said, "if we can't be sure we'll get to the gig on time—or at all."

Worksheet I: Yours
INDIVIDUAL GOALS

Short-term	Middle- & Long-term
1.	1.
2.	2.
3.	

Worksheet I: Example
Valerie Nichols
INDIVIDUAL GOALS

Short-term	Middle- & Long-term
1. Guitar	1. Home
2. Microwave Oven	2. Furniture
3. Dog	

WHY MANAGE MONEY?

Worksheet II: Yours
INDIVIDUAL GOALS

Short-term

1. New Car
2. Vacation
3. Clothes

Middle- & Long-term

1. Home
2. Update Stereo System

Worksheet II: Example
James Nichols
INDIVIDUAL GOALS

Short-term

1.
2.
3.

Middle- & Long-term

1.
2.

They surprised themselves by finding that on both their lists of long-term goals, buying a house had absolute top priority.

The primary objective

Everything in your financial plan is directed to a single goal: the accumulation of capital, or money. This calls not only for good definition of goals but for follow-through on their details. If your top short-term goal is to accumulate a down payment for a home, now is the time to estimate what it will cost, at least in today's dollars. Make the effort to get actual figures on the kind of house you have in mind. Just getting the figures could switch this goal from short-term to middle-term (but not necessarily!). If it does, then be sure to keep tabs on costs so you can update the figures once a year.

This kind of planning and figuring can help you avoid waking up one day to find that you have to borrow to meet a goal because its price crept up while you weren't looking.

Goals and needs are subject to change. Check them over at least once a year. *Important:* Never feel you must stay locked into a specific goal. Your interests can change. Your needs can change.

Tip: Never use the money set aside for a middle- or long-term goal to pay for something you want now. That's robbing yourselves.

How you benefit from setting goals

Setting goals forces you both to examine your values, to clarify them, to reach understanding and agreement with each other. It forces you to devise ways to use your resources to attain your goals. It gives you control. And it makes you aware that each partner's pattern of behavior for attaining goals—just how you go about reaching them—must be compatible with the other's and both must be consistent with the goals. Otherwise you're headed for conflict and trouble.

In fact, classic confrontations between husbands and wives have occurred because either or both have not let their goals be known. It is imperative that you talk about values and goals with each other. Talk, then talk some more. Set up a system that gives you time to talk when you are both fresh and up to it—not at bedtime, not when you are tired after work, not at dinner with drinks. Make it early in the day, or over brunch on Saturday or Sunday. Give yourselves a reward for good talk about finances—the brunch itself, a place to go, a show to see.

Make money talk fun. It can be. Handling money can be fun and interesting and rewarding, as I hope this book will demonstrate. But you need a system to make it so, to help you deal with any possible conflicting values and find solutions.

Think of such a system as a continuous circular process involving these steps:

1. Identify the problem together. Talk about it openly until you agree on just what it is.
2. Discuss possible solutions. Don't try to settle on any particular solution now—just put every possible (or even remotely possible) solution out on the table.
3. Set it all aside for a while. For at least several hours. Maybe several days or a week.
4. Go back to it and discuss solutions again.
5. Negotiate a resolution together.

HOW THE BUCKS NEGOTIATED BETWEEN BLOOMIES' AND THE MARKET...

Jane and Chris Buck ran smack into a major goal conflict when they were furnishing their apartment, about a year after their wedding.

Chris came home from work one evening with his head full of big plans to get them started investing in Wall Street. Turned out he had been building castles of dreams for weeks, based on their combined income.

That was the very day that Jane had spent a long lunch hour at Bloomingdale's, lining up about $2,500 worth of furnishings that would complete the decoration of their apartment. Dinner wasn't a meal—it was a head-on collision. They talked and argued

Worksheet III: Yours
SAVING FOR A SPECIFIC GOAL

A. GOAL _____

B. DATE NEEDED _____

C. NUMBER OF YEARS TILL GOAL _____

D. AMOUNT NEEDED _____

E. MONEY ALREADY SET ASIDE _____

F. AMOUNT MONEY SET ASIDE WILL GROW TO AT _____ % _____

G. AMOUNT STILL NEEDED _____

H. AMOUNT TO BE SAVED PER YEAR AT _____ % INTEREST _____

---

half the night, but eventually they were communicating and a few days later they had figured out how they could order some of the most important items from Bloomies' and still have some money to start a small investment program in the market.

Chuckling about it afterward, they realized they had turned a no-win situation for either one of them into a "win-win" situation for both of them.

THE NICHOLSES ARE DYING TO OWN A HOUSE . . .

Buying their own home means more than anything else to Valerie and James—maybe because it would give them the stability they can't seem to find as performers in the world of music.

Having set that goal, they have socked away every penny they could possibly spare through the first year of their marriage. When they stopped in at a local bank recently and talked about a mortgage, the loan officer was astounded to learn that they had accumulated more than $3,000 in six months even though neither of them has what bankers call "steady" income.

"We don't entertain," says Valerie. "We don't drink. We don't go to the movies."

It hasn't been all that easy to get a mortgage, and they don't have one lined up yet. The loan officer wanted them to find a cosigner—a parent or older relative who would sign with them and be responsible for payments if they failed to keep them up.

**Worksheet III: Example
James & Valerie Nichols
SAVING FOR A SPECIFIC GOAL**

A. GOAL _____A house_____

B. DATE NEEDED _____1985_____

C. NUMBER OF YEARS TILL GOAL _____1_____

D. AMOUNT NEEDED _____8,000_____

E. MONEY ALREADY SET ASIDE _____3,000_____

F. AMOUNT MONEY SET ASIDE WILL GROW TO AT __10__ % _____3,312_____

G. AMOUNT STILL NEEDED (D.-F.) _____4,688_____

H. AMOUNT TO BE SAVED ~~PER YEAR~~ *Monthly* AT __10__ % INTEREST _____370.35_____

They decided to wait until they accumulate a larger down payment, in another few months. This will provide even stronger evidence of their dependability.

To help them focus on their goal of home ownership, Valerie and James put down their plan on paper. Worksheet III, **Saving for a Specific Goal,** was the result. It identified for Valerie and James precisely what they needed to do to reach their goal. The figure in line H is the amount that they have to save each year, assuming a 10 percent interest. This figure comes from the Financial Compound Interest and Annuity Tables. (Check with your bank, insurance agent, or accountant who has ready access to this particular book.)

Sit down together and fill out the blank copy of Worksheet III for one of your specific mid- or long-term goals, and you'll see how it concentrates your attention on what you need to do *now* to achieve what you really want *later.*

WHY MANAGE MONEY? 13

WHO'S GOING TO MANAGE THE MONEY? 3

The next logical question after "Why manage money?" is "Who's going to do it?" And right after that comes "How is it done?" This takes us to *budget*—but I'm getting too far ahead of the story. The three questions are very closely tied together and they obviously overlap in many ways. They are broken into three chapters only for purposes of discussion and clarity.

Some questions to ask one another

Before you can set up a budget, you need to talk out some basic points:

- Who is going to pay for what? What is a workable method of paying bills and putting away savings? Will one of us be in charge of all bill paying? Should we take turns?
- Are we going to try to pay for day-to-day living expenses—food, utilities—out of one salary?
- Will we reserve the other paycheck for savings, investments, and extras?
- Should we pool all our income into a single account, paying all bills and setting aside savings from it?
- Or should we maintain separate accounts and each take responsibility for certain expenses?
- Or—a third way—should we set up a joint account for fixed expenses, with separate accounts for other expenses and individual use? This means we must decide how much we will each contribute to the joint account.
- Is one of us better than the other at handling money? This is really the *key* question.

There are no absolute answers to these questions. You have to put your heads together and decide what is best for you *together*, in your situation. And your decision must also fit what is best for each of you *individually*.

Some factors that affect your decisions

In the rare cases where you both earn nearly the same amount, a single pooled account can work out fine. But if one of you earns a good deal more than the other, you may want to keep individual accounts and contribute proportionately to a joint account for paying the day-to-day expenses (more on this in subsequent chapters).

To help keep the chores fairly divided, you might want to split them this way: One of you handles the checkbooks and bill paying, while the other does the record keeping—posts the income and outgo in your budget book, takes care of the filing, and also handles the tax returns. This gives you a sort of mini-auditing system, so you have some checks and balances in your financial partnership. It's not a bad idea from several standpoints: If one of you feels less good at this kind of work than the other, you can learn from your partner. If the check writer and bill payer is straying from systems or goals you agreed on, it will be discovered and you can openly discuss how to fix the problem. And once you have established this system and both know how it all works, you can switch responsibilities if and when you get bored or just feel it's time for a change.

Important: If you set up such a system, make sure responsibilities are clearly assigned and kept separate. Don't fall into a situation where both of you are casually writing the checks and keeping the records, because sooner or later one of you will think the other did something—paid some bill, filed some cash register tape—that neither of you did.

Eventually, the best system for handling the money will evolve. From working together you'll see which one of you is better at handling money and actually enjoys it more. You'll find out who has more time for it, or who can take care of it more quickly.

Your job situations can be a factor, too. If one of you is traveling a lot, the other probably should be the money manager.

Checks and checkbooks

In most cases, I recommend that each person maintain a separate checking account. Even a non-working spouse should keep an account, if that spouse is handling the food budget, for instance, and may be able to save some of it.

Separate accounts give each of you control over your own income. As long as you know and agree on who is responsible for what, you have no particular need to account to each other for what is in your own accounts. If either of you is able to save a little in your own account, it is yours to do with as you please. If the grocery buyer can save something on the food budget, as mentioned above, there should never be any complaints as long as you are both eating well right through to the last day of the month. *This concept is very important.*

If you are maintaining separate accounts and a joint "household" account, you might want to tie into the new system of telephone bill-paying services that many banks now offer. This can cut down on check writing time and give you an easy way to pay rent, mortgage, utilities, American Express card accounts, department stores—even, in some communities, the garbage collector.

Orderly checkbooks are vital—whether for separate accounts or for a joint account. An excellent habit to get into is that of writing the check stub *first*, before you write the check. Be sure to put down what the check is for, not just to whom it is payable, on the stub. This will be important for your budgeting process. (See also Chapter 7, Banks, Bankers, and Banking.)

Tip: Try using colored markers to put a mark or an asterisk on each stub—maybe red for medical expenses, yellow for charitable contributions, and so on—so that at the end of the year you can quickly go through your checkbook to pull together income tax information.

While you are thinking together about who is going to manage the money, you should at the same time start to put together your budget. The two considerations—who manages money and *how* you manage it—go hand in hand.

HOW TO MANAGE THE MONEY: YOUR BUDGET 4

Nobody likes the word *budget*. It means discipline. It means harsh reality. It means a very firm "yes" or "no" when you are considering an expenditure.

But nothing could be more important in a two-income family. Your budget is your guide, your control, your hand on the throttle. If one of the two paychecks is temporary—if, for instance, one of you plans to quit work for a period of several years once a child comes along—then I suggest you try to live on one income right now. Salt away the other.

In fact, even if you think both incomes are "permanent," don't spend them both up to the limit. There are too many unpredictables out there: a temporary layoff, a disability, any number of unforeseen expenses.

What a budget is

A budget is a worksheet. A road map. A resume. It depicts your lifestyle and shows what you need to do to manage it. It shows you how to get to where you want to be.

The fun of it is, you make your own rules. Like gourmet meals? Budget for them. Enjoy the theater? Budget for it. Want to see faraway places with strange-sounding names? Budget for them. Want a knockout wardrobe, closets so full you seldom wear the same thing twice to the office? Budget for it.

The point is that the money is yours. No one can tell anyone else how to spend their money. *You* decide on the priorities that will make *your* lifestyle.

Your budget—a road map

Think of your budget as just that: a road map. Its purpose is to show you where you are going and how to get there. But it can be used, like any good road map, to show you where you can *sensibly* and safely get off the road when you must, then get back on again without losing direction or missing your destination. It is important for you both to realize that you can do that. You can change your route to cope with an emergency or a change in plans that may delay reaching your planned destination. There's

FINANCIAL FITNESS FOR NEWLYWEDS

nothing wrong with that if you do have your map to guide you and remind you of your goal and the route you structured for reaching it.

Your budget is valuable not only as a road map. It is the key to knowing how much credit you can safely afford to carry. Millions of Americans constantly face the problem of paying for what they bought yesterday while feeling the urge to buy something more today. Only a well-tended budget can answer the nagging question, can we afford the payments?

Every budget has two sides

Getting and spending. Income and outgo. Revenue and expenses. Every budget has two sides, one for money arriving, the other for money departing. The two sides are basic to every budget in creation—a household budget for two of you, or the budget of a giant transnational corporation with worldwide production, employees and sales.

Start with your revenue budget. (See Worksheet IV on pages 17–18, headed **Sources of Income**.)

On this sheet, for each of you, write down *all* your income, by category: what you earn as wages or salary; extra money you take in from part-time work, moonlighting, hobbies, whatever; interest you get from savings accounts; dividends from investments; regular gifts from parents; rent from any property you own or from roomers or boarders; payments from unemployment insurance or disability insurance. Look at your paycheck stub and note deductions for Social Security, taxes, and any fringe benefits.

Tip: Be brutally honest. Do not count unhatched chickens. A pay raise is not a pay raise until it comes home in your paycheck. Your budget is always *now*. It is never what might be: what you hope it will be next month, or even what promises lead you to think it is going to be.

Now look at the expense side of your budget.

Two kinds of expenses: fixed and flexible

Fixed expenses are those you must pay regularly—every month or every quarter or once a year. They are expenses you cannot escape or change to any

Worksheet IV: Yours
SOURCES OF INCOME

EARNED INCOME	Husband	Wife	Joint	Total	Monthly
Salary & Wages					
Self-Employment Income					
Bonus					
INVESTMENT INCOME					
Interest on Savings					
Interest from Bonds					
Capital Gains					
Dividends					
Rental Income					
Trust Income					

	Husband	Wife	Joint	Total	Monthly
PENSIONS & ANNUITIES					
Social Security					
Employer's Pension					
Private Pensions					
Other					
OTHER INCOME					
Family Contributions					
Gifts					
Unemployment, Disability Insurance					
Alimony & Child Support					
Gross Income					

DEDUCTIONS

	Husband	Wife	Joint	Total	Monthly
TAXES					
Federal					
State					
Local					
SOCIAL SECURITY					
BENEFITS					
OTHER					
NET INCOME					

TIPS ON SOUND SPENDING HABITS

You can learn to spend your money efficiently and, as a result, save money. Here are a number of tips:

1. Watch the non-essentials. How much are you spending for a magazine you don't read, a milk shake, a taxi ride when the bus would get you there, seeing a movie you didn't want to see just because another couple was going?

2. Guard against sales. If you really need the item, buy it. If a blouse "was such a bargain, I couldn't resist," you may be in for adding a skirt or shoes to match. Note when certain items go on sale every year—January white sales, Christmas cards at half price right after the holidays (but don't buy them in January unless you really will use them the following December).

3. Never charge a sale item on a credit card on which you are making time payments. The finance charges will cost you what you saved on the sale.

4. Make shopping lists—and stick to them. The supermarkets thrive on impulse buying by people who don't have firm lists. Probably you seldom go to the grocery store without a list. But make lists for all other shopping, too.

5. Why buy tools you don't often use? You can rent them more cheaply than owning them. Need a leaf blower once or twice a fall? Rent it. Ski once or twice a year? Rent the skis. You can find furniture, stereos, TV sets, plants, clothing, dishes, tableware—just about anything—for rent. Look in the telephone book yellow pages.

6. If you're in a neighborhood where a number of people could use a leaf blower or snow blower or a special lawn mower, buy it together. But be sure someone takes responsibility for maintenance.

7. Barter. Or swap services. You could babysit for a neighbor in exchange for a ride to work every day. You might change the oil in a neighbor's car as a trade for use of a lawn mower. You can think of a zillion ways to gain services by trading your own.

8. Avoid shopping with a friend. Especially with someone who makes more than you do or has different spending habits. A fancy shop where you would never go alone? And now you're in there buying something because your friend shops there? No way! Don't ever feel ashamed to say, "No, thanks."

9. Buy at discount stores. Look over the ones near you. Some are better than others, in terms of the quality of the merchandise. All give you good price breaks.

10. Save your small change. Empty pockets or purse of all coins every night. You will fill a coffee can before you know it. Keep hands out of this pot and lug it to the savings bank. (Most savings banks have machines that will count up your coins in just a few minutes.)

11. Think energy when you think budget. Can you ride a bike or walk to work, and save on gasoline? Do you turn off the lights when you leave a room? Should you have a day-night thermostat installed?

12. Save on long-distance phone calls. Check your phone book for the difference in rates during various time periods. If you make a lot of long-distance calls, consider signing up with one of the budget long-distance companies.

13. Watch lunches out. If you are both working, keep a close eye on spending for pickup meals, whether fast-food or gourmet.

14. Think long-range savings. A microwave oven may or may not be a luxury. If you use it regularly to reheat leftovers that you would otherwise throw out, it could be worth the initial expense.

great degree: the rent or mortgage payment, insurance premiums, taxes, monthly payments on credit obligations, utilities. (Of course, you can reduce utility bills by disciplining telephone use, turning off lights, lowering the thermostat.)

To be sure you always have the money to pay these, make a payment every month to a *fixed-expenses account*. To determine how much you need for this account every month, line up all your fixed expenses for the year, writing them in on Worksheet V (pages 22–24) for each month. Some you have to pay every month (rent or mortgage, for example), some quarterly (insurance premiums, probably), some semi-annually (real estate taxes), some annually (example: personal property taxes). Total each category, then figure out its monthly average. Now total the monthly averages to see how much must go into your fixed-expenses account each month. Hard as it will be—*at first*—you must start immediately to put in that amount every month. And no matter how enticing the sale or how tight the money seems, you must fight off the urge to dip into your reserves for fixed expenses. (More in a moment on practical ways to handle the money—literally.) Be sure the checkbook for this account does not go to the market but stays home in the desk drawer.

Once you have established the habit of putting that monthly average into the fixed-expenses account, you will find it is painless to maintain. With the system functioning well, you will always be able to pay a tax bill or the insurance premium when it comes due.

Think of *savings* as a fixed expense. The first kind of savings you need is a payment to yourselves for an *emergency fund*.

How much goes into it? At any one time, your emergency fund should contain the equivalent of from three to six months' net income. If you are both working, if car and appliances and house are new and not likely to cry for major repairs soon, it is safe to have a minimum of three months' income stashed away. Later on, especially as your family grows, you will feel a lot more comfortable when you maintain a six-month cushion for emergencies.

So figure how much your emergency fund should be, and start now to put it away.

After your emergency fund has built up to a safe level, be sure to keep replenishing it regularly.

Use this cash reserve for just that: emergencies. A major medical expense not covered by insurance, a major car or household repair, a stretch of unemployment—such emergencies, without the reserves on hand to pay for them, could send you to a bank or some other lender to sign for a loan. That, in turn, would add to your fixed obligations each month, giving you more to pay out, more to worry about, and less to have for flexible expenses and discretionary spending. Your savings each month should also include the amount you have determined is necessary to reach specific goals.

"Do we really need this?"

When you want to buy something, ask yourselves, "Do we really need this?" The question can help you control impulse buying. Having taken a good hard look at your priorities as you analyze your cash flow, you will find yourselves distinguishing between buying for pleasure and buying for need. By making this distinction every time you make a significant expenditure—and only you two know what's significant for you—you will stay financially fit.

Tip: To test your real need to buy something, write out a check for its purchase price. Look at the check. Do you need that amount now, to buy groceries or pay a department store bill? If you do, you don't need the item you are considering. Can you make up the amount by skipping several trips to the movies, putting off a holiday trip, not dining out a few times? Better to do so than to make the purchase and then find out you cannot pay for basic flexible expenses or discover yourselves dipping into money you need for fixed expenses.

Of course, you have to make trade-offs. That's inevitable. But you can establish limits for large expenses. You can agree in advance that you won't spend more than a certain amount for a car or to furnish a room.

Above all, remember that money is not an end in itself. It is a tool to help you enjoy life and reach your goals. So spend realistically and save carefully in ways you can be comfortable with.

And let your budget be your guide—your road map. Review it at least once a year. See where it needs adjusting, where goals have been met, where new goals should be set. When you have successfully cut costs or gained a short-term goal, you can even reward yourselves with a special dinner out or—if the numbers are right—a weekend away.

> ### IMPORTANT BUDGETING DON'TS
>
> - Don't dictate. You must work out the budget together, with full mutual agreement.
> - Don't rush. You can't work out a budget in one evening. It takes time. Go back to it after you have both thought about it.
> - Don't go by what others spend (don't keep up with the Joneses).
> - Don't look for miracles. Your budget is a management tool. It will not, all by itself, give you more money or cut your spending.
> - Don't nickle and dime it. Round figures up or down to the nearest dollar, and big figures to the nearest ten dollars.
> - Don't overdo the paper work. Report the essentials, that's all.
> - Don't be inflexible. Remember that a budget must have room for give and take. Circumstances will change. Income will grow, but so will outgo. Children will arrive. Interests will shift. Be ready to review, evaluate, revise, and adjust as your lifestyle changes.

Handling flexible expenses

What are flexible expenses? They are those you spend for regularly but that may vary in amount depending on what you're doing, how you're feeling, what you need. Food, of course. Clothing. Medical care. Cars and travel. (The cost of regular commuting by train, subway, or bus, however, is a fixed expense; it should be calculated in your fixed-expense total.) Entertainment and recreation. Ordinary household maintenance (such non-emergencies as cleaning services). Laundry and dry cleaning. Magazine subscriptions.

Tip: How to "handle" your money so you are fair to each part of your budget? The best way is to set up three separate bank accounts:

1. A savings account for your emergency fund.
2. A checking account for your fixed expenses. (Some people who have immense self-discipline find that they can keep their emergency-fund money and their fixed-expenses money in the same account. I admire such Spartans, but I am not one of them. My recommendation: Set up separate accounts.)
3. A checking account for your flexible expenses. There's another system. People used to use it all the time. Some still do. It's the *envelope system*. It gives you immediate feedback, so you know where you stand. You mark envelopes for each of your basic flexible-expense items—food, entertainment, clothing, etc. Into each envelope you put the amount you have budgeted for that expense. If by the 20th of the month the entertainment envelope is empty, you know you have spent your budget and you watch TV. If the food envelope is empty by the 20th, you'll find yourself doing some frantic borrowing from other categories and you'll be more cautious in the supermarket next month. The chief disadvantage of the envelope system: You're keeping more cash in the house than it's wise to.

How much to budget per category?

How do you know how much to budget for each category of flexible expenses—especially if the two of you have not lived together before or budgeted before?

Your best guide is what you spent last year, if you kept records. If you did not keep records, start today to keep some.

Record keeping is easy. There are only three ways you can pay for something: with cash, by check when you buy it, or by charge account paid later. Always get a receipt, whether you are paying by cash, check or charge. If you cannot get a receipt (not even a cash register tape), make your own note of date, item, and amount; note the sales tax, too—handy for computing sales tax totals when you do your income tax return.

Put all receipts on a spindle at home—or in a large envelope, filed chronologically. When you pay

Worksheet V: Yours
FIXED & FLEXIBLE EXPENSES

	SAVINGS	JAN	FEB	MAR	APR	MAY	JUN	JUL	AUG	SEP	OCT	NOV	DEC	TOTAL
1	Emergency Fund													
2	Short-term Goal													
3	Other Goal													
4														
5	**TOTAL SAVINGS**													
	FIXED EXPENSES													
1	Rent/Mortgage													
2	Fuel													
3	Electricity													
4	Telephone													
5	Water													
6	Homeowners Insurance													
7	Automobile Insurance													
8	Disability Insurance													
9	Medical Insurance													
10	Life Insurance													
11	Life Insurance													
12	Life Insurance													
13	Personal Property Taxes													
14	Real Estate Taxes													
15	Income Taxes													
16	Automobile Loan													
17	Loan Repayment													
18	Loan Repayment													
19	Other Debt													
20	Other													
21														
22														
23	**TOTAL FIXED EXPENSES**													
24	Monthly Average													
25	Difference (Amount to be left in													
26	fixed expense account)													
27														
28														
29														
30														
31														

FLEXIBLE EXPENSES	JAN	FEB	MAR	APR	MAY	JUN	JUL	AUG	SEP	OCT	NOV	DEC	TOTAL
1 Food/Beverage													
2 Clothing													
3 Laundry/Cleaning													
4 Home/Office Supplies													
5 Animals													
6 Personal Care Toiletries													
7 Periodicals													
8 Recreation													
9 Entertainment													
10 Travel/Vacations													
11 Gifts													
12													
13 **Household Maintenance**													
14 Lawn & Snow Removal													
15 Maid													
16 Garbage													
17 Repairs													
18 Home Furnishings													
19 Major Appliance Purchases													
20													
21 **Transportation**													
22 Gas/Oil													
23 Repairs													
24 Licenses & Registration													
25 Commutation, Parking													
26													
27 **Children's Expenses**													
28 Allowances													
29 Lessons													
30 Camp													
31 Recreation/Sports													
32 Child Care—Baby sitting													

HOW TO MANAGE THE MONEY: YOUR BUDGET

		JAN	FEB	MAR	APR	MAY	JUN	JUL	AUG	SEP	OCT	NOV	DEC	TOTAL
33	**Education**													
34	Tuition													
35	Room/Board													
36	Books & Supplies													
37	Travel													
38														
39	**Medical Expenses**													
40	Doctor													
41	Dentist													
42	Drug													
43														
44	**Contributions**													
45	Church/Synagogue													
46	Other Charity													
47	Total Flexible Expenses													
48														
	TOTAL SAVINGS													
	TOTAL FLEXIBLE EXPENSES													
	TOTAL FIXED EXPENSES													
	TOTAL EXPENSES													
	NET INCOME													
	PROFIT (LOSS)													

by check, be sure to note on your checkbook stub for what (and for whom) the purchase was made.

In tallying charge accounts against your budget, be sure to categorize what is actually charged, not what you are paying on your total charge bill, as you may be paying it off in installments.

Now, total all the columns on your expense sheets (Worksheet V). Are your total expenditures higher than your income? If they are, don't be discouraged. Overspending gives you a good reason for doing an analysis, taking a good hard look at priorities, cutting down here or there.

A TIGHT BUDGET IS A MUST FOR THE NICHOLSES...

Income is never the same two weeks in a row—let alone month after month—for Valerie and James. As musicians, they not only see it rise and fall constantly, but they also have no sure way to base their budget for the future. So they took what they earned together in their first year of marriage and made that the base for their budget in the second year.

Since they are both self-employed, they get *all* their pay. No employer does any withholding. That means they have to include income taxes and Social Security payments in the amounts they budget, and pay them quarterly on an estimated basis.

Before arriving at net earnings on which to base the payments of estimated taxes, they deduct all expenses related to their profession: musical instruments, telephone, automobile, costumes.

"Our fixed and flexible expenses come to a little over $13,000 a year," says James. "That's about $1,085 a month. We put all our paychecks into a savings account. Then we transfer $1,000 into our checking account every month—more if we have a big bill, like an insurance bill. The balance sits right in that money market account so it can earn some extra, and we use it to pay the taxes, buy the musical equipment we need, cover emergencies, and, best of all, give us that house we want—next year, we hope."

Valerie smiles. "We had just one big emergency. A blown-out tire. No problem. The system really has been working. We won't touch those savings for anything we don't really have to have."

Worksheet IV: The Nicholses
SOURCES OF INCOME

	JAN	FEB	MAR	APR	MAY	JUN	JUL	AUG	SEP	OCT	NOV	DEC	TOTAL
Valerie	482	300	800	745	1,065	400	1,140	1,420	1,350	1,350	1,250	1,560	11,862
James	519	607	737	704	950	1,120	1,546	1,345	1,435	1,350	1,450	1,650	13,413
Interest Income	2,400	60	65	500	70	85	500	85	80	475	90	90	4,500
Total	3,401	967	1,602	1,949	2,085	1,605	3,186	2,850	2,865	3,175	2,790	3,300	29,775

Worksheet V: The Nicholses
FIXED & FLEXIBLE EXPENSES

	SAVINGS	JAN	FEB	MAR	APR	MAY	JUN	JUL	AUG	SEP	OCT	NOV	DEC	TOTAL
1	Emergency Fund	60	60	60	60	60	60	60	60	60	60	60	60	720
2	Short-term Goal ⟩ house	370	370	370	370	370	370	370	370	370	370	370	370	4,440
3	Other Goal INCOME TAX	400	400	400	400	400	400	400	400	400	400	400	400	4,800
4														
5	TOTAL SAVINGS	830	830	830	830	830	830	830	830	830	830	830	830	9,960
	FIXED EXPENSES													
1														
2	Rent/Mortgage	320	320	320	320	320	320	320	320	320	320	320	320	3,840
3	Fuel													
4	Electricity	30	25	30	28	27	35	40	55	60	25	30	28	423
5	Telephone	40	25	35	29	31	40	35	31	40	35	38	31	410
6	Water		125											125
7	Homeowners Insurance													
8	Automobile Insurance			125			125			125			125	500
9	Disability Insurance													
10	Medical Insurance	200			200			200			200			800
11	Life Insurance													
12	Life Insurance													
13	Life Insurance													
14	Personal Property Taxes													
15	Real Estate Taxes													
16	Income Taxes													
17	Automobile Loan	137	137	137	137	137	137	137	137	137	137	137	137	1,644
18	Loan Repayment													
19	Loan Repayment													
20	Other Debt													
21	Other													
22														
23	TOTAL FIXED EXPENSES	727	632	647	714	515	657	732	543	682	727	525	641	7,742
24	Monthly Average	645	645	645	645	645	645	645	645	645	645	645	645	549
25	Difference (Amount to be left in		13			130			102			120	4	
26	fixed expense account)													
27														
28														
29														
30														
31														

FINANCIAL FITNESS FOR NEWLYWEDS

	FLEXIBLE EXPENSES	JAN	FEB	MAR	APR	MAY	JUN	JUL	AUG	SEP	OCT	NOV	DEC	TOTAL
1	Food/Beverage	150	140	135	160	150	135	140	155	155	140	160	175	1,795
2	Clothing	100		85		75	50	45	80	175	120		50	780
3	Laundry/Cleaning	25		10			40		30		10	8	5	128
4	Home/Office Supplies													
5	Animals — FOOD - vet	25		50		35	70	10	60		70	35	20	365
6	Personal Care Toiletries		60			50	20		45		35		50	270
7	Periodicals	10	10	10	10	10	10	10	10	10	10	10	10	120
8	Recreation	125			35			125			40			325
9	Entertainment	25	30	40	25	30	25	40	27	30	25	50	75	422
10	Travel/Vacations													
11	Gifts		30	25	15	25							75	170
12														
13	**Household Maintenance**													
14	Lawn & Snow Removal													
15	Maid													
16	Garbage													
17	Repairs													
18	Home Furnishings		600			300								900
19	Major Appliance Purchases													
20														
21	**Transportation**													
22	Gas/Oil	75	100	85	60	70	75	50	65	80	75	70	75	880
23	Repairs						75	80				50		205
24	Licenses & Registration													
25	Commutation, Parking													
26														
27	**Children's Expenses**													
28	Allowances													
29	Lessons													
30	Camp													
31	Recreation/Sports													
32	Child Care—Baby sitting													

HOW TO MANAGE THE MONEY: YOUR BUDGET

		JAN	FEB	MAR	APR	MAY	JUN	JUL	AUG	SEP	OCT	NOV	DEC	TOTAL
33	**Education**													
34	Tuition													
35	Room/Board													
36	Books & Supplies													
37	Travel													
38														
39	**Medical Expenses**													
40	Doctor			25					35					85
41	Dentist		60						30			30		120
42	Drug													
43														
44	**Contributions**													
45	Church/Synagogue													
46	Other Charity													
47	Total Flexible Expenses	535	1,030	490	305	745	500	500	537	450	525	413	535	6,565
48														
	TOTAL SAVINGS	830	830	830	830	830	830	830	830	830	830	830	830	9,960
	TOTAL FLEXIBLE EXPENSES	535	1,030	490	305	745	500	500	535	450	525	413	535	6,565
	TOTAL FIXED EXPENSES	727	632	647	714	515	657	732	543	682	727	525	641	7,742
	TOTAL EXPENSES	2,092	2,492	1,967	1,849	2,090	1,987	2,062	1,910	1,962	2,082	1,768	2,006	24,267
	NET INCOME													
	PROFIT (LOSS)													
	BUSINESS - MUSICAL													
	P.A. SYSTEM	30		25			40		30		60		35	220
	INSTRUMENTS		1,000											1,000
	PUBLIC RELATIONS				500				300			1,000		1,800
	OFFICE SUPPLIES	40	50		30		80			40	50			220
			80				25			60		35		270
	TOTAL EXPENSES	2,162	3,622	1,992	2,379	1,790	2,132	2,062	2,240	2,062	2,192	2,803	2,041	27,477

HOMEOWNERS CATHY AND PATRICK McQUARTER...

... put saving for their house into their budget from day one of their marriage. They started by saving $200 a month, then increased it as their salaries increased. Now, as they look for their house, they have $18,000 in savings.

"I guess we could have saved even faster," says Cathy, "but it's really tough to work a full day and then come home and cook, so we do eat out quite a lot—or buy pickup food to take home. But we never go any place very expensive."

Cathy and Patrick are like most two-income families in that respect. The growth in the number of working couples has been accompanied by growth in restaurant dining and sales of prepared food.

Worksheet IV: Example Two
The McQuarters
SOURCES OF INCOME

EARNED INCOME	Husband	Wife	Joint	Total	Monthly
Salary & Wages	$20,000	$15,000		$35,000	$2,917
Self-Employment Income					
Bonus					
INVESTMENT INCOME					
Interest on Savings			$1,600	$1,600	$133
Interest from Bonds					
Capital Gains					
Dividends					
Rental Income					
Trust Income					

HOW TO MANAGE THE MONEY: YOUR BUDGET

	Husband	Wife	Joint	Total	Monthly
PENSIONS & ANNUITIES					
Social Security					
Employer's Pension					
Private Pensions					
Other					
OTHER INCOME					
Family Contributions					
Gifts					
Unemployment, Disability Insurance					
Alimony & Child Support					
Gross Income					

DEDUCTIONS

	Husband	Wife	Joint	Total	Monthly
TAXES					
Federal					
State					
Local					
SOCIAL SECURITY					
BENEFITS					
OTHER					
NET INCOME					

Worksheet V: Example Two
The McQuarters
FIXED & FLEXIBLE EXPENSES

	SAVINGS	JAN	FEB	MAR	APR	MAY	JUN	JUL	AUG	SEP	OCT	NOV	DEC	TOTAL
1	Emergency Fund													
2	Short-term Goal	300	300	300	300	300	300	300	300	300	300	300	300	3,600
3	Other Goal I.R.A.				1,000									1,000
4														
5	TOTAL SAVINGS	300	300	300	1,300	300	300	300	300	300	300	300	300	4,600
	FIXED EXPENSES													
1														
2	Rent/Mortgage	300	300	300	300	300	300	300	300	300	300	300	300	3,600
3	Fuel	45	30	35	38	45	90	80	85	90	35	30	37	640
4	Electricity													
5	Telephone	50	20	25	30	25	24	19	20	22	24	35	19	313
6	Water													
7	Homeowners Insurance Renters							166						166
8	Automobile Insurance	150				300		150			300			900
9	Disability Insurance													
10	Medical Insurance		50			50			50			50		200
11	Life Insurance													
12	Life Insurance													
13	Life Insurance													
14	Personal Property Taxes													
15	Real Estate Taxes													
16	Income Taxes													
17	Automobile Loan	95	95	95	95	95	95	95	95	95	95	95	95	1,140
18	Loan Repayment Refrig	22	22	22	22	22	22	22	22	22	22	22	22	264
19	Loan Repayment													
20	Other Debt													
21	Other													
22														
23	TOTAL FIXED EXPENSES	657	517	477	485	837	531	832	572	529	776	532	473	7,218
24	Monthly Average	602	602	602	602	602	602	602	602	602	602	602	602	602
25	Difference (Amount to be left in fixed expense account)	65	125	117		71		30	73		70	129		
26														

HOW TO MANAGE THE MONEY: YOUR BUDGET

	FLEXIBLE EXPENSES	JAN	FEB	MAR	APR	MAY	JUN	JUL	AUG	SEP	OCT	NOV	DEC	TOTAL
1	Food/Beverage	160	175	180	175	190	150	165	150	175	160	180	250	2,110
2	Clothing	300	150	75	75		75	40	55	200	175		150	1,295
3	Laundry/Cleaning	15		25		75			15		15	25	30	200
4	Home/Office Supplies													
5	Animals													
6	Personal Care Toiletries	75		25	50	40	60	75	115	70	85	15	40	650
7	Periodicals	10	10	10	10	10	10	10	10	10	10	10	10	120
8	Recreation			85		125		25	25	40	75	80		480
9	Entertainment	150	175	250	200	150	150	75	75	175	110	250	300	2,060
10	Travel/Vacations				900			300						1,200
11	Gifts		25				60						250	360
12														
13	Household Maintenance													
14	Lawn & Snow Removal													
15	Maid													
16	Garbage													
17	Repairs													
18	Home Furnishings	80		125				85			175		225	690
19	Major Appliance Purchases													
20														
21	Transportation													
22	Gas/Oil	105	150	115	95	105	85	145	120	120	110	100	155	1,405
23	Repairs			75	180		65			50		80	110	560
24	Licenses & Registration													
25	Commutation, Parking													
26														
27	Children's Expenses													
28	Allowances													
29	Lessons													
30	Camp													
31	Recreation/Sports													
32	Child Care—Baby sitting													

FINANCIAL FITNESS FOR NEWLYWEDS

		JAN	FEB	MAR	APR	MAY	JUN	JUL	AUG	SEP	OCT	NOV	DEC	TOTAL
33	**Education**													
34	Tuition													
35	Room/Board													
36	Books & Supplies													
37	Travel													
38														
39	**Medical Expenses**													
40	Doctor		75			40		25			40			205
41	Dentist		40						40		80			160
42	Drug	25				25								90
43														
44	**Contributions**													
45	Church/Synagogue	10		10									25	55
46	Other Charity	5					25	10		10			10	50
47	Total Flexible Expenses	935	825	975	1,685	810	680	955	630	850	1,050	740	1,555	11,690
48														
	TOTAL SAVINGS	300	300	300	300	300	300	300	300	300	300	300	300	4,600
	TOTAL FLEXIBLE EXPENSES	935	825	975	1,685	810	680	955	630	850	1,050	740	1,555	11,690
	TOTAL FIXED EXPENSES	657	517	477	485	837	531	832	572	529	776	532	473	7,218
	TOTAL EXPENSES	1,892	1,642	1,752	2,470	1,947	1,511	2,087	1,502	1,679	2,126	1,572	2,328	23,508
	NET INCOME	2,025	2,025	2,025	2,025	2,025	2,025	2,025	2,025	2,025	2,025	2,025	2,025	24,300
	PROFIT (LOSS)	133	383	273	(445)	78	514	(62)	523	346	(101)	453	(303)	792

HOW TO MANAGE THE MONEY: YOUR BUDGET

THE BUCKS ARE STUCK . . .

. . . with a severe strain on the budget, thanks to the amount of credit payments they have to make every month. The car is $250, the furniture $75, VISA and MasterCard are $50 each, and Bloomingdale's department store adds another $35—making a total of $460 that must go to repay debts every single month. By the time they pay a healthy rent check and make expenditures for food, clothing, and entertainment to keep up their lifestyle, nothing is left for savings. Comparing budgets with the Nicholses and McQuarters shows that the Bucks will be the last of the three couples into a home of their own—yet they need the tax advantages of home ownership more than the other two couples.

Worksheet IV: Example Three
The Bucks
SOURCES OF INCOME

EARNED INCOME	Husband	Wife	Joint	Total	Monthly
Salary & Wages	$24,000	$18,000		$42,000	$3,500
Self-Employment Income					
Bonus					
INVESTMENT INCOME					
Interest on Savings			$150		$13
Interest from Bonds					
Capital Gains					
Dividends					
Rental Income					
Trust Income					

	Husband	Wife	Joint	Total	Monthly
PENSIONS & ANNUITIES					
Social Security					
Employer's Pension					
Private Pensions					
Other					
OTHER INCOME					
Family Contributions					
Gifts					
Unemployment, Disability Insurance					
Alimony & Child Support					
Gross Income	$24,000	$18,000	$150	$42,150	$3,513

DEDUCTIONS

	Husband	Wife	Joint	Total	Monthly
TAXES					
Federal	$4,200	$3,400		$7,600	$633
State	$2,100	$1,200		$3,300	$275
Local					
SOCIAL SECURITY	$1,608	$1,206		$2,814	$235
BENEFITS					
OTHER					
NET INCOME	$16,092	$12,194		$28,286	$2,357

Worksheet V: Example Three
The Bucks
FIXED & FLEXIBLE EXPENSES

	SAVINGS	JAN	FEB	MAR	APR	MAY	JUN	JUL	AUG	SEP	OCT	NOV	DEC	TOTAL
1	Emergency Fund													
2	Short-term Goal													
3	Other Goal													
4														
5	TOTAL SAVINGS													
	FIXED EXPENSES													
1														
2	Rent/Mortgage	400	400	400	400	400	400	400	400	400	400	400	400	4,800
3	Fuel													
4	Electricity	50	58	53	48	48	50	65	75	85	50	40	55	677
5	Telephone	56	40	50	38	40	55	25	60	50	45	55	38	552
6	Water													
7	Homeowners Insurance													
8	Automobile Insurance	250			250			250			250			1,000
9	Disability Insurance	90			90			90			90			360
10	Medical Insurance													
11	Life Insurance													
12	Life Insurance													
13	Life Insurance													
14	Personal Property Taxes													
15	Real Estate Taxes													
16	Income Taxes													
17	Automobile Loan	250	250	250	250	250	250	250	250	250	250	250	250	3,000
18	Loan Repayment	75	75	75	75	75	75	75	75	75	75	75	75	900
19	Loan Repayment MasterCard	50	50	50	50	50	50	50	50	50	50	50	50	600
20	Other Debt Visa	50	50	50	50	50	50	50	50	50	50	50	50	600
21	Other Bloomies	35	35	35	35	35	35	35	35	35	35	35	35	420
22														
23	TOTAL FIXED EXPENSES	1,306	958	963	1,286	948	965	1,290	995	995	1,295	955	953	12,909
24	Monthly Average	1,076	1,076	1,076	1,076	1,076	1,076	1,076	1,076	1,076	1,076	1,076	1,076	1,076
25	Difference (Amount to be left in	118	113	128	111	81	81	121	123					
26	fixed expense account)													

FINANCIAL FITNESS FOR NEWLYWEDS

	FLEXIBLE EXPENSES	JAN	FEB	MAR	APR	MAY	JUN	JUL	AUG	SEP	OCT	NOV	DEC	TOTAL
1	Food/Beverage	200	175	225	210	200	175	100	155	180	175	250	300	2,345
2	Clothing	450	120	250		550	85	300		600	65	175	600	3,195
3	Laundry/Cleaning	80	75	85	85	65	180	75	75	65	70	60	150	1,030
4	Home/Office Supplies													
5	Animals	85	25		75	25	150			125		75	150	760
6	Personal Care Toiletries	30	55	40	60	40	55	40	40	50	40	50	75	575
7	Periodicals	225		150		175		225		185		95		1,055
8	Recreation	300	350	380	150	225	475	380	350	300	400	150	500	3,930
9	Entertainment						500							500
10	Travel/Vacations			250			250			250			800	1,550
11	Gifts													
12														
13	**Household Maintenance**													
14	Lawn & Snow Removal													
15	Maid													
16	Garbage													
17	Repairs		250			75			120		85		120	650
18	Home Furnishings													
19	Major Appliance Purchases													
20														
21	**Transportation**													
22	Gas/Oil	100	100	100	100	100	100	100	100	100	100	100	100	1,200
23	Repairs				350		120			250		80		800
24	Licenses & Registration													
25	Commutation, Parking	100	100	100	100	100	100	100	100	100	100	100	100	1,200
26														
27	**Children's Expenses**													
28	Allowances													
29	Lessons													
30	Camp													
31	Recreation/Sports													
32	Child Care—Baby sitting													

HOW TO MANAGE THE MONEY: YOUR BUDGET

		JAN	FEB	MAR	APR	MAY	JUN	JUL	AUG	SEP	OCT	NOV	DEC	TOTAL
33	**Education**													
34	Tuition	250								250				500
35	Room/Board													
36	Books & Supplies													
37	Travel													
38														
39	**Medical Expenses**													
40	Doctor					55			85					140
41	Dentist			45			45				45	45		180
42	Drug													
43														
44	**Contributions**													
45	Church/Synagogue													
46	Other Charity													
47	Total Flexible Expenses	1,820	1,275	1,495	1,045	1,635	2,335	1,320	1,025	2,455	1,080	1,180	2,895	19,610
48														
	TOTAL SAVINGS	0	0	0	0	0	0	0	0	0	0	0	0	0
	TOTAL FLEXIBLE EXPENSES	1,820	1,275	1,495	1,045	1,635	2,335	1,320	1,025	2,455	1,080	1,180	2,895	19,610
	TOTAL FIXED EXPENSES	1,306	958	963	1,286	948	965	1,290	995	995	1,295	955	953	12,909
	TOTAL EXPENSES	3,126	2,233	2,458	2,381	2,583	7,300	2,610	2,020	3,450	2,375	2,135	3,848	32,519
	NET INCOME	2,360	2,360	2,360	2,360	2,360	2,360	2,360	2,360	2,360	2,360	2,360	2,360	28,320
	PROFIT (LOSS)	(766)	127	(98)	(21)	(223)	(940)	(250)	340	(1,090)	(15)	225	(1,488)	(4,199)

FINANCIAL FITNESS FOR NEWLYWEDS

YOU AND THE LAW: WHO OWNS WHAT? 5

"Husband and wife are one . . . and that one is the husband."

That is what common law once held. A woman lost not only her name but her financial identity when she married.

Marriage is a legal union recognized by society through the government. In the United States, each state government sets regulations on wedlock, applying considerations of what is called "public policy." Public policy can and does vary according to current understandings of what society wants or thinks is good for itself. Public policy changes as time goes by.

Take property rights. Until the mid-1800's, public policy decreed that women lost control over their property when they entered into wedlock. Then, late in the 19th century, the Married Women's Property Acts were passed, giving women the right to own property in their names even though they were married.

Only in very recent years have women retained their own names upon marriage. A separate legal identity was extremely rare for a woman.

Today the status of women is changing. It is common to read in a wedding announcement that "the bride will retain her own name." And for the past several generations women have been able to own property without their husbands' say-so.

Generally speaking, each spouse owns whatever he or she brings into the marriage. The man and the woman each have the right to buy or sell "separate property," or to borrow money against it. However, you can lose control of separate property. For instance, if you put your money into a joint bank account it is then presumed, in most states, to belong to both of you—and either of you can take it out of the account.

Community-property laws in eight states

In certain states, however, everything (or almost everything) is fifty-fifty. They have passed community-property laws that say that all money and property—salaries and assets including real estate, furniture, books, or whatever—acquired during marriage are considered the joint community property of both husband and wife. The only exceptions are money and property acquired through inheritance or a gift from a third party. What's more, community property in these states does not carry the right of survivorship. When one spouse dies, the other does not automatically assume full ownership. Each spouse must make disposition of his or her half by a legal will. If there is no will, the laws of the state take over.

Which states have community-property laws? Arizona, California, Idaho, Louisiana, Nevada, New Mexico, Texas, and Washington. Their laws are not all the same, however, so it is important if you live in one of these states to know its particular community-property rules.

It is also possible for you to own community property in a state that does not have such laws. If you once lived in a community-property state and acquired property while there, it remains community property even after you have moved to a "common-law" state. The opposite is not true, however. If either of you owned property while living in a common-law state, and you move to a community-property state, the property does not become community property—worth knowing if either of you works for a big company that is likely to move you around from place to place as your career advances.

Four types of ownership

Whether you are acquiring a house, stocks, bonds, or a bank account, you have a choice, in all common-law states, of any one of these four kinds of ownership:

1. *Separate.* Any individual, whether married or not, may hold title and full ownership. A spouse has no claim on the property. Upon death, it is passed on by the owner's will or by the state's intestate laws if there is no will.
2. *Joint tenant with right of survivorship.* Two or more people jointly hold title and ownership. On the death of any one of the joint tenants, that person's entire interest in the property passes automatically to the survivor or survivors. It does not take a will to make this happen. It is instant and automatic.
3. *Tenants by entirety.* This is a special form of joint ownership between husband and wife. It gives either tenant the right of survivorship upon the death of the other. But there is an important difference: This tenancy can be ended only by mutual consent or by the termination of the marriage. A joint tenancy with right of survivorship, on the other hand, can be ended by any one of the tenants acting unilaterally.
4. *Tenants in common.* This form of ownership involves two or more tenants, each with some proportion of the ownership. Each may sell or donate his or her share, or dispose of it by will.

Which type of ownership is right for you, as a couple? You have to decide. Choosing the right one is important, for it can affect your future. The more property you own, the more attention you should pay to how it is owned. *Note:* You do not have to put all your property into the same type of ownership. Joint tenant with right of survivorship is an easy form and is, of course, the ultimate sign of togetherness.

Tip: If you are setting up Individual Retirement Accounts (IRA's), and if you are *both* working, you will want *separate* ownership rather than *spousal* or *joint* ownership. That way, acting as individuals, you can each put in up to $2,000 each year (as against a total of $2,250 yearly in a spousal account). Another example is the stock market. If you both want to invest in the market, do so under your separate names rather than buying any given stock jointly.

Advantages and disadvantages of joint ownership

You can get a nice cozy feeling of security from jointly owned property. One important advantage is that it permits property to bypass probate. In some states, jointly owned property may be exempt from seizure by creditors of a deceased person. But it has some disadvantages:

- Control is not clear. One spouse may be able to dispose of jointly owned property without the other knowing about it in advance. Obvious example: a joint checking account, against which either party may write checks.
- To sell property, consent is needed. When assets are to be disposed of, both partners are often required to sign documents or approve action. If a spouse becomes disabled or mentally ill, or just plain says "no," this can become sticky. The property can be tied up and you can find yourself going to court to get some kind of legal partition. This can happen with the sale of a house or of stocks and bonds.
- The death of a spouse can create problems. In many states, banks must tie up joint accounts upon the death of either party. Jointly held safe-deposit boxes may be sealed, pending settlement of the estate. The laws vary from state to state, so it's smart to know whether accounts and boxes could be frozen where you live; it could make sense to keep separate bank accounts.

Some people think joint ownership means you will save on estate taxes. Not necessarily. Under the Economic Recovery Tax Act of 1981, one half of all jointly held property is included in the estate of the first spouse to die, regardless of who paid for it. The law also provides an unlimited marital deduction, however, so there are no estate taxes on the amount you leave to your spouse, no matter the size of the estate. However, some states do limit marital deductions, so you should check on the law in the state where you live.

As your assets increase and you acquire a home, more furniture, cars, stocks and bonds and other investments, the question of who owns what will become more and more important. *Choosing the right kind of ownership can become difficult.* A lawyer or accountant who knows the federal and local estate and property laws will be able to help you make the right decisions.

Note: Because credit laws are so extensive and varied, they have not been discussed in this chapter. (See Chapter 7 on Banks, Bankers, and Banking.)

You can change later

The way you set up ownership at the start of your marriage does not mean that everything is set in concrete. You can change later. Even the deed on your house can be changed. If one of you already owns a house, for example, you can make your spouse a joint owner when you marry.

Tip: Before making any change in the kind of ownership you are using, check the tax consequences. Talk with a lawyer or accountant who knows tax law and who can look at the specifics of your situation and tell you which kind of ownership gives you the greatest advantages.

Do you need a premarital financial agreement?

It all depends. It depends on the answers to questions like these:

- Does either of you own stocks or bonds or real estate that have market value?
- Is either of you the owner or part owner of a business?
- Is either of you already well along in a career with a company that has vested you in a pension plan?
- Do you have other assets—substantial savings, collectibles, quality furniture—that you are bringing to the marriage?

Most couples getting married in their early to mid-twenties do not have enough assets to justify a premarital agreement. Most couples in their upper twenties or early thirties do have enough—especially if it is a second marriage for either partner.

WHEN VALERIE AND JAMES NICHOLS GOT MARRIED . . .

. . . all the assets they had together in the entire world fit into Valerie's beat-up ten-year-old Volvo. Stereo, musical instruments, clothing, wedding gifts, kitchen utensils—they didn't need a premarital financial agreement to haul the stuff to their first home.

CATHY AND PATRICK McQUARTER WERE IN THE SAME BOAT . . .

In their Chicago apartment that first three months, their assets consisted of a camp stove and an ice chest. Later, Cathy inherited family heirloom furniture from her grandmother. If she had had that furniture before they were married, it would have been a good idea to work out a premarital financial agreement that made it clear—and legal—that it was all hers and would remain hers regardless of future conditions.

THE BAROMETER OF FINANCIAL FITNESS: YOUR NET WORTH

6

Before you can begin to plan anything, you've got to know just where you stand—right now. And then as you move along in the future, you will need to know where you are financially.

This chapter is to help you see where you are now and to show you how to keep track of where you are over all the years of your marriage and financial partnership.

The two key words are: *net worth*. They sound like something bookkeepers and accountants talk about when they figure out how a business stands. They also make up a phrase that life insurance sales people use when they are analyzing what kind of coverage they recommend.

Why is it important for a newly married couple to know their net worth? Let me answer that by explaining exactly what your net worth is. It is the difference between your assets and your liabilities or debts: the difference between all the money and tangibles that you possess and all the unpaid bills, outstanding loans, taxes, and other obligations you may have. You'll get descriptive details on all that in this chapter. But the basic point I want to make, up front, is that if you don't know your net worth you haven't got a marriage or financial partnership.

So what you've both got to figure out is: Just what is our net worth? What is the difference between what we have and what we owe?

You can do this as individuals or as a couple—or both ways. For the purposes of this chapter, let's consider your net worth as a couple.

Some tough questions

Ask yourselves questions like these:

- Are we saving any money? Are our savings growing?
- Have we started making any investments? Are *they* growing?
- Are our investments producing income?
- Are we in debt? How much? Too much?
- Are we keeping up with inflation? Or ahead of it?

You cannot answer such questions unless you know your net worth. It is the basis for any sound strategy for savings and investment. And in the years ahead it will be the basis for your retirement planning and estate planning—two subjects that may seem far in the future but that you will want to start thinking about before too long.

Knowing your net worth at any time can give you real security both now and in the future. Why? Because, if it shows positive signs, you know you have a realistic basis on which to make financial decisions about investments, home buying, raising a family. And if it shows negative signs, you know where you must reduce debt, change investments, or hold off on decisions that cost money.

As I said, your net worth is the difference between your assets and your liabilities, or debts. Let's talk first about assets.

What are all your "pluses"?

Turn to Worksheet VI on pages 45–46. As accurately as you can, write down the actual value of all your assets—money in checking accounts, savings accounts, money market funds; or such securities as stocks, bonds or mutual funds.

> *Note:* Except for regular checking accounts, these are all *income-producing assets*. They pay you *interest* or *dividends* on a regular periodic basis (usually quarterly), and at a fixed rate of percentage.

Next, write down the value of any real estate you own. This should be the current market value if you were to sell it today. Put down the cash value of any whole life insurance policies (see Chapter 10) you have (not the "face value" that the policy would pay in case of death, but the amount you would get back if you simply turned in the policy today and stopped paying for it; this is shown in a table in the policy itself). And add any other long-term assets, as shown on the worksheet.

Personal property comes next. This is the value of your car—even if it's a Rustbucket Special—your furniture, clothing, jewelry, collections, whatever.

> *Note:* These are *non-income-producing assets*. Unlike savings or investments, they just sit there.

But, it is to be hoped, some—such as silver or precious gems (diamonds, for example), or collections (books or stamps maybe)—will increase in real value as times goes by. They are *appreciating*.

Some thoughts about assets

- *Income* is a key word when you talk about assets. Always be sure you know whether an asset is going to produce income and, if so, how much. If it is definitely a non-income-producing asset, be aware of whether it does, nevertheless, appreciate over time. Some boats, for instance, actually appreciate. Most automobiles do not. Houses usually do, as does most real estate.
- *Needs* change. What you are doing at various stages of life will dictate what you want your assets to do for you. At times your income from wages or salary will be all you need. But when your children hit college age, or when you retire, extra income from assets may come in handy—very handy. Assets have to be evaluated as needs and circumstances change.
- *Insurance* is a bargain when you're young. See Chapter 10 for details on insurance, but let's say here and now that if you buy insurance at a young age you not only buy protection against bad news but you start to build up cash surrender values that will be important future assets. Some parents have paid for entire college educations by borrowing on cash surrender values in insurance policies they bought when the college students were babes in arms.
- *Income-producing assets* may not be your thing right now. Probably you are both working and producing two salaries, but chances are you find it important to spend what you can on non-income-producing assets for the time being—until you have the home and furnishings you want, for instance, or until you've got the car or have done the traveling that you had planned. But do think about the insurance, because those rates go up just as regularly as your birthdays come around.
- *Planning* is vital. Think and talk together about what assets you want and what you want them to give you—your home, those college educations.

Worksheet VI: Yours
NET WORTH STATEMENT

Date_____

ASSETS	Monetary Value	Owner of Asset

Current Assets

Checking Account_____ _____

Savings Account_____ _____

Credit Union Accounts_____ _____

Money Market Funds_____ _____

CD's_____ _____

Treasury Bills_____ _____

Treasury Notes_____ _____

Securities

Stocks_____ _____

Bonds_____ _____

Mutual Funds_____ _____

Real Estate

Residence_____ _____

Recreational Property_____ _____

Income Property_____ _____

Long Term

Insurance_____ _____

Annuities_____ _____

Pensions_____ _____

Profit Sharing Plans_____ _____

Individual Retirement Accounts_____ _____

Business Interests_____ _____

THE BAROMETER OF FINANCIAL FITNESS: YOUR NET WORTH

Personal Property	Monetary Value	Owner of Asset
Home Furnishings		
Automobiles		
Clothing & Furs		
Jewelry		
Antiques		
Stamp Collection		
Coins		
Fine Art		

TOTAL ASSETS _____

LIABILITIES OR CREDIT OBLIGATIONS

Current Liabilities:	Amount Due	Obligator
Medical & Dental		
Current Bills		
Charge Accounts		

Unpaid Taxes

Capital Gains		
Federal		
State		
Local		

Real Estate (see 8.)

Residence		
Recreational		
Income Property		

Other Dept or Installment Debt (see 8.)

Automobile Loans		
Home Improvement Loans		
Education Loans		
Life Insurance Loans		
Margin Accounts		
Bank Loans		
Credit Cards		

TOTAL ASSETS _____
TOTAL LIABILITIES _____
NET WORTH _____

- *Assets are not set in concrete.* There's no law against selling off certain assets. You don't have to stay in the same house, hold onto the same collectibles, stick with the same securities. If assets are large, your insurance, retirement insurance, and retirement assets can be smaller. If all other assets are small, your insurance and retirement accounts should be larger. Since no two couples are in quite the same boat, you have to analyze your own situation and make your own decision.
- *How much are things worth?* A dealer or appraiser can tell you the current value of a car, a diamond, a rare stamp, an antique doll. A reputable specialized magazine may include listings you can depend on. Your daily newspaper will tell you today's market value of stocks, bonds, and mutual funds. A reliable real estate broker can give you a pretty good fix on the value of your home, if you already own one. And check your local paper for ads giving prices for comparable houses.

How much do you owe?

Now for the liabilities. Start with current bills. List everything you have been billed for but have not yet paid—as of today. Put down any taxes that are unpaid, including all that have not been deducted from your paycheck (federal or state income tax), any capital gains tax, real estate taxes, personal property taxes on a car or boat.

If you now own a house or condominium or vacation home, write down the unpaid balance on the mortgage. What about installment debt? Whatever you currently owe to MasterCard, VISA, American Express, or other rotating charge accounts should be listed. Add the unpaid balances on loans for a car, home improvement, education, or life insurance, or other personal loans.

Check and double-check. Make sure you have listed every asset and every liability that exists in your lives.

Now total each column—assets and liabilities. Subtract the liabilities from the assets. The result is your net worth as of today.

Note: If your liabilities turn out to be greater than your assets, you have a "negative net worth"—a precarious situation that should command your immediate attention.

Repeat—how often?

You can't go back and redo your Net Worth Statement weekly or even monthly to reflect the fluctuations that are bound to occur. But you should remember to revise it whenever your major needs and situations change. When you buy a new car, sign for a mortgage on a house or condo, inherit securities, become vested in an employee profit-sharing plan, put savings into an IRA, you should dust off the Net Worth Statement and see how it all stacks up under the new conditions.

By all means, review it at least once a year. It is indeed the barometer of your financial situation. Before you make any major decision, a look at your Net Worth Statement can give you a sound basis for figuring out which way to go.

THE McQUARTERS' NET WORTH . . .

In the five years of their marriage, Cathy and Patrick have been able to put some $18,000 into savings. All of it has been kept in their money market account, ready to use in buying their house. They still owe $2,000 on the car they bought a couple of years ago, but the refrigerator that was their first big purchase together has long since been paid off.

. . . AND THE BUCKS' . . .

Jane and Chris are realizing what "negative net worth" means. Their assets, counting the small amount of cash in the bank and the market value of their furniture and car, come to $10,500. Current bills now sitting on top of the desk add up to $950. Outstanding debts? Plenty. Some $10,800 counting their credit card accounts and bank loan.

And, of course, their assets are entirely in non-income-producing things—not in savings or investments that produce income. They have not saved a penny. Their negative net worth is $1,250.

Worksheet VI: Example One
The McQuarters
NET WORTH STATEMENT

Date __4/15/84__

ASSETS	Monetary Value	Owner of Asset
Current Assets		
Checking Account	750	joint
Savings Account	500	joint
Credit Union Accounts		
Money Market Funds	3,000	joint
CD's		
Treasury Bills		
Treasury Notes		
Securities		
Stocks		
Bonds		
Mutual Funds		
Real Estate		
Residence	57,000	joint
Recreational Property		
Income Property		
Long Term		
Insurance		
Annuities		
Pensions		
Profit Sharing Plans		
Individual Retirement Accounts	1,000	Patrick
Business Interests		

Personal Property	Monetary Value	Owner of Asset
Home Furnishings	5,000	joint
Automobiles	5,000	Cathy
Clothing & Furs		
Jewelry		
Antiques		
Stamp Collection		
Coins		
Fine Art		

TOTAL ASSETS 72,250

LIABILITIES OR CREDIT OBLIGATIONS

Current Liabilities:	Amount Due	Obligator
Medical & Dental		
Current Bills	800	joint
Charge Accounts		

Unpaid Taxes

Capital Gains		
Federal		
State		
Local		

Real Estate (see 8.)

Residence	45,000	joint
Recreational		
Income Property		

Other Dept or Installment Debt (see 8.)

Automobile Loans	2,000	Cathy
Home Improvement Loans		
Education Loans		
Life Insurance Loans		
Margin Accounts		
Bank Loans		
Credit Cards		

Total Liabilities 47,800
TOTAL ASSETS 72,250
TOTAL LIABILITIES 47,800
NET WORTH 24,450

THE BAROMETER OF FINANCIAL FITNESS: YOUR NET WORTH

Worksheet VI: Example Two
The Bucks
NET WORTH STATEMENT

Date_____

ASSETS	Monetary Value	Owner of Asset
Current Assets		
Checking Account	500	joint
Savings Account		
Credit Union Accounts		
Money Market Funds		
CD's		
Treasury Bills		
Treasury Notes		
Securities		
Stocks		
Bonds		
Mutual Funds		
Real Estate		
Residence		
Recreational Property		
Income Property		
Long Term		
Insurance		
Annuities		
Pensions		
Profit Sharing Plans		
Individual Retirement Accounts		
Business Interests		

Personal Property	Monetary Value	Owner of Asset
Home Furnishings	8,500	joint
Automobiles	1,500	Chris
Clothing & Furs		
Jewelry		
Antiques		
Stamp Collection		
Coins		
Fine Art		

TOTAL ASSETS 10,500

LIABILITIES OR CREDIT OBLIGATIONS

Current Liabilities:	Amount Due	Obligator
Medical & Dental		
Current Bills	950	joint
Charge Accounts		

Unpaid Taxes

Capital Gains		
Federal		
State		
Local		

Real Estate (see 8.)

Residence		
Recreational		
Income Property		

Other Dept or Installment Debt (see 8.)

Automobile Loans		
Home Improvement Loans		
Education Loans		
Life Insurance Loans		
Margin Accounts		
Bank Loans	10,800	joint
Credit Cards		

TOTAL ASSETS 10,500
TOTAL LIABILITIES 11,750
NET WORTH (1,250)

THE BAROMETER OF FINANCIAL FITNESS: YOUR NET WORTH

BANKS, BANKERS, AND BANKING   7

Chances are, the two of you are starting a new relationship with a bank. Maybe in a new city or town, where you are unknown.

How do you decide on a bank?

Shop around. Ask people what bank they use. Are they satisfied with the service in general? Does their bank make many goofs? Are the lines long on Friday? Do they get service from knowledgeable tellers and people "on the platform" (i.e., the area where the bank officers' desks are) or are they shunted around from one person to another before getting answers to questions?

Take time to go into two or three banks that you are considering. You'll discover there really is a difference among banks—in service, in courtesy, in atmosphere and attitude.

Get to know your banker

It is important to establish a relationship not just with your bank but with a banker in your bank. When you are opening an account or considering opening one, ask to meet an assistant vice president. Call and make a business appointment by phone. Dress appropriately, and be sure to take along any papers, such as paycheck stubs, that can show your credit worthiness. After you get to know an officer, keep in touch with him or her regularly. This relationship will come in handy when:

- you need a loan or want to get an all-purpose credit card (such as VISA or MasterCard)
- you seek a "bridge" loan to cover the down payment on a new home but cannot provide it because your old home has not yet been sold
- you want the bank to waive a penalty charge on an overdrawn account
- you seek credit with foreign banks
- you want to buy travelers' checks.

What kind of account?

While you are looking over several banks, find out about their charges for checking accounts. Some offer "free" or "no-strings" checking. But this may mean you have to maintain a monthly minimum balance if you want to avoid a service charge. That could mean your money is in a non-interest-bearing account, so that in reality you would be losing interest that the money could earn. Some banks charge a monthly service fee plus a charge for each check you write.

Try to figure out how much you will use the checking account—how many checks you are likely to write each month, how many deposits will be coming in—so you can predict what your costs will be and thus figure out which kind of account will serve you best and cost you least.

Two important angles to know about:

1. *The NOW (for Negotiable Order of Withdrawal) account.* This account pays interest on the money you have in it—but there are strings attached. You have to maintain a minimum balance. (How much? That depends on the account you select when you set it up.) If you fail to maintain that balance, the bank charges you a service charge. In fact, most banks automatically check your balance at the end of each day, and charge you the service fee if the balance is below the minimum even for that one day. The fees vary from bank to bank: Some charge you for each check written during the month when your balance dropped below the minimum, others charge the fee only on those checks written while your balance was low. Some pay no interest during all of, or some part of, the period when your account was below the required minimum. Obviously, the way to avoid all service charges is to keep the required minimum balance in your NOW account.

Example: Say you set up a NOW account on which you are to maintain a $1,000 minimum balance and the bank is to pay five percent. But you drop below the minimum and your average balance is $900. This would earn you $3.75 per month ($900 × 5% ÷ 12). If the bank's service charge were $5, you would lose $1.25. Better to be in a checking account that pays no interest or has a small service charge.

Note: Some people set up a NOW account in addition to a savings account that pays a higher yield (i.e., more interest). Then, if the NOW account falls below its minimum required balance, they transfer money into it from the higher-yield account. This doesn't make an awful lot of sense, however, because they then lose interest that the high-yield account would have paid.

2. *Cash reserve.* Banks have various names—some cute and clever—for this system. What happens is this: The bank checks your credit rating and issues you a "line of credit" in connection with your checking account. If you overdraw your account, whether inadvertently or on purpose, you dip into the cash reserve. In effect, you instantly borrow from the bank to cover the amount you have overdrawn. Your cash reserve will have a limit, determined by your discussion with the bank officer when you set it up and the bank's judgment of how much they think you can safely be allowed to borrow. The bank charges you a finance charge and expects you to pay back a certain percentage of your total "cash reserve in use" each month.

Cash reserve can come in mighty handy. It can enable you to take advantage of a bargain price on a major item when you find it on sale. It can help you cover an emergency situation—for example, having to buy an airline ticket because someone suddenly becomes ill, and you have to make a trip you had not planned for. But if you are using cash reserve every month to pay monthly bills—a habit and a trap that many, many people have fallen into—you are overextending yourselves.

Tip: Check on how different banks set up cash reserve accounts. Some lend you the exact amount of the overdrawn check, then repay it in full, and charge you interest, out of your next deposit. Say you have zero in your checking account. You write a check for $125. As soon as that check gets back to your bank, the bank pays it—advancing you the $125. Then you come along and make a deposit of $200. The bank immediately repays itself the $125 plus interest covering the time while the $125 was borrowed. Now you have your full line of credit again.

Other banks lend you your cash reserve in increments of $100. So if you write the check for $125, the bank automatically lends you $200 as soon as your check comes in. It may also expect you to repay in monthly amounts of $25. Thus the bank makes you borrow more than you need and repay over a longer period. **Result:** You pay more interest. You do, of course, have the choice of paying back the borrowed amount in full at any time.

Don't ignore a bank statement

Some people chuck each bank statement into a desk drawer as soon as it arrives, figuring they will get around to it sooner or later. When later comes—maybe several months later—you can find a pile of bank statements and a situation that is puzzling, confusing, and maybe even costly. Sometimes no one pays attention to the statement until a notice arrives saying the account is overdrawn. This means paying a service charge for each overdraft and going through a highly embarrassing process of corrections.

Your bank gives you 10 days to let them know if you do not agree with the statement. So it is important to spend a few minutes each month making sure that neither you nor your bank has made any mistakes. Here's what to do:

1. Look at the lower right-hand corner of every check and make sure the bank has encoded the same amount you wrote the check for. The encoded amount is in those funny-looking computer numbers printed in magnetic ink. This is one of the few places where human error can creep into the process, since human eyes have to look at what you wrote on the check, then record that amount correctly; after that, your check is just a piece of paper flying through complex computerized equipment that deducts the amount from your balance and prints out your statement.

2. Make sure the amount of each deposit has been entered correctly on your statement. This is just about the only other place where human error can sneak in.

3. Line up the checks in order according to their numbers (some banks that have sophisticated equipment put them in sequence in your statement envelope; most banks still leave them in the order in which they arrived in the bank).

4. Put a mark on each stub in your checkbook for each check that has come back.

5. On the back of your bank statement (almost all banks imprint a form for this purpose) list all checks that are outstanding (i.e., checks not returned with your statement).

6. Add up the amounts of all outstanding checks.

7. To the balance shown on the bank statement, add any deposits you have made that are shown in your checkbook but were not in time to appear on this statement.

8. Deduct the total of checks outstanding. This gives you your current balance from the bank's viewpoint.

9. From the balance in your checkbook, deduct any service charge or finance charge (if, for instance, you have used cash reserve). This gives you your balance from your checkbook's point of view.

10. See if the bank and your checkbook agree. If they do not, you should talk with someone "on the platform" at the bank.

Important: Don't forget your dealings with Automatic Teller Machines (ATMs). When you withdraw money from the hardware in the wall, it's easy to forget to enter that withdrawal in your checkbook. Consternation and misery can result. (See exhibits 1 and 2 on pages 55 and 56.)

That machine in the wall

As a matter of fact, the ATM, combined with the EFT (Electronic Fund Transfer) and your PIN (Personal Identification Number) can take you right through the looking glass into the wonderland of the checkless society. You can, if you want, do all your banking without ever talking to or dealing with a teller. Make deposits, get cash, pay bills, transfer funds from one account to another—it's all possible with the ATM.

(Footnote to banking history: In 1983, Citibank in New York tried to impose on its customers a rule that, if they kept less than a certain minimum balance in checking accounts, they would be *required* to use only the ATM to handle the transactions they had always done with tellers over the banking counter, and would be refused the services of tellers. This was a public-relations goof of the first magnitude, as customers reacted vigorously with protests over this "inhuman" treatment. Citibank soon lifted the restriction on dealing with real live tellers.)

Tips on using the ATM:

1. Enter every ATM transaction in your checkbook, the sooner the better. This is a *must*. If you find you are the type who just can't keep track of

Exhibit 1
BANK STATEMENT

FROM 7/24/83
TO 8/24/83
PAGE

Valerie and James Nichols

STATEMENT OF ACCOUNTS

BEGINNING BALANCE		DEPOSITS AND ADVANCES TOTAL AMOUNT	NO		CHECKS AND PAYMENTS TOTAL AMOUNT	NO		SERVICE CHARGE		ENDING BALANCE
100.00	+	1,260.00	3	−	820.75	11	−	3.20	=	536.05

Refer to reverse side for explanation of identification codes (ID)

DEBITS — CHECKS, WITHDRAWALS & TRANSFERS

CHECK NO.	DATE	AMOUNT	ID	ACTIVITY CHARGE
594	8/1	36.75		
595	8/3	62.50		
596	8/4	81.20		
597	8/6	44.36		
598	8/8	320.00		
599	8/12	136.64		
600	8/18	30.50		
601	8/20	24.80		
ATM	8/21	25.00		
ATM	8/22	40.00		
603	8/24	19.00		
b.c.	8/24	3.20		

Money Market Savings Account 109204376
Average monthly Interest Rate 9.02%

CREDITS — DEPOSITS & TRANSFERS
DAILY BALANCE LISTED IN DATE ORDER

DATE	AMOUNT	ID	BALANCE	ID
OPENING BALANCE			100.00	
			63.25	
8/3	425.00		425.75	
			344.55	
8/6	375.00		675.19	
			355.19	
			218.55	
			188.05	
			163.25	
			138.25	
			98.25	
8/23	460.00		539.25	
			536.05	
7/24			4,536.09	
8/3 deposit	425.00		4,961.09	
8/10 deposit	375.00		5,336.09	
8/15 deposit	250.00		5,586.09	
8/20 deposit	450.00		6,036.09	
8/24 interest	45.37		6,081.46	

BANKS, BANKERS, AND BANKING 55

Exhibit 2
Reconciling Your Checking Account

Before you start, make sure that all checks, withdrawals and deposits appear on this statement as you have them in your checkbook.

In your checkbook, subtract any automatic withdrawals, service or other charges that appear on this statement. Also, add in any automatic deposits and, if applicable, NOW account interest shown on this statement.

Then proceed as follows:

1. At the right, enter the **Ending Balance** shown on this statement.

2. List in **Deposits Not Credited** any deposits you have made that do not appear on this statement. Total them and add to the Ending Balance in the space provided.

3. List in **Unpaid Checks** any checks you have written and automatic teller withdrawals you have made that do not appear on this statement. Total them and subtract from the Total above.

4. The resulting **Balance** should agree with your checkbook balance.

Ending Balance $ __536.05__

Deposits Not Credited

Amount	Amount

Enter Deposit Total and add to above   (+) _____

TOTAL _____

Unpaid Checks

Check Number	Amount	Check Number	Amount
602	60.00		

Checkbook Balance $499.25
service charge   3.20
* $496.05*
outstanding
check   +60.00
* $556.05*

Enter Check Total and subtract from above   ( ) __60.00__

Balance $ __476.05__

THE CONNECTICUT BANK AND TRUST COMPANY, N.A.

---

such things, do not use the ATM. Stick to plain old-fashioned check writing.

2. Take your receipt when the machine spits it out. Keep it in a safe place—a box or large envelope. It is your only record of the transaction.

3. If you are using EFTs, be sure to reconcile your bank statement. It is a) your proof of payment to the other party, b) your record for tax purposes, and c) your way of checking and reconciling those EFT transactions and your bank balance. If you find any discrepancy between your bank statement and your checkbook that results from an EFT, you must notify the bank within 60 days after your statement is mailed. If you fail to do so, and if the bank can show that it could have prevented the loss if you had contacted it, you may have to take the loss. In other words, the checkless society puts the burden of monitoring the system on you, the customer of the bank.

4. If you lose your ATM card or if you think it may have been stolen, you will be liable for no more than $50 of loss *if you contact the bank within two business days*. Otherwise, you can be held responsible for losses up to $500.

5. Never lend anyone your ATM card. That's asking for trouble.

FINANCIAL FITNESS FOR NEWLYWEDS

Savings accounts

Money in a checking account is like cash in your pocket. It burns a hole. It will be spent.

Having at least one savings account is a must. Open one when you open your checking account or accounts. And start the habit of paying yourself immediately after payday by putting money into your reserve for emergency fund and fixed expenses.

1. *Passbook savings.* This is the old standby. Its chief advantage is that your money is available any time you want it, without your paying any penalty for taking it out. Its disadvantage is that it doesn't pay as much interest as other types of accounts, so the idea is to save in a passbook account until you have enough saved to move it into a *money market account*—minimum balance, $2,500. Not all passbook accounts are alike, so:

- Shop around to see where you can get the best deal on interest.
- Watch out for evaporation: Some banks impose a $5 service charge every month on accounts with less than a $300 balance (if you have $100 in a passbook account in such a bank and you forget it for a year, you will have $40 in the account).
- Ask how interest is credited: Is it compounded annually, semiannually, quarterly, or daily? The answer tells you where you will get the highest *effective yield*, or total interest paid on the account. (How do you figure out *compound interest?* To your balance, or principal amount, you add the interest earned for the period—year, half-year, month, or day—to get a new principal amount. Then calculate the interest on *that*, and add it, for still another new principal. Obviously, the more frequently the interest is compounded, the higher the effective yield. What you want, ideally, is interest compounded daily from day of deposit to day of withdrawal.)
- Check also on *when* interest is credited. In some banks, even though compounding is daily, the money earned may not be credited to your account until the end of a three-month period. If you withdraw money before it is credited, you can lose the interest on it for the entire three-month period. Again, day-of-deposit to day-of-withdrawal compounding is what you want.

2. *Money market account.* Once you have accumulated $2,500 in a regular passbook account, transfer it to a money market account. Introduced in December 1982, these accounts require, by law, a minimum balance of $2,500. Key points to be aware of:

- You will be permitted only six withdrawals per month—a maximum of three checks and three automatic transactions.
- You have instant access to the account and you incur no penalties.
- Banks may determine their own rates of interest, based on what they consider to be market conditions, so careful shopping around is called for.
- Banks may not *guarantee* a rate of interest for longer than one month. Most guarantee by the week; this keeps them competitive with the popular money market funds on Wall Street.
- The chief advantage is that you can have your money market account in the same bank as your checking account and transfer funds when you need them, thus earning interest until you need to use the cash.
- If your balance in the money market account drops below the $2,500 minimum, the rate of interest paid by the bank will be at the level of its passbook savings rate.

3. *CD's or TD's.* Certificates of deposit or time deposits are also worth considering. With these, you are committed to keeping a certain amount of money on deposit for a minimum period. These fixed-term savings were deregulated on Oct. 1, 1983. Every bank may now set its own minimum investment size and interest rate; and while there used to be specific time limits, you may now purchase a certificate for virtually any term you want—from three months to 10 years. You may also decide on the maturity date you want. Want a certificate to mature on your wedding anniversary or on a child's birthday? Just say so when you're buying it. You may select the term or the interest rate and the bank will design a certificate to match what you want.

Deregulated investments demand close scrutiny.

Take the time to read the bank advertisements and ask hard questions. The choices are many, and so are the decisions you will have to make.

Tip: with deregulation, the penalties that used to be imposed if you withdrew your money before the maturity date have been relaxed. They are far less severe.

Four checking and savings tips

1. Find the checking account that best suits you . . . and be sure you both agree on it. Probably best: a regular non-interest checking account, where you maintain a low balance and transfer money from savings as you need it.

2. Establish the account that fits your personalities and lifestyle. If you know you are likely to dip into a savings account that you have set up for your mid-term goals, put the money in a different bank from the one where your checking is, or that is far enough away to make it inconvenient. Then force yourselves to deposit but not withdraw.

3. Remember: You are a valuable customer. You may feel like "just a small depositor," but, as your earnings increase and your borrowing power increases, your relationship with a bank will be valuable not only to you but to the bank. If the relationship is good, chances are that the bank will be where you apply for your mortgage, future business loans, auto loans, and so on.

4. Remember that the U.S. government insures each account for $100,000. It insures all accounts owned by an individual "in the same capacity and the same right." This means you can actually obtain several times that $100,000 of insurance by opening accounts in various capacities and rights at the same bank. Here's how you can stretch the coverage to five accounts insured for $500,000:

Husband (account in own name)	$100,000
Wife (account in own name)	100,000
Husband & wife (joint account)	100,000
Husband, in trust for wife	100,000
Wife, in trust for husband	100,000
	$500,000

Exhibit 3
COMPOUND INTEREST CHART

Investing small amounts of money over time can prove to be very profitable. The chart below shows the effect of $1,200 per year ($100 per month) invested at varying rates compounded annually.

End of Year Values	8%	10%	12%
5th year	$7,603	$8,059	$8,538
10th year	18,774	21,037	23,586
20th year	59,307	75,602	96,838
30th year	146,815	217,131	324,351
40th year	335,737	584,222	1,030,971

Exhibit 4
CHECKBOOK REGISTER

RECORD ALL CHARGES OR CREDITS THAT AFFECT YOUR ACCOUNT

NUMBER	DATE	DESCRIPTION OF TRANSACTION	PAYMENT/DEBIT (−)	√T	FEE (IF ANY) (−)	DEPOSIT/CREDIT (+)	BALANCE $100.00
594	8/1	✓ Pet Shop	36 75			425 00	36 75 / 488 25
595	8/3	✓ Food Store	62 50				62 50 / 425 75
596	8/4	✓ Clothing Mart	81 20			375 00	81 20 / 719 55
597	8/6	✓ A.B.C. Corp.	24 36				24 36 / 695 19
598	8/8	✓ Rent	320 00				320 00 / 375 19
599	8/12	✓ Car Payment	136 64				136 64 / 238 55
600	8/18	✓ Electric	30 50				30 50 / 208 05
601	8/20	✓ Telephone	24 80				24 80 / 183 25
ATM	8/21	✓ Cash - lunches	25 00				25 00 / 158 25
602	8/22	Oil Co. - Car	60 00				60 00 / 98 25
ATM	8/23	✓ Cash - dinner - movie	40 00				40 00 / 58 25
603	8/24	✓ Pizza Joint	19 00			460 00	19 00 / 499 25
604	8/26	Food Store	35 00				35 00 / 464 25

REMEMBER TO RECORD AUTOMATIC PAYMENTS/DEPOSITS ON DATE AUTHORIZED.

COMPOUND INTEREST IS HELPING BUY THE McQUARTERS' HOUSE...

They started saving $200 a month soon after they were married. They've been really self-disciplined about not touching that savings account, and they've upped their own ante whenever either of them got a raise. Now, five years later, and after an average effective yield of 10 percent each year, they have $18,000 ready for down payment and closing fees.

BANKS, BANKERS, AND BANKING

Exhibit 5
CHECK ENCODING MISTAKE

VALERIE NICHOLS HAS A SHARP EYE FOR FIGURES . . .

. . . but she couldn't figure out what was wrong when her bank statement showed a deduction of $44.36 although she had not written any check for $44.36. Filling out the back of the statement, she found that her balance was $20 off—she had $20 less than she thought she should have. After slowly going bananas for most of an evening, she took checkbook and statements around to the bank the next day. There a service assistant found that check number 597, written to the ABC Corporation, had been incorrectly encoded by a clerk in the bank's "back room." Instead of imprinting $24.36 in magnetic ink in the lower right-hand corner of the check, the clerk had imprinted $44.36, and from there on the computerized check-reading and posting equipment blithely took $20 more from Valerie's account than it should have.

---

60   FINANCIAL FITNESS FOR NEWLYWEDS

DEBT: HOW TO GET INTO IT, AND OUT AGAIN— WITHOUT GETTING HURT

8

It's all so beautiful and shiny and fresh. You have unwrapped the wedding gifts and set them out to admire. Your eyes feast on the crystal bowls, the toaster, the automatic coffee maker, the bone china, the stainless steel. Lovely!

But the surroundings: the apartment you had before you got married, the hand-me-down sofa that your folks used in their first apartment!

After a few days or weeks in this setting, you are leafing together through the magazines, dreaming over beautiful new furniture. On Saturday, it's easy to make a trip through the shopping mall "just to look." Then comes the dialogue:

"I'd really feel better about entertaining if that living room looked better."

"We could just do the living room—and still sleep on the mattress on the floor in the bedroom. And those bureaus your brother bought at Goodwill his freshman year—we can live with those for a while."

"Why not use some of the wedding money? We can charge the rest."

New sofa, chairs, tables, lamps, a special unit for the stereo and TV, draperies, and a beautiful new carpet—it all makes the living room look great and the bedroom look worse than ever. Result: by the time the new bed moves in, with his and her chests and a couple of bedside tables, the goal of a vacation next year is out the window. Monthly payments now go to paying off the furniture. Nothing goes into savings. The dialogue now goes like this:

"We just got caught up in the decorating. We forgot about tomorrow."

"We thought we could find a way to handle the payments. But it doesn't look like we can."

This is the kind of trap into which many newlyweds have fallen. It has been easy to fall into it— the trap of overextended credit—because the world has been on a spending spree throughout your lifetimes. At least, the world you and I know has—the world of the U.S. dollar. Credit has been easy to get. Anyone who wants to buy now and pay later has been welcome to do so, and in fact everyone has been encouraged to do just that. I won't bore you with a litany of the instant gratifications of de-

DEBT: HOW TO GET INTO IT, AND OUT AGAIN—WITHOUT GETTING HURT 61

sires that we have all become used to. It's a world in which you can have what you want when you want it and somehow find a way to pay the price.

Credit is nothing new. Debt goes back hundreds of years. Shakespeare talked of borrowers and lenders. Dickens saw Mr. Micawber in and out of debtors' prison. But *consumer* credit as a system of borrowing and repaying really began in this country in 1856 when Isaac Singer hit upon the idea of time payments—$5 down and $5 a month—to sell his $125 sewing machines at a time when the average American's annual income was $525.

Singer's system generated sales that never could have been achieved if people had had to pay cash. Over the years, buying big-ticket items "on time" and paying for them while you used them became standard for millions of Americans. It also created a vast industry that includes bank loan departments, credit unions, General Motors Acceptance Corporation, loan sharks, and countless others.

For the purposes of this chapter, by the way, credit means credit as handled by such organizations as I've just mentioned. I'm *not* talking about home mortgages.

All-purpose credit cards are a more recent phenomenon. Diner's Club started it all, in 1950. The total outstanding debt of American consumers then stood at $21.5 billion. Thirty years later—with American Express, VISA, MasterCard and many others in line with Diner's Club—the figure had reached over $300 billion.

Renting money

What is credit? It is a means of renting money when you need it and for as long as you need it. It is just as practical as renting a car or a U-Haul trailer or a chain saw. Rental firms charge a rental fee; credit firms charge you interest. When interest rates rise, you pay the lender more for the money you borrow, just as you would pay more for the trailer or chain saw if the rental company raised its rates.

There are two basic types of consumer credit:

1. *Open-ended or "revolving" credit.* This is the type you can use over and over again, usually up to a certain borrowing limit that is arranged in advance. It includes such credit cards as VISA, MasterCard, American Express and Diner's Club; department store charge cards; and cash reserve on your checking account. *Note:* VISA and MasterCard, and perhaps some others, have a way of sending you a notice, after you have proved that you are a dependable repayer, informing you that because you are so good they have increased the amount you are permitted to charge at any one time. Be wary of this trap. Make your own decisions about what your limits are.

2. *Installment loan credit.* Here you borrow a specific amount for a specific purpose and pay it back over a specific period, with due dates agreed upon. This type of loan is used for big-ticket items: automobiles, boats, mobile homes or recreation vehicles, home improvements.

Where can you borrow?

- *Small loan companies.* Also known as consumer finance companies, these specialize in loans with limits ranging from a few hundred dollars to thousands of dollars. These companies will make loans for almost any conceivable purpose.
- *Credit unions.* These are "co-ops." Usually tied into a labor union at the place where you work, they make loans to their members (all borrowers must be shareholders in the credit union) for any reasonable purpose. Greatest advantage: The credit union rate of interest is usually lower than that of other financial institutions.
- *Commercial banks.* Traditionally, their credit customers were business people and farmers. In the past 30 years, however, they have moved into the area of personal loans in a big way, showing more rapid growth than any other type of lending institution.
- *Savings and loan associations.* While their business is mainly making mortgage loans out of the capital they amass from savings deposits, they are permitted, in many states, to make consumer loans as well. Compare your local S & L's versus commercial banks and savings banks.
- *Life insurance companies.* If you are buying life insurance that builds up savings, you can borrow the cash surrender value from the insurance company or use the policy as security

on a loan from a bank. (See Chapter 10 on Insurance.) Usually after a policy has been in force for a few years, it has built up a cash surrender value, and you can either surrender the policy and accept a lump sum in cash, or borrow out a specific amount and keep the policy in force.

Secured versus unsecured loans

If your loan is "secured," it means you must pledge something of value as collateral—an automobile, a savings account, or some other personal property—which the lender is legally entitled to take away from you if you do not repay the loan. An "unsecured" loan demands no collateral. You pay a higher rate of interest for an unsecured loan.

What does credit cost?

Prices vary. But whatever the cost, the creditor must tell you, under the Truth in Lending Law—in writing and before you sign any agreement—exactly what is the annual percentage rate (APR) and just how much the total finance charge will be for the period over which you are borrowing the money.

The *finance charge* is the total *dollar* amount you may pay in order to use credit. It can include not only the cost of interest but service charges, and some credit-related premiums, such as credit life insurance or appraisal fees.

The *annual percentage rate* (APR) is the relative cost of credit on a yearly basis, expressed as a *percentage* reflecting all costs of your loan. It is the key to comparing costs between one lender and another. Figuring their APRs involves complex mathematical computations, but all lenders have tables that do the work. In essence, let me describe the situation this way: If you borrow $1,000 from me for a year at 10 percent, you'll pay me back $1,000 plus interest a year later. But if you go to a bank and borrow the $1,000 you will repay it in 12 equal monthly installments that include the interest. This means you won't really have the use of the entire $1,000 for the entire year. In effect, you'll get to use less and less of it each month, and the APR will be more than a simple 10 percent.

Note: Interest limits are set by state governments. Some permit higher limits than others. The finance charges on credit cards such as VISA and MasterCard are set by the bank that issues the card, not by the card company. So a bank offering VISA in Connecticut, for instance, may set its finance charge only as high as 18 percent, while a bank in South Dakota may charge its VISA customers up to 25 percent.

How do you get credit?

If you have never borrowed money or bought anything on credit, how do you "get credit" in the first place?

The situation is a Catch-22. You cannot get credit until you prove you can be depended on to pay your debts, and you cannot get debts to pay until someone takes the risk of extending credit to you.

If you are applying for your first credit card—either singly or for a joint card—you may have a tough time at first. A lender will ask you to fill out an application form. The creditor is looking for three things:

1. Do you have the capability of repaying? What is your present income from all sources—including dividends on investments or part-time employment?
2. What are your assets?
3. Do you have the willingness to pay? If you have no previous history of repayments, this is the Catch-22. For example, when my daughter first applied for a credit card in her own name, she didn't have enough income to qualify for the card, so I was asked to be a cosigner for her. This meant that my income and credit history were used to enable her to qualify, and I was as liable for payments on her account as she was. Yet the card was in her name and was reported to credit bureaus as such, so that she began to establish a credit identity of her own.

What can you do, if you are refused credit on your own the first time you apply—and if you cannot find a cosigner? Try these suggestions:

- Insist on finding out which credit bureau has reported on you and how accurate they are. Recently the Federal Trade Commission reported that one of the nation's largest bureaus, the Trans Union Credit Information Com-

pany, had been making a "significant" number of errors in its reports on consumers. Mix-ups included sending a file with the correct name but the wrong address, ZIP code, or Social Security number to credit granters.
- Open checking and savings accounts at a local bank in your own name (as we discussed in Chapter 7). Get to know your banker.
- When you have a savings account established, borrow against it. A savings account shows you are in the habit of saving. A bank that is considering your application for a personal loan, for instance, should look favorably on this, and would use the balance in your savings account as security. This would mean, of course, that you could not withdraw from your savings the amount the bank considered security until the loan was repaid.
- Apply for a charge account at a local store. Pay it promptly each month.
- Establish an installment loan at a local store, purchasing something on the layaway plan rather than simply charging.
- Apply for a small bank loan—even if you don't need it. Put the money in a savings account. Withdraw enough each month to make the payments on the loan.
- Try obtaining a credit card (VISA or MasterCard) through the bank where you have established your checking account and where the banker now knows you and knows you are OK.

How the lender views it

Whether it is a bank, a store, American Express, Diner's Club—whatever the firm—it is taking a chance on *you*, based on *your* current income and circumstances, when it agrees to let you have credit. So the creditor has the right to know whether or not you are a good risk—whether you have a savings account and/or a checking account, whether you rent your living space or own it, how long you have been at that location, how long you've worked for the same employer. From all this information, the lender decides how much of a chance he or she is taking on you.

SHOPPING AROUND HELPED THE NICHOLSES . . .

When Valerie's elderly car collapsed, they wanted to buy an $8,000 automobile. They had $3,000 for the down payment, thanks to wedding gifts. So they needed $5,000.

Working over their budget, Valerie and James figured that $140 was the most they could pay per month on a car. They shopped several banks until they found one that would lend them the money at 14 percent—lower than most auto loans. This meant monthly payments of $136.64 for 4 years—just within their budget.

THE BUCKS COULDN'T GET CREDIT . . .

Chris and Jane figured they would just have to get another loan so they could buy a day-sailer to race on Barnegat Bay this summer—something several of their friends were doing, and something they had talked about, but not saved for, ever since they were married.

The loan officer at the bank took their application. In a few days, he sent them a credit rejection. The credit bureau the bank checked with showed that the Bucks had been late with payments on VISA (three months behind), MasterCard (two months late), and Bloomingdale's (also two months late).

The banker pointed out that, even though their total income before taxes is $42,000, they are carrying $10,800 in current debts. They are making monthly payments of $460, and clearly they are having trouble making ends meet. Their debt ratio is just too high.

Your credit record

Once you have acquired credit, remember that it is an obligation that you have agreed to pay back. Never abuse it. List this monthly obligation as a fixed ex-

Exhibit 6 page 1

CREDIT APPLICATION — INDIVIDUAL

Financial Statement Of: 5/1/84 (Date)

Name: Jane and Chris Buck   Home Phone No.: 555-1212

Home Address: 987 Main Street Big City, N.Y. 00001

Social Security No.: 044-56-0334   Age: ___   Number of Dependents: 1

Occupation: Accountant   Business Address: 460 S. Park

To: State Bank, Big City, N.Y.

For the purpose of procuring credit and/or any other accommodations or benefits which may be requested, direct or otherwise, from you from time to time, the undersigned hereby furnishes you with the following as being a true and correct statement of the financial condition of the undersigned and of all facts herein set forth, and for such purpose agrees that you may at any time assume that the condition and affairs of the undersigned have continued and are substantially as good as herein set forth and that there has been no change materially reducing the ability of the undersigned to pay all claims and demands against the undersigned, unless you are notified in writing to the contrary by the undersigned, and for such purpose the undersigned further agrees immediately to notify you in writing of any substantial change in the condition or affairs of the undersigned.

In consideration of the granting of such credit, the undersigned agrees that if the undersigned at any time stops payment, makes a bill of sale, a mortgage, assigns any accounts or transfers of a considerable portion of the undersigned's property without due notice to you, or should the undersigned's stock be attached, or should the undersigned make an assignment for the benefit of creditors, or should a petition in bankruptcy be filed by or against the undersigned or if any of the representations made below prove to be untrue, or if the undersigned fails to notify you of any material change as before agreed; then in any of such cases all of the undersigned's obligations held by you shall immediately become due and payable without demand or notice, and the same may be charged against the balance of any deposit account kept by the undersigned with you, the undersigned hereby giving a continuing lien upon such balance of deposit account from time to time existing to secure all obligations of the undersigned held by you.

It is further agreed that the exercise of or omission to exercise such option in any instance shall not waive or affect any other or subsequent right to exercise the same.

ASSETS		LIABILITIES AND NET WORTH	
Cash on hand and in banks (A)	$500	Notes due Bank (A)	$
Marketable Securities (B)		Notes due Relatives & Friends (G)	
Other Securities (C)		Notes due Others (G)	
Accounts & Notes Receivable		Accounts or Bills Due (G)	
Relatives & Friends		Income Taxes Due	
Others (D)		Other Taxes Due	
Real Estate (E)		Real Estate Mortgages Payable (E)	
Automobiles	1,500		
Cash Value—Life Ins. (F)		Brokers Margin Accounts	
Other Assets (Describe)		Other Debts (Itemize)	
Home Furnishings	8,500	Total Liabilities	$11,750
		Net Worth	$(1,250)
Total Assets	$10,500		

CONTINGENT LIABILITIES		ANNUAL INCOME	
Endorser, Co-maker, Guarantor	$	Salary	$42,000
Surety		Commissions & Bonuses	
On Contractual Obligations		Dividends & Interest	
Legal Claims		Rent (Net of Expense)	
Other—List		Other Income:	

YOU ARE NOT REQUIRED TO DISCLOSE INCOME FROM ALIMONY, CHILD SUPPORT, OR MAINTENANCE PAYMENTS. HOWEVER, IF YOU ARE RELYING ON INCOME FROM ALIMONY, CHILD SUPPORT OR MAINTENANCE PAYMENTS AS BASIS FOR REPAYMENT OF THIS OBLIGATION, PLEASE COMPLETE THIS SECTION.

(A) Cash in Banks and Notes Due to Banks (Specify If Joint)

Name of Bank	On Deposit	Due Banks	Maturity	Collateral (if any)
STATE BANK	$500	$		

Form MS-1056 Rev 9/78 BB

DEBT: HOW TO GET INTO IT, AND OUT AGAIN—WITHOUT GETTING HURT

Exhibit 6 page 2

(B) Marketable Securities

No. of Shares or Face Value (Bonds)	Description	Registered Owner	Cost	Market Value
			$	$

(C) Other Securities

No. of Shares or Face Value (Bonds)	Description	Registered Owner	Cost	Market Value
			$	$

(D) Accounts and Notes Receivable

Borrower and Address	When Due	Balance Due	Original Amount	Collateral (if any)
		$	$	

(E) Real Estate

Description	Date Acquired	Cost	Title in Whose Name	Present Value	Mortgage Amount	Monthly Payment	Mortgage Holder
		$		$	$	$	

(F) Life Insurance

Face Value	Insuror & Address	Owner	Beneficiary	Cash Surrender Value	Loans
$			$	$	

(G) Notes and Accounts Due

Owed to & Address	Balance Due	Payment Terms	Collateral
National Bank	$ 4,000		
Decorators Furn.	3,000		
Visa	1,200		
MasterCard	1,500		
Bloomingdale's	1,100		
Current Bills	950		

The undersigned further represents that there are no encumbrances against any of the foregoing property except those specifically disclosed above.

Chris Buck
Signature

Jane Buck
Signature

_____
Date

FINANCIAL FITNESS FOR NEWLYWEDS

Exhibit 7
CREDIT REJECTION

July 27, 1983

Jane & Chris Buck
987 Main
Big City, New York

Retail Merchants
Assn
306 W. Market St
Big City, N.Y.

Dear Customer:

Your recent application for a loan is appreciated, and your request has been given careful consideration.

In processing this application, we requested information from the above referenced credit bureau. Unfortunately, the information furnished will not allow us to approve the issuance of a loan for the principal reason(s) indicated below:

Delinquent credit obligations.

If you question this information, you may wish to contact the credit bureau referenced above to discuss your credit record personally. Should you find this information to be in error or that your credit situation has changed, we would welcome the opportunity to reconsider your application.

Very truly yours,

MANAGER - CREDIT

JGK:HK

SEE FEDERAL EQUAL CREDIT OPPORTUNITY ACT NOTICE ENCLOSED.

---

pense on your budget sheet, and repay it just as you pay your rent, utilities, and other fixed expenses.

Now you are building up your credit record. Next time you seek credit, the lender will be able to obtain a "credit report" on you from a *credit bureau*— any one of some 2,000 firms in the United States that act as clearinghouses for information about consumers' debts and bill-paying habits. Banks, finance companies, stores, and other creditors feed information about their customers into these credit bureaus.

Should you worry about your credit profile? Not

unless you are refused credit for no apparent reason, or unless you have failed to keep up with payments and are in trouble with some account somewhere.

Some things you should know about credit bureaus:

- They do not assign credit ratings or make judgments on your ability to repay. They simply sell creditors a look at your profile, which then speaks for itself. It is the bank, store, gasoline company, or other lender who determines whether you are worthy of its credit.
- The best way to keep your credit standing is to pay your debts on time.
- Under the law, you are entitled to see any credit report on you that has been prepared by a credit bureau and to challenge any items in the report that seem incorrect. The credit bureau is obliged to make an investigation and correct any errors. This is especially important if the information or evidence could be misleading.
- Any time you are denied credit by any organization to which you have applied, you are entitled to receive a copy of your credit history free of charge. If you simply want to check into what a local credit bureau has on you in its files, the bureau may insist on a fee for issuing a copy of your report. Usually the fee is less than $10. You can find your local credit bureau by looking in the yellow pages under "Credit Reporting Agencies."

Two important credit laws

If you have any complaints about how a lender treats you, two key laws may help:

1. *The Fair Credit Billing Act*. This law sets up a procedure for correcting billing mistakes, for promptly crediting your payments, and for your refusal to make credit card payments on defective goods.

The law defines a billing error as:

a. any unauthorized charge from which you received no benefit
b. any charge for a wrong amount or a wrong date
c. any charge that is not correctly identified
d. any charge for which you want to see an explanation or clarification (i.e., you want to see the creditor's documentation)
e. any charge for goods or services that were not delivered to you or were not accepted by you in accordance with your agreement with the seller (e.g., a department store delivers the right sofa in the wrong color)
f. any failure to credit a payment to your account promptly
g. any errors in arithmetic (e.g., the creditor incorrectly computes the finance charge)
h. any additional finance charge or minimum payment due that results from failure by the creditor to deliver the bill to your current address (remember, however, that when you move you must notify the creditor at least 10 days before the closing date of the billing cycle involved).

What do you do if you don't agree with a bill? Procedures are outlined under the law, including:

- Notify the creditor *in writing* within 60 days after the bill was mailed. Be sure to include your name, account number, the reasons why you believe the bill contains an error, and the suspected amount of the error or the item you want explained.
- Pay all parts of the bill that you do not dispute. While you are waiting for a reply, you do not have to pay the amount in question or any minimum payments or finance charges that apply to the disputed amount.
- If it turns out that the creditor has made a mistake, you do not have to pay any finance charges on the disputed amount. Your account must be corrected, and you must be sent an explanation of any amount you still owe.
- If the creditor cannot find an error, he or she must promptly send you an explanation of the reasons for saying there is no mistake, and a statement of what you owe; this may include any finance charges that have accumulated and any minimum payments you may have missed while you were disputing the bill.

Note: It is unlawful for a creditor to threaten your credit rating while you are resolving a billing dis-

TRW CREDIT DATA — UPDATED CREDIT PROFILE

Exhibit 8 page 1

CONFIDENTIAL

TCR2

INQUIRY INFORMATION

DFD2 9999999ABC BUCK, CHRIS.,
S-548926847, 987 MAIN ST BIG CITY, NY 10001

PAGE	DATE	TIME	PORT	HV	CONSUMER		02-999999/99
1	08-01-84	15:19:14	AL11	A14			

CHRIS BUCK
987 MAIN
BIG CITY, NY 10001

A & B ACC'T
460 S. PARK
BIG CITY, NY 10001

SS# 044-56-0334

YOB-1956

ACCOUNT PROFILE			SUBSCRIBER NAME/COURT NAME			SUBSCRIBER #/COURT CODE	ASSN CODE	AMOUNT	BALANCE	ACCOUNT NUMBER/DOCKET		PAYMENT PROFILE — Number of months prior to balance date
POS	NON	NEG	STATUS COMMENT	DATE REPORTED INQUIRY	DATE OPENED	TYPE	TERMS			BALANCE DATE	AMOUNT PAST DUE	1 2 3 4 5 6 7 8 9 10 11 12
A			NATIONAL BANK CURR	6/15/84	7/82	AUT	2 48	$7,000	$4,000	402245 7/1/84		CCCCCCCCCCCC
	M		DECORATOR'S FURN CURR WAS 30-3	6/15/84	1/82	CHG	2 60	$5,000	$3,000	892941 7/15/84	$75	C1CC1CC11CC1
		A	VISA CURR 60 PAS		9/81	CHG	2 REV	$2,000	$1,200	32214 6/20/84	$70	CCC11CCCC1C1
		A	MASTER CURR 60 PAS		7/81	CHG	2 REV	$2,500	$1,500	41221 6/30/84	$100	1CCC1CC1CC11
A			BLOOMING-DALE'S CURR ACT		10/81	CHG	2 REV	$1,500	$1,100	12211 7/10/84		CCCCCCCCCC1C

© *TRW* INC. 1971, 1978

DEBT: HOW TO GET INTO IT, AND OUT AGAIN—WITHOUT GETTING HURT

Exhibit 8 page 2

NAME OF CREDIT GRANTOR | TO THE ATTENTION OF

SIGNATURE: ______________ DATE: ______________

EXPLANATION OF INFORMATION ON FORM

TRW *CREDIT DATA* — ***UPDATED CREDIT PROFILE*** — ***CONFIDENTIAL***

INQUIRY INFORMATION [1]				
PAGE	DATE	TIME	PORT	H V
[2]				

ACCOUNT PROFILE [3]			SUBSCRIBER NAME COURT NAME [4]			SUBSCRIBER # COURT CODE [5]	ASSN CODE [6]	AMOUNT	[14]	ACCOUNT DOCKET NUMBER [7]		PAYMENT PROFILE MONTHS PRIOR TO BALANCE DATE [17]											
POS	NON	NEG	STATUS COMMENTS [8]	DATE REPORTED [9]	DATE OPENED [10]	TYPE [11]	TERMS [12]	[13]	BALANCE	BALANCE DATE [15]	AMOUNT PAST DUE [16]	1	2	3	4	5	6	7	8	9	10	11	12

1. Information used to obtain this Credit Profile abbreviated in computer language.
2. Your name and most recent address and reporting subscriber number, your employment on the date shown, and year of birth or age, if on file.
3. These columns provide an abbreviated description of the status of the items in your profile. POS(Positive) Generally viewed as favorable by credit grantors. NEG(Negative) Generally viewed as unfavorable by credit grantors. NON(Nonevaluated) May be viewed positively, negatively or indifferently depending on each credit grantor's policy and experience. A and M indicate the method by which the credit grantor reports information to TRW. (M) Manual; Manually prepared form. (A) Automated: Automated tapes prepared from the credit grantor's computer.
4. Name of credit grantor, lienholder or court name.
5. A TRW assigned identification number.
6. An association code describes your legal relationship with an account. (See below)
7. The number assigned to your account by the credit grantor or court docket number.
8. Abbreviated description of the account status. (See Explanation of Status Comments to the right.)
9. The status comment shown in 8 is as of this date.
10. Month account opened or month credit transaction took place. 5-Y or 10-Y indicates open prior to 5 years or 10 years respectively.
11. Credit grantor's abbreviated description of the nature of the credit extended. (See chart below)
12. Terms are the periods within which extensions of credit are to be repaid. Charge accounts are stated as REV meaning revolving. Terms for account types R/E, R/F, R/V and R/C (See #11) are stated in years and for all other account types the terms are stated in months.
13. This amount will be either the amount of the original (or revised) credit established, or the highest amount owed.
14. Balance owning on date stated under balance date (#15) or the name of judgement creditor.
15. Date of the balance (#14).
16. Dollar amount past due on balance date (#15), if any.
17. This information is read from left to right. This column reflects the status of the account for each of the 12 months preceding the balance date (#15). A blank space indicates we do not maintain a payment history of this account. A symbol appearing under one of the numbers (1 through 12) means that the account had such a status (as defined below) in that month under which the symbol appears. The following symbols are used in this column:
   - C = current
   - 1 = 30 days past due
   - 2 = 60 days past due
   - 3 = 90 days past due
   - 4 = 120 days past due
   - 5 = 150 days past due
   - 6 = 180 days past due
   - - = no history has been reported for that particular month
   - Blank = no history maintained, see status comment.

EXPLANATION OF STATUS COMMENTS

BK ADJ PLN	Debt included in or completed through Bankruptcy Chapter 13.
BK LIQ REO	Debt included in or discharged through
CHARGE OFF	Unpaid balance reported as a loss by credit grantor
CLOS INAC	Closed inactive account
CLOS NP AA	Credit line closed/not paying as agreed
COLL ACCT	Account seriously past due/account assigned to attorney, collection agency or credit grantor's internal collection department
CO NOW PAY	Now paying, was a charge-off
CR CD LOST	Credit card lost or stolen
CR LN CLOS	Credit line closed/reason unknown or by consumer request/there may be a balance due
CR LN RNST	Account now available for use and is in good standing. Was a closed account
CURR ACCT	This is either an open or closed account in good standing. If the account is a credit card or charge account, it should be available for use and there may be a balance due. If the account is closed, there were no past due amounts reported and it was paid
CUR WASCOL	Current account was a collection account
CUR WAS DL	Current account was past due
CUR WASFOR	Current account. Foreclosure was started
CUR WAS 30	Current account was 30 days past due
CURWAS30-2	Current account was 30 days past due twice
CURWAS30-3	Current account was 30 days past due three times
CURWAS30-4	Current account was 30 days past due four times
CURWAS30-5	Current account was 30 days past due five times
CURWAS30 + 6	Current account was 30 days past due six times or more
CUR WAS 60	Current account was 60 days delinquent
CUR WAS 90	Current account was 90 days delinquent
CUR WAS120	Current account was 120 days delinquent
CUR WAS150	Current account was 150 days delinquent
CUR WAS180	Current account was 180 days or more delinquent
DECEASED	Consumer deceased
DELINQ 60	Account delinquent 60 days
DELINQ 90	Account delinquent 90 days
DELINQ 120	Account delinquent 120 days
DELINQ 150	Account delinquent 150 days
DELINQ 180	Account delinquent 180 days
DEL WAS 90	Account was delinquent 90 days/now 30 or 60 days delinquent.
DEL WAS120	Account was delinquent 120 days/now 30, 60 or 90 days delinquent
EDU CLAIM	Claim filed with government for insured portion of balance on an educational loan
FORECLOSURE	Credit grantor sold collateral to settle defaulted mortgage
FORE PROC	Foreclosure proceeding started
INQUIRY	A copy of the credit profile has been sent to this credit grantor at their request
INS CLAIM	Claim filed for payment of insured portion of balance
NOT PD AA	Account not being paid as agreed
PAID ACCT	Closed account/zero balance/not rated by credit grantor
PAID SATIS	Closed account/paid satisfactory
PD BY DLER	Credit grantor paid by company who originally sold the merchandise
PD CHG OFF	Paid account/was a charge-off
PD COLL AC	Paid account/was a collection account, insurance claim or education claim
PD FORECLO	Paid account. A foreclosure was started
PD NOT AA	Paid account. Some payments were made past the agreed due dates
PD REPO	Paid account/was a repossession
PD WAS 30	Paid account/was past due 30 days
PD WAS30-2	Paid account/was past due 30 days 2 or 3 times
PD WAS30-4	Paid account/was past due 30 days 4 times
PD WAS30-5	Paid account/was past due 30 days 5 times
PD WAS30 + 6	Paid account/was past due 30 days 6 times or more
PD WAS 60	Paid account/was delinquent 60 days
PD WAS 90	Paid account/was delinquent 90 days
PD WAS 120	Paid account/was delinquent 120 days
PD WAS 150	Paid account/was delinquent 150 days
PD WAS 180	Paid account/was delinquent 180 days or more
REDMD REPO	Account was a repossession/now redeemed
REFINANCED	Account renewed or refinanced
REPO	Merchandise was taken back by credit grantor; there may be a balance due
SCNL	Credit grantor cannot locate consumer
SCNL NWLOC	Credit grantor could not locate consumer/consumer now located
SETTLED	Account legally paid in full for less than the full balance
TRANSFERRED	Account transferred to another office
VOLUN REPO	Voluntary repossession
30 DAY DEL	Account past due 30 days
30 2 TIMES	Account past due 30 days 2 times
30 3 TIMES	Account past due 30 days 3 times
30 4 TIMES	Account past due 30 days 4
30 5 TIMES	Account past due 30 days 5 times
30 6 + TIMES	Account past due 30 days 6 times or more
30 WAS 60	Account was delinquent 60 days/now 30 days

COURT CODES

CIR	CIRCUIT
CITY	CITY
CVL	CIVIL
CO	COUNTY
CT	COURT
DIS	DISTRICT
IRS	INTERNAL REVENUE SERVICE
JUS	JUSTICE
MUN	MUNICIPAL
REG	REGISTRAR
ST	STATE
SPR	SUPERIOR
SUP	SUPREME

TYPE OF ACCOUNT

ABBREV	EXPLANATION
AUT	Auto
UNS	Unsecured
SEC	Secured
P/S	Partially Secured
H/I	Home Improvement
FHA	FHA Home Improvement
ISC	Installment Sales Contract
CHG	Charge Account
R/E	Real Estate Specific Type Unknown-term in years
SCO	Secured by Co-Signer
BUS	Business
REC	Recreational Merchandise
EDU	Educational
LEA	Lease
COM	Co-Maker (not borrower)
C/C	Check Credit or Line of Credit
F/C	FHA Co-Maker (not borrower)
M/H	Mobile Home
CRC	Credit Card
R/F	FHA Real Estate Mortgage-terms are in years
NTE	Note Loan
NCM	Note Loan with Co-Maker
HHG	Secured By Household Goods
H + C	Secured By Household Goods & Other Collateral
ASL	Auto
R/V	VA Real Estate Mortgage-terms are in years
R/C	Conventional Real Estate Mortgage-terms are in years
R/O	Real Estate Mortgage-with or without other collateral Usually a second mortgage-terms are in months Amount shown in $100.00 increments
SLC	Co-Maker (not borrower)
REN	Rental Agreement
SUM	Summary of Accounts with same-status
UNK	Unknown
DCS	Debt Counseling Service
CCP	Combined Credit Plan
OST	Account review by credit grantor
A/M	Account monitor by credit grantor
RVW	Account review by credit grantor
EMP	Employment
PSC	Solicitation

ASSOCIATION CODES WITH DEFINITIONS

ASSOCIATION WITH ACCOUNT CURRENTLY ACTIVE . . . . ASSOCIATION TERMINATED AS OF DATE REPORTED

0 . . . . UNDESIGNATED . . . . A

Reported by TRW Credit Data only.

1 . . . . INDIVIDUAL . . . .

This individual is the only person associated with this account.

2 . . . . . JOINT ACCOUNT-CONTRACTUAL RESPONSIBILITY . . . . . B

This individual is expressly obligated to repay all debts arising on this account by reason of having signed an agreement to that effect. There are others associated with this account who may or may not have contractual responsibility.

3 . . . . AUTHORIZED USER-JOINT ACCOUNT C

This individual has use of this joint account for which another individual has contractual responsibility.

4 . . . . JOINT ACCOUNT . . . . D

This individual participates in this account. The association cannot be distinguished between Joint Account-Contractual Responsibility or Authorized User.

5 . . . . CO-MAKER . . . . E

This individual has guaranteed this account and assumes responsibility should maker default. This code only to be used in conjunction with Code 7-Maker.

6 . . . . ON BEHALF OF . . . . F

This individual has signed an application for the purpose of securing credit for another individual, other than spouse.

7 . . . . MAKER . . . . G

This individual is responsible for this account, which is guaranteed by a co-maker. To be used in lieu of Code 2 and 3 when there is a Code 5-Co-Maker.

ITEMS OF PUBLIC RECORD

CH 7—FILED	Voluntary or Involuntary Petition in Bankruptcy Chapter 7 - (Liquidation) filed
CH 7—DISCH	Voluntary or Involuntary Petition in Bankruptcy Chapter 7 - (Liquidation) discharged
CH 7—DISM	Voluntary or Involuntary Petition in Bankruptcy Chapter 7 - (Liquidation) dismissed
CH 11—FILE	Voluntary or Involuntary Petition in Bankruptcy Chapter 11 - (Reorganization) filed
CH 11—DISC	Voluntary or Involuntary Petition in Bankruptcy Chapter 11 - (Reorganization) discharged
CH 11—DISM	Voluntary or Involuntary Petition in Bankruptcy Chapter 11 - (Reorganization) dismissed
CH 13—FILE	Petition in Bankruptcy Chapt. 13 (Adjustment of Debt) filed
CH 13—DISM	Petition in Bankruptcy Chapt. 13 (Adjustment of Debt) dismissed
CH 13—COMP	Petition in Bankruptcy Chapt. 13 (Adjustment of Debt) completed
CITY TX LN	City Tax Lien
CITY TX REL	City Tax Lien Released
CONSEL SER	Debt Counseling Service
CO TAX LN	County Tax Lien
CO TAX REL	County Tax Lien Released
FED TAX LN	Federal Tax Lien
FED TX REL	Federal Tax Lien Released
JUDGMENT	Judgment
JUDGMT SAT	Judgment Satisfied
JUDG VACAT	Judgment Vacated or Reversed
MECH LIEN	Mechanic's Lien
MECH RELE	Mechanic's Lien Released
MN MTG FIL	Manual Mortgage Report (Developed credit report prepared for this credit grantor, copy attached.)
NT RESPON	Not Responsible Notice, e.g., husband or wife claims not responsible for debts incurred by spouse.
STAT TX LN	State Tax Lien
STAT TX REL	State Tax Lien Released
SUIT	Suit
SUIT DISMD	Suit Dismissed or Discontinued
WAGE ASIGN	Wage Assignment
W/A RELEASE	Wage Assignment Released

pute. Your creditor is not permitted to report you as delinquent, close out your account, or deduct money from other accounts to pay the disputed amount. If after the matter is settled (from the creditor's standpoint) you still disagree, write again. The creditor must report to the credit bureau that you have challenged the bill, and must give you the name and address of each person who has received information about your account. After the matter is finally settled, the creditor must report the outcome to each person who has received information about you. In addition, you are entitled to put your side of the dispute in writing in your credit history on file at the credit bureau.

The Fair Credit Billing Act also obliges your creditor to credit payments to your account on the day the payment is received at the specified address, so that you do not run up finance charges after you have sent in your payment. The creditor must also mail your bill at least 14 days before the payment is due, if your account is the type that gives you a period in which to pay before finance charges are added.

2. *The Equal Credit Opportunity Act.* Before this law was passed in 1975, there was much discrimination based on sex and marital status. It was common to deny credit to a married couple whose joint income was more than enough to carry the loan, on the grounds that the woman was of childbearing age, might become pregnant and quit work, and thus the couple's income would drop.

The act does not guarantee that you or anyone else will be issued credit. But it does prohibit discrimination based on sex, marital status, race, color, religion, national origin, age, and other factors. It requires every creditor to apply the same standards of "creditworthiness" equally to all applicants. Its most important rules:

- You cannot be denied credit because you are a woman. Before this act was passed, women had difficulty getting credit. Bankers and other creditors believed that a woman would ignore her debts when she got married, and that her income would disappear after marriage because she would leave the work force to have children.
- Single, married, separated, divorced, or widowed—none of these states can be a reason for denying you credit.
- A creditor may not refuse you credit because you depend on income from alimony or child support.
- A woman who is deemed creditworthy is not required to have her husband cosign an account (except in certain instances where property rights are involved).
- If your marital status changes, a creditor may not require you to reapply for credit, change the terms of your account, or close your account—unless there is some clear indication that you are no longer willing or able to repay your debt. In the case of a separation, divorce, or death, a creditor may ask you to reapply if your spouse's income was needed to support your credit. Thus, getting married does *not* mean that either of you must give up your own accounts or your own credit history.
- If both husband and wife use an account or are liable for it, the names of both must be carried on reports to credit bureaus (formerly, accounts were reported only in the name of the husband).
- Your creditor has just 30 days after your application has been completed in which to notify you of approval or denial. If you are denied credit, the notice must be in writing and must tell you why.
- If your account is closed, you have the same rights: You must be notified in writing, with the reason clearly stated.

Note: If you are denied credit, be sure to find out—and *understand*—why. Some possible reasons: You may have asked for more money than the creditor feels you can repay on your income and considering your other obligations . . . you may not have lived in the community long enough, or been on your job long enough . . . you don't have a credit record or history.

Important: If you have reason to believe you have been discriminated against, cite the law. And dig in and fight.

How much credit is too much?

Your budget answers this question. It will tell you how much credit you can safely afford to carry. To start using credit without setting up a working budget is foolhardy. If you aren't watching where your money is going, you can get into trouble before you know it.

"Over-extended" is the term the banker types like to use. The scenario goes like this: Your checking account balance drops to zero. Your wallet or purse is empty. You want to—or need to—buy something. Out comes the credit card and up goes your credit-card balance. Each month your payment gets larger. Your balance tops out at the limit originally approved by your bank. You apply for more credit. Or you go to other stores and open new accounts.

Eventually in this scenario, your minimum payments plus the finance charges on a number of accounts get to be one of your major monthly items of expense, cutting ever more deeply into each month's available cash for discretionary and other uses. You miss a monthly payment or two, because now you're juggling—paying this account this month, that account next month. Past due notices are arriving regularly in the mail. Next: phone calls and notices from collection agencies.

You don't have to be a $100,000-a-year executive to find yourself playing out this ulcer-producing scene. Plenty of $14,000-a-year secretaries and assistant managers have debts as high as their annual pay. It's no fun.

And here are some of the possible consequences. Your creditor can:

- repossess the merchandise—come and haul away furniture or drive away the car; they are not yours until *all* payments have been made
- take away the collateral you put up to secure the loan
- garnishee your wages—get a legal lien that forces your employer to give your creditor up to 10 percent of your pay each pay period until the debt is repaid
- tell the credit bureau—providing negative information about you that the credit bureau will show to other creditors.

How do you determine how much credit you *can* handle? You must find out what your *debt ratio* is, and see whether it is comfortably low, safely just about right, or uncomfortably high—and, if it's too high, work to get it down.

Turn to Worksheet VII, marked **Lists of Debts**, and to Worksheet VIII, **Personal Debt Ratio**. Fill in all debts that are current (your total indebtedness is on your Net Worth Statement; your monthly obligations are included under credit repayment on your fixed-expense sheet).

Use the Debt Ratio sheet to figure out a ratio for yourselves, based on total take-home pay and installment obligations. Your debt ratio is a percentage of your total take-home pay (the net income you have on your budget sheet, after all payroll deductions) that is committed to repaying your debts.

Most people are in danger if they commit more than 15 or 20 percent of net income to repaying debt. If the ratio goes higher, you may find yourselves sliding into the scenario of robbing Peter to pay Paul and charging items that have a life span less than the time it takes to pay for them.

Here's a good standard to apply: Can all your debts be paid off in 18 to 24 months? If not, your debt ratio is too high.

At any particular time, you should know the ratio of all your debts to your total net income. It will change, of course, when you pay off a loan—and you can then decide whether it is safe to borrow again, and how much it makes sense to borrow.

Turn to the completed Worksheets VII and VIII for the Bucks on pages 75 and 76. Look at the Bucks' Personal Debt Ratio. At 19.4 percent, it's obvious why the loan officer at their bank refused to grant them a loan for that sailboat. They were already pressing the upper limit of the safe zone! One more loan could put them in real trouble. Chris and Jane may not have realized it, but the bank was doing them a favor by refusing to grant them that loan.

Tip: Resist the inclination, when you have just paid off a loan that had an obligation of $50 a month, to take on another with a $65 monthly payment. You say to yourselves, "What's another $15 a month—we can handle that." But if you have other expenses that are rising, and if inflation is creeping up, what looks like "a mere $15" can be disastrous. Adding a new debt that is higher than the old one each time is a sure way to get into a dangerous debt ratio. Keeping debt within your means, on the other hand, will give you

**Worksheet VII: Yours
LISTS OF DEBTS**

Date _____

CREDITOR'S NAME	TYPE OF LOAN	DATE OF LAST PAYMENT	MATURITY DATE	MONTHLY PAYMENT From Budget	TOTAL AMOUNT DUE From Net Worth Statement

TOTAL MONTHLY PAYMENTS $ _____

TOTAL AMOUNT OWED $ _____

DEBT: HOW TO GET INTO IT, AND OUT AGAIN—WITHOUT GETTING HURT

> **Worksheet VIII: Yours**
> **PERSONAL DEBT RATIO**
>
> Your ratio is based on take-home pay. You have figured out the amount of debt that you owe for installment loans. Is this too much for you?
>
> | | | Monthly | Yearly |
> |---|---|---|---|
> | 1. | Your total take-home pay | $ | |
> | 2. | Use 20% (maximum for most consumers). Divide income by 5. If you feel this is too high, use 15% or divide by 6.7. | $ | |
> | 3. | Your present installment obligations | $ | |
> | 4. | Your present safety margin—subtract line 3 from line 2. | $ | |
> | 5. | Your personal ratio—divide your installments obligation (line 3) by your take home pay (line 1). | | |
>
> It might be wise to use both the 15% and 20% figures to see the difference in your own situation.

more spendable dollars as you avoid paying out a large amount for interest.

The spending habit: Can you kick it?

It's tough, but you can do it. Your best way is to go cold turkey. If your budget, your cash flow analysis, and your debt ratio all show that you have just plain got to cut back on expenses in order to pay off debt, make an agreement with each other that you will not—absolutely and positively will not—add any new debts for at least one year.

You might even take your charge cards and put them in a friend's safe-deposit box. Or cut them in half and return them to the creditor, with a note of explanation.

Then cast a cold eye on your budget. Cut out—or at least cut down on—every living expense that is not an absolute necessity. Open another savings account and put a certain amount in every day, using this account for debt reduction and *only* for debt reduction.

Sounds impossible? I've seen it work time and again. With this kind of regimen, you can learn—together—to manage on the amount of money you have.

What about bankruptcy?

I don't want you even to think about it. But this book would be incomplete if it did not explain the basics. Some facts, tips, and suggestions:

- If you're in deep trouble, you can find lending institutions that will consolidate all your debts, lending you enough to pay back everyone you

FINANCIAL FITNESS FOR NEWLYWEDS

Worksheet VII: Example
The Bucks
LISTS OF DEBTS

Date _____

CREDITOR'S NAME	TYPE OF LOAN	DATE OF LAST PAYMENT	MATURITY DATE	MONTHLY PAYMENT From Budget	TOTAL AMOUNT DUE From Net Worth Statement
National Bank	Auto Loan	4/1/84	6/1/86	$250.00	$4,000
Decorator's Furniture	Charge	2/1/84	12/31/87	75.00	3,000
Visa	Revolving Act	1/1/84		50.00	1,200
MasterCard	" "	2/15/84		50.00	1,500
Bloomingdale's	" "	2/20/84		35.00	1,100
				TOTAL MONTHLY PAYMENTS $460.00	
				TOTAL AMOUNT OWED	$10,800

DEBT: HOW TO GET INTO IT, AND OUT AGAIN—WITHOUT GETTING HURT

Worksheet VIII: Example
The Bucks
PERSONAL DEBT RATIO

Your ratio is based on take-home pay. You have figured out the amount of debt that you owe for installment loans. Is this too much for you?

		Monthly	Yearly
1.	Your total take-home pay	$ 2,369	28,428
2.	Use 20% (maximum for most consumers). Divide income by 5. If you feel this is too high, use 15% or divide by 6.7.	$ 474	5,686
3.	Your present installment obligations	$ 460	5,520
4.	Your present safety margin—subtract line 3 from line 2.	$ 14	166
5.	Your personal ratio—divide your installments obligation (line 3) by your take home pay (line 1).	19.4%	19.4%

It might be wise to use both the 15% and 20% figures to see the difference in your own situation.

owe. You then pay back that lender over an extended period. The trouble is, it's expensive, as this type of loan may involve a substantial amount of interest. But it gives you a lower amount to pay each month—lower than the total of paying all those separate accounts—for debt reduction.
- If you're into that kind of debt reduction plan—consolidating all your debts—don't make the mistake of starting to use your plastic cards all over again before the big consolidated loan is paid off. If you do, you'll start the cycle again and, within a few months or a year or two, you'll be signing for another consolidation loan. This is the path to bankruptcy.
- Congress passed the Bankruptcy Reform Act of 1978 to ease the burdens of going bankrupt and to make it easier to repay a substantial portion of one's debt. The law recognizes the fact that people often get themselves into economic situations that are beyond their control. The "ripple effect" of inflation, for example, is tough on those who are overextended. The Bankruptcy Act has resulted in a tremendous increase in the numbers of personal bankruptcies, with creditors losing about $6 billion.
- Talk with a lawyer before you decide to declare personal bankruptcy. Get yourselves informed on various "chapters" of the Bankruptcy Act. Some details you'll learn:

  - You must get petitions filled out.
  - Chapter 7 covers a "straight bankruptcy" in which the court collects, sells and distributes debtors' assets.
  - Chapter 13 encourages debtors to repay their loans.
  - Chapter 13, the so-called "wage-earner

plan," allows you to consolidate debts and repay a court-approved percentage of them over three years.
- Creditors must suspend charges for interest or late payments on most debts.
- Creditors are barred from continuing any action against the debtors.
- If you use Chapter 13 and then default on payments, the court will throw you into Chapter 7 proceedings.

How to stay out of credit trouble

Keep these points in mind:

1. Debt must be paid off; paying a loan is a fixed expense.
2. Deferred spending is often avoided spending. Ask yourselves: Would we buy this if we had the cash in hand to buy it?
3. Good axiom about small purchases: If you can't afford to pay cash, you can't afford to buy it on credit.
4. Always shop around before signing for a loan.
5. Avoid impulse shopping. If you have to buy something to "lift your spirits," keep within reason.
6. Never put everyday expenses on credit.
7. Watch credit card purchases closely. Make sure you both put credit card slips in one place immediately after any purchase. There's nothing worse than opening a monthly credit card bill to learn for the first time that your spouse has added a large purchase.

Almost "free" money

Your credit cards can be the closest thing you will ever have to "free" money. Here's how.

The best way to use credit cards is to pay the full amount due every month. Usually your credit card allows a grace period of 25 to 30 days from the date when you are billed until you will be assessed interest or a finance charge. So if you make a purchase immediately after your billing date (which is imprinted on your bill), and if you pay in full when you pay, you can gain free credit for almost two months. *Example:* Suppose your billing date is July 1. If you buy something on July 2, it will not appear on your bill until August, and you will then have until September 1 (or the stated due date) to pay for that purchase. If you pay the full amount of your new balance by September, no interest will be charged. You will have had free use of your July 2 purchase until the first of September.

Understanding finance charges

Finance charges are added to any credit card bill if the amount due is not paid in full. The charges can be calculated by any number of methods.

The most common method is the *average daily balance method with newly billed purchases included*. This method does not allow the grace period for newly purchased items that I talked about in describing "almost 'free' money." Under this method, it is important to note that the finance charge is based on the average amount you have charged during the month. As soon as your latest purchase goes into the computer, your average changes and your finance charge increases. The finance charge then continues to be calculated on your latest average daily balance until it again changes. Therefore, if your creditor is using this method, it is better to pay as soon as you receive the bill, rather than waiting (as you might have done when paying in full) until the end of the month. In other words, if you decide to leave part of a bill unpaid for just one month, you will be charged interest.

The cost of stretching out payments

If you make only partial payments month after month, you are using a very costly method of repaying your debts. Here's why.

Whatever amount you pay, the creditor takes the full finance charge out before crediting anything to your account. This means that if you pay only the minimum due, you reduce the actual amount you owe by that amount *less* the finance charge. Say you send in the minimum payment of $50 called for on your monthly statement. If the finance charge on the *total* you owe is $10, the creditor will take $10 to pay that finance charge and thus deduct only $40 from the total you owe. So if the balance you owe is quite large, your required minimum payment may be mostly interest (i.e., finance charge) month after month. The principal amount you owe will be reduced ever so slowly—much too slowly for you to consider it sound money management.

Tip: One practical way to use multipurpose cards (VISA, MasterCard) is to put all big-ticket items on one, and all small-cost items on the other. Then be sure to pay the card with the small-cost items in full every month. That gives you the convenience of buying the shirt or the lipstick with plastic—while you're paying for the stereo over the long haul. *Caution:* This system works only if you pay up—promptly and in full—on the small-cost account every month.

Student loans—and Sallie Mae Options

Is either of you—or are you both—repaying a student loan? Are the repayments using up most of your debt ratio? If so, you must put the brakes on other debt obligations *and* get a good understanding of student loans.

First, some background. If you borrowed for college or graduate school under the Guaranteed Student Loan Program (GSL), National Direct Student Loans (NDSL), or Federally Insured Student Loans (FISL), you were allowed very low interest rates through a bank or credit union. The loans were insured either by the federal government or the guarantee agency in your state. Your rate of interest was set with the first loan you received, and all your subsequent loans stayed at that rate even if interest rates rose. Your maximum repayment period was to be either 10 years or 15 years from the date of your first loan. If student loans are, in fact, a heavy part of your debt ratio, that's a long haul.

Now, meet Sallie Mae. That's a nickname for the Student Loan Marketing Association (SLMA, or Sallie Mae). In 1981, Sallie Mae set up a program called OPTIONS to help former students stretch out their repayment of student loans. The Sallie Mae OPTIONS program:

- consolidates all your loans (perhaps one a year for several college years) into a single debt
- gives you a lower monthly payment
- gives you a choice: equal payments over the years, or graduated payments that increase as your earning power increases
- gives you up to 20 years to repay
- lets you wait until six months after you leave college before you must start payments
- restricts eligibility to loans that are not delinquent or in default, but lets you become eligible by bringing payments up to date
- lets you apply for options at any time
- may be used on any loan or combination of loans that is more than $7,500
- may be used if your loans total more than $5,000 from more than one lender (i.e., you attended two or more different schools).

Suppose you owe a total of $12,000 in student loans. Under the regular payment plan, the term is 10 years and your monthly payment of interest and principal is $140. Under the Sallie Mae OPTIONS program, you have these choices:

Option 1. Equal payments during the repayment term. Your debt would be extended to 16 years, with monthly payments reduced to about $104. Good for keeping the budget under control.

Option 2. Graduated payments, starting at a low level and increasing. Maximum period would also be 16 years, but payments would increase every two years, from $79 a month at the start to about $152 in the final years. Helpful if you're just starting on your career.

Option 3. Payments accelerating more rapidly than in Option 2. Maximum period would be 13.3 years, with payments increasing every two years—from $79 at the start to about $189 at the end. Great if you expect your income to rise fast.

For each option, the interest rate is fixed at seven percent annually. If your interest rate is now less than seven percent—for instance, on a National Direct Student Loan—the Sallie Mae OPTIONS program could cost you more while giving you a longer time to pay. If you have a nine percent Guaranteed Student loan, you would save on interest.

Sallie Mae can be a big help. The reduction in monthly expenses it can provide may make it possible for you to borrow to buy a car, for instance, or simply add to the flexibility of your budget.

So weigh the options. Decide whether it is better

to extend the time of repayment, despite greater interest charges, in order to keep the size of monthly payments within your budget.

Then, if you want to apply for a Sallie Mae OPTION, write to:

> Sallie Mae
> Student Loan Consolidation Center
> P.O. Box 973
> Beltsville, MD 20705

Include information on who your lenders were, which programs you are in (GSL, NDSL, or FISL), the amount you now owe on each, the date repayment on each began or will begin, the total number of loans you have signed for (and total number of lenders), and the total amount you owe.

You can get a lot of benefits from credit. It lets you go places and buy things you might otherwise never be able to see or own, or that it would take you years to save for. But you must handle credit carefully. Budgeting is your most valuable tool for knowing how much credit you can comfortably afford to carry, and it is the only way to control credit abuse and—if abuse occurs—take charge and get it back under control.

It boils down to this: You control credit or credit controls you. Take your choice.

YOUR JOB AND YOUR FRINGE BENEFITS   9

Almost any older couple you ask will tell you that job changes are a part of life when you are young and especially, it seems, when you are newly married. It's a time when you are looking for opportunities to connect—to land the ideal spot in the ideal company in the field you have chosen, or maybe even to move into a related field.

When you are considering a job change or actually starting a new job, fringe benefits can make a big difference. These are all the "extras" that most employers offer in addition to your regular pay, and include life insurance and medical insurance, dental plans, and retirement plans. You need to check them carefully, for you can get burned just as easily as you can come out far better than on your last job. A beautiful pay increase, for instance, could be offset by a real loss in fringe benefits. Moving from a company that pays all Blue Cross premiums in full to one that deducts them from your paycheck could be a mistake if you don't pick up enough of a pay increase to cover the difference. In fact, a top-notch fringe benefit package can be worth the equivalent of hundreds of thousands of dollars more in compensation, over the long haul. Some companies that pay low salaries are extremely generous with fringe benefits. They find it's one good way to keep turnover down.

Let's take a look at some of the items that are included in a fringe-benefit package.

Insurance

Most companies carry several types of insurance for their employees, deducting the premiums (or a percentage of them) from the regular paycheck. By putting all its employees together in a single group, the company gets a rate, or price, that is much lower than any individual could get. Typical coverage includes:

- *Life insurance.* Most employers provide life insurance. Usually your coverage is one to two times your annual pay. In some companies, you can buy additional coverage at the low group rate, with the premium deducted from your paycheck. This could be extremely valuable if, for example, you have a medical problem that makes you uninsurable or necessitates extra premium riders on life insurance policies, for, if you are in a company group, you do not have to pass an individual physical examination to determine your eligibililty.

Important: When you leave your company for another job, you leave your group life insurance behind. Usually, however, you are entitled to convert your group policy within a month to an individual policy for which you pay the insurance company directly—again, without a physical exam but at a higher premium.

- *Health and dental insurance.* Probably there are more variations among company attitudes on these fringes than on life insurance. Some companies, for instance, pay Blue Cross in full for their employees, while others pass the full cost along through payroll deductions (you get an advantage, nevertheless, because you are paying your share of a group premium rather than an individual policy premium). Some companies pay for the employee's coverage but not for his or her dependents. Others pay for Blue Cross but not for major-medical coverage. Some questions to ask:

How much, if anything, do employees themselves have to pay?
Must the employee pay for dependents?
What is the deductible allowed for the employee and family?
Is there a maximum yearly limit on the dollar amount of claims—or on their number?
Are there any medical problems that this kind of insurance does not cover?
Just what does the dental plan cover? (Some may not include routine cleaning by a dental hygienist; most pay less than the standard fees charged by most practicing dentists for bridges and for orthodontic work—i.e., braces.)

- *Disability insurance.* Most people give very little thought to short-term disability coverage, yet you need only one accident to understand its importance. The chances of becoming disabled for several weeks or for three months or more are high. If your company does not offer disability coverage, you can buy a policy on your own.

Note: All of the foregoing on insurance is discussed here simply to give you the basics of insurance *as a fringe benefit.* (See Chapter 10 for details on types of insurance, how much you should buy, how long-term and short-term disability plans work, and many other practical tips.)

Savings plans

The payroll system where you work can help you to save. Many companies offer a straight payroll savings plan. This sets aside a certain amount to be deducted from every paycheck, or once a month, and put directly into a savings account.

One plan gives you a way to save money and actually get more take-home pay at the same time. Called a *salary reduction plan,* it permits you to deduct part of your salary every year, up to a maximum of $30,000, *before* the company pays any withholding taxes on it. Thus the money saved is pre-tax, rather than after-tax, dollars. The money put into this type of account (called a 401k) is deferred on a tax-sheltered basis so it can accumulate until you leave the company or retire.

Here's how it works: Say you are earning $25,000 a year. You choose a six percent salary reduction. The company sets aside $1,500 ($25,000 x 6%) over a year and figures your withholding taxes on the basis of a salary of $23,500. The salary reduction plan:

- reduces state and city income taxes
- can grow rapidly if your employer kicks in (as many do) 50 percent of the amount you are contributing
- is not sealed in concrete; if you get into a jam and need the money that's been put away, you can take advantage of the plan's hardship provision
- means that you get favored tax treatment when you ultimately do take your money out of savings.

Retirement benefits

You may think the last thing you want to be concerned about now is retirement plans. But this is one very important benefit. You should understand it. Find out, first of all, whether you are covered by your company's retirement plan. Some companies limit their plans to those who have certain jobs and work a certain specified number of hours, or those who have been with the company for a certain period of time or have reached a certain age. You can also be included in a plan but not yet eligible to receive any benefits from it. For example, take "vesting." When you are vested in a pension plan, it means that the money credited to your name is legally yours, without question or qualification. You will get it when you retire, and if you should leave your job before then you will be entitled to take it all or, in some cases, a percentage depending on how many years you have been vested. In most companies, you become *fully* vested only after you have worked a certain number of years (e.g., 10 years); and you start to be *partially* vested at various percentages over a number of years, starting sooner (e.g., after five years). Suppose vesting starts at your fifth year, but the company has been putting money in since the end of your second year. And suppose a job offer from another company turns up just at the end of your fourth year. You might figure out that it would be better to wait a couple of years before changing jobs, in order to be able to take with you the money that will then be vested for you.

Some employers have "non-contributory" plans, meaning that you do not have to contribute anything; the company puts in all the money. Others use "contributory" plans, in which you must make contributions through payroll deductions. The number and types of plans are bewildering, but all fall into two basic types:

1. *Defined benefit plan.* This type specifies in advance the benefits you will receive. They may be based on the amount of your earnings over a specified period of service with the company. Or they may be a fixed dollar amount paid for each year of service.

2. *Defined contribution plan.* Here, a predetermined formula may set a fixed dollar amount as the contribution each year. Or the employer's contribution may vary from year to year as profits of the firm vary.

"Cafeteria" benefits

Here's a new breed of cat. Some companies are beginning to let employees pick and choose certain benefits—the idea growing out of the increasing number of both-spouses-working families, where certain benefits (such as Blue Cross) are often duplicated by the employers of each. Under the "cafeteria" plan, if your wife or husband is covered for a medical plan, you might decide to drop your own medical but pick up a dental plan, an extra week's vacation, additional life insurance, or maybe even cash. An employee who is young might pass up contributions to a pension plan, under the cafeteria system, and add vacation time, while an older employee might want to increase medical coverage and payments into the pension plan. You can see the possibilities—especially if you don't need many of the benefits offered where you work, because your spouse gets them for both of you at his or her place, and if you're given the option of taking cash. Not bad.

Tips:
- Always evaluate fringe benefits carefully before you start a job or change jobs.
- Investigate the "benefit" dollars as well as the "paycheck" dollars you're being offered.
- Remember that a large pay increase may well be offset by a loss of important fringe benefits.
- Fringe benefits do not usually increase your tax bill the way a salary increase will.

THE McQUARTERS ARE BOTH COVERED BY BENEFITS . . .

. . . with a lot of duplication. Both their employers provide major-medical and Blue Cross/Blue Shield, and Pat's TV station has a good dental plan that covers Cathy as well. But it has no retirement plan. So Pat has opened an Individual Retirement Account (IRA) and is thinking about looking for a job with a station that does provide a retirement plan.

Meantime, Cathy's teaching job in the public school system means that she is eligible for a Tax-Sheltered Annuity plan (TSA), which enables her to put before-tax dollars into a retirement plan (that is, her employers withhold income-tax money only on the part of her pay that is left *after* she has contributed to her TSA). Currently she is putting five percent of her pay into the plan. It buys an annuity contract each year.

INSURANCE: HOW MUCH DO YOU NEED? WHAT KIND SHOULD YOU GET?

10

I have to admit that I never knew much about insurance—*any* kind of insurance—until long after I was grown and married. When I was in high school, I put a few dents in the family car. I couldn't understand why my parents weren't paid the entire cost of repairs by the insurance company. When I was in college, my stereo was stolen. I fully expected my folks to collect the total cost of replacement from the insurance company.

Eventually I learned about the principles of insurance—how the idea is to spread the risk, with insurance premiums paid by a large number of people who are exposed to similar risks . . . how "deductibles" save the insurance company (and thus all those who are sharing the risks) the costs of paying countless very small claims that could eat up the reserves needed to pay more substantial claims.

Insurance covers many risks: the chance that someone will die and a productive source of income will disappear . . . the chance that something may be stolen or accidentally destroyed . . . the chance that health will fail and medical bills will have to be paid . . . the chance that someone will hold you responsible for personal injury or damage to property . . . the chance that fire will damage or destroy property, or will kill or injure people.

As newlyweds, you will probably find yourselves thinking about insurance—all kinds of insurance—in a way you hadn't thought about it before. Until now, you may have had an "if anything happens, well, it won't matter all that much" attitude toward life insurance or even toward fire and theft and liability insurance. But now that you're a twosome, you find yourselves concerned about what the effect of loss, disability, or death would be on the other person.

The following discussion will cover all kinds of insurance and how they work. You must then decide on what insurance you need—and how much—for yourselves, your family, your situation. Let's start with the most important kind: life insurance.

Protecting income

The main purpose of life insurance is to protect the income part of your budget. Life insurance exists to replace the income that stops if the earner dies. But it does have another purpose: to accumulate savings.

The key word in thinking about life insurance is *now*. Now is not 10 years from today, and it is not last year. Yet countless people carry life insurance that was right last year or will be right 10 years from now. The fact is that as your life changes your insurance needs will change. It is important, in planning life insurance, to make it fit what you need *now*—maybe even more important than making it fit what you will need at some time in the future.

This does not mean you need to revise your life insurance coverage every year. But do be sure to review your needs and your coverage at least every five years. Otherwise you could be wasting money on insurance—or not buying enough.

The basic types of life insurance

The insurance world is loaded—in fact, it is overloaded—with variations on types of policies. It seems as if every insurance company has its own. But all fall into one of four basic types:

1. *Term insurance.* As the name implies, this means you are buying life insurance for a specific term or period of time—usually one to five years. This is low-cost insurance. In fact, term is the cheapest form of life insurance you can buy. If pays off if you die. But it does not build up any savings or other benefits. If provides nothing but protection. When the term ends, you have nothing—but during the term you have been protected. If you renew for another term, the cost is higher because you are older and the likelihood of death is greater as you get older. If you keep buying term insurance, you will find that by the age of 45 or 50 the premium cost is rising rapidly—much faster than in earlier years—and it is no longer "low-cost" insurance. But by the time you reach that age, you should not be buying term anyway, or you certainly should be buying less of it.

Term insurance is really ideal for a young couple. It gives you greater amounts of protection at less cost than whole or straight life insurance.

Tip: If you are buying term, be sure the policy you get can be renewed without your having to pass another physical examination. Also be sure it contains a clause that permits you to convert it into a whole policy without a physical—and at a guaranteed rate. These factors—renewability and convertibility—can be vitally important if your health changes during the term and you become uninsurable or become a high risk, which would send the cost of a policy up to a prohibitive rate.

2. *Whole or straight life insurance.* With this type, you get more than protection. You build up savings. At the time you buy the policy, the insurance company determines the amount of the premium by your age and state of health. The premium then stays the same as long as you keep the policy in force. Therefore, the younger you are when you buy a whole or straight policy, the less it costs you. During the first few years, the insurance company credits only a small amount of your total premium payments to savings. Then, as time goes on, the savings build up. This amount is yours if you cancel the policy. Or you can borrow the amount that is in savings, paying interest on it (at an interest rate you will find stated in your policy) to the insurance company. When you "borrow against the policy," you continue to pay the premium, keeping the policy in force. However, if you die, the insurance company deducts the amount you borrowed from the "face amount" of the policy before it pays your beneficiary. For example, if you are buying a $25,000 policy but have borrowed $8,000 on it, the company will pay only $17,000.

This "policy loan" provision is a valuable right. In enables you to draw upon the "cash value" that has built up in your policy in order to meet financial needs.

3. *Endowment policy.* This is the ultimate in savings types of life insurance. It states a designated sum that will accumulate from the premiums you pay and the dividends the insurance company will pay. When the policy matures at the end of its specified period (say, 20 years, in a "20-year endowment policy"), the face amount is paid to the beneficiary you have named. If that beneficiary is no longer living, it goes to your contingent beneficiary, if you named one in your will. If you did not, it goes into your estate. The premium amount stays the same for the life of the policy.

4. *Universal life.* This one combines term insur-

ance with a tax-deferred investment program that earns interest at bond market rates. When you set up the policy with the insurance company, you decide how much of the premium you want to go toward buying insurance protection and how much you want put into investments.

Which type of policy to buy?

You have to weigh the advantages and disadvantages of each kind of policy. The first question to ask yourself is: How much coverage do we really need right now? The second question: How much can we afford? If you are depending on both your incomes to maintain the household, think about near possibilities, too—such as what would happen if one of you died soon after you started a family. Tough question. But one you have to think about seriously. How much insurance would be needed by the spouse and child who were left?

Tip: When you are considering life insurance policies, weigh whether you are being sold on a whole or straight life policy, which costs more, when what you really need is a larger amount of protection, which you could buy for the same price by taking a term policy. If youth is on your side, you can buy a lot more insurance for a few years when you need the protection, by buying term. Just don't keep term going for too many years, because it will cost more and more.

How to decide how much you need

You should never buy any more life insurance than you need. How do you know how much you need? Worksheets are the only way. You can calculate exactly what's needed on Worksheet IX, filling in some of the information from the other worksheets you've already completed. Look at your budget worksheets. What income will be available to your spouse if you die? Here are the possibilities:

- Spouse's income, if he or she works or can return to work.
- Social Security payments, if the spouse is eligible for them.

A surviving spouse is eligible for benefits only if there are children under 18 and only as long as the spouse does not remarry.

Note: You should know what you are getting for those Social Security payments they deduct from your paycheck. It takes 10 years for you to become "fully insured" in the eyes of Social Security so that you are entitled to all its benefits in your retirement years. However, if a breadwinner has paid in during a total of six quarters, during any three calendar years before death, then he or she is "currently insured" and entitled to death benefits.

- Dividends and interest from investments (see Worksheet IV, **Sources of Income**).
- Benefits from a pension plan.
- Proceeds from insurance you already have in force or included in coverage where you work.

Next, look at the expense side of your budget. If you die, which expenses will decrease for your spouse and family? Probably food, clothing, transportation, and life insurance premiums. The rule of thumb is 75 percent: Figure that a family in which either parent dies still needs at least three-quarters of its previous take-home pay in order to cover expenses and maintain its lifestyle. Imagine how tough it would be to plan insurance needs accurately if you did not have a good picture of what it costs you to live!

It's important to figure out the cash that would be needed, and that insurance should cover, if the breadwinner (or *either* breadwinner) died. Some of this necessary amount you have already listed on your Net Worth Statement. Be sure to include:

- Current debts (unpaid bills as well as installment loans and mortgage).
- Expected education expenses. If you already have children, it's important (no matter how young they are) to know what it is going to cost to educate them. When you receive the proceeds from a life insurance policy, earmark enough for college, and invest it at a rate of return that would keep up with the ever-increasing costs of college.
- Final expenses that a death brings. These include administration of the estate, probate costs,

Worksheet IX: Yours
HOW MUCH LIFE INSURANCE?

A. ANNUAL FAMILY LIVING COSTS (from Budget form) _____

B. SOURCES OF INCOME AVAILABLE

- Spouse's Income _____
- Social Security Benefits _____
- Income from Income-Producing Assets (from Budget form) _____
- Income from Proceeds of Existing Life Insurance Policies (use an assumed rate of interest)

  6%—multiply amount of insurance by .06
  10%—multiply amount of insurance by .10
  12%—multiply amount of insurance by .12

  _____ × .10 = _____

- Other Sources of Income _____

  TOTAL SOURCES OF INCOME _____

C. ADDITIONAL INCOME NEEDED (subtract B from A) _____

D. AMOUNT OF MONEY TO MAKE UP SHORTAGE (at an assumed rate of interest)

  6%—multiply by 6
  10%—multiply by 10
  12%—multiply by 12

  _____ × 10 _____

E. ADDITIONAL CASH REQUIREMENTS

  Final Expenses _____

  Education for Children _____

  Liabilities (including Mortgage) _____ _____

F. INSURANCE NEEDS (D plus E) _____

FINANCIAL FITNESS FOR NEWLYWEDS

Worksheet IX: Yours
HOW MUCH LIFE INSURANCE?

A. ANNUAL FAMILY LIVING COSTS (from Budget form) _____

B. SOURCES OF INCOME AVAILABLE

• Spouse's Income _____

• Social Security Benefits _____

• Income from Income-Producing
Assets (from Budget form) _____

• Income from Proceeds of Existing Life Insurance Policies
(use an assumed rate of interest)

  6%—multiply amount of insurance by .06
10%—multiply amount of insurance by .10
12%—multiply amount of insurance by .12

_____ × .10 = _____

• Other Sources of Income _____

TOTAL SOURCES OF INCOME _____

C. ADDITIONAL INCOME NEEDED (subtract B from A) _____

D. AMOUNT OF MONEY TO MAKE UP SHORTAGE
(at an assumed rate of interest)

  6%—multiply by 6
10%—multiply by 10
12%—multiply by 12

_____ × 10 _____

E. ADDITIONAL CASH REQUIREMENTS

Final Expenses _____

Education for Children _____

Liabilities (including Mortgage) _____

F. INSURANCE NEEDS (D plus E) _____

INSURANCE: HOW MUCH DO YOU NEED? WHAT KIND SHOULD YOU GET?

attorney's and accountant's fees, appraisal fees, taxes, final medical expenses that are not reimbursed from major medical or other insurance plans, and funeral expenses. Allow two to five percent of the total estate, plus up to $5,000 for funeral expenses, to cover these.

With so many variables, you can see how the amount of insurance you need can change as life changes. When you're buying a home and raising young children, your needs keep increasing. When the mortgage is paid off and the children finish college, your needs decrease. At least once every five years, look over your needs and the insurance you have been buying to cope with them. And remember that Financial Fitness does not demand that you be overinsured. Plan carefully and buy the amount of coverage you need—not the amount an agent wants to sell you. To help guide you, your **Net Worth Statement** and **Budget** Worksheets will tell you which assets will produce income, which liabilities should be paid off with proceeds from life insurance, and what it will cost either of you to maintain your lifestyle if you lose your spouse.

Tip: Many young couples figure bad news is something that always happens to someone else. Let me urge you to be hardheaded and practical—but certainly not morbid—in your thinking. I can promise you that, once you have gone through this tough thinking and made sensible plans that are workable for your situation, you will be able to feel relaxed about the future.

What happens if an insured person dies?

There are several ways, called *settlement options*, in which an insurance company pays out the policy after the death of the insured person. When you are buying the policy, the agent may try to get you to pick one of these options so it can be specified in the policy. You do not have to decide then, however, and in fact it is unfair to ask you to decide then because it is impossible for you to know, when the policy is created, what will best serve your family's needs some time in the future. A few intervening years can change too many things. If you are pressured to decide among the options, hold your ground firmly.

Pressure can also come immediately after the death of the insured person. If you are the beneficiary, the insurance company is likely to ask you for a decision right away, but you can ask them to hold the proceeds of the policy until you have had time to weigh the options. Take your time, and don't let anyone rush you into it or make the decision for you. The options are:

1. *Lump sum.* This means you get a check immediately for the full amount of the policy (less any amount that may have been borrowed out). If you are into investments and are already knowledgeable about them (or if you have good advice and are willing to learn), this can be a good option. If interest rates are running high, you should be able to get a better return on investment than the insurance company can provide.

2. *Interest only.* This means the insurance company holds the principal amount but pays you the interest it is earning—a good holding position while you decide what to do with the proceeds.

3. *Fixed installments.* Here, the insurance company agrees to pay you a fixed amount at regular intervals, until the money is all gone. Meantime, it also pays interest on the remaining balance it is holding.

4. *Fixed period.* The company sets a period of time over which it will pay out the proceeds, plus accrued interest. The size of each check depends on how long a time you choose to have the proceeds spread over.

Tips:
- If you choose the fixed installment or fixed period, be sure you have the right to change your mind and withdraw the entire sum at a later date.
- If you are going to buy an annuity (an investment the purpose of which is to pay you a fixed income for a fixed number of years) you do not *have* to buy the annuity through the insurance company. Check what the company offers and compare it with other annuity contracts. Get the highest monthly income possible for each $1,000 you have available to set up the annuity.

- If you have a mortgage, be cautious about paying it off. Even if the proceeds from an insurance policy make it possible to pay off a mortgage, that may not be the best thing to do. For instance, you might be able to take the money you would use to pay it off and invest it at higher rates of interest.

Practical details of life insurance policies

A life insurance policy is a legal contract. Every policy has three parts:

1. *The summary.* This contains the essential details of what you and the insurance company have agreed between you. You agree to pay a stipulated premium on a regular basis. The premium is based on your age and condition of health. In return for your paying the premium, the company agrees to pay the face amount (less any loans that have been made to you, if it is a whole or straight life policy), provided the policy is in force at the time of your death. Usually two additions are made to the summary, if you elect to have them: a) waiver of premium, which means that if you become permanently disabled and unable to earn income the company will continue the policy without your paying for it, and b) an accidental-death "rider" by which the company usually doubles the face value of the policy (e.g., if you are insured for $10,000 and die as the result of an accident, the company pays $20,000 to your beneficiary).

2. *The details.* This is the nitty-gritty: the date your premium payments will be due (you choose from quarterly, semiannual, or annual payments); the grace period (how long you are allowed to go without paying the premium before a penalty will be imposed or the policy canceled—usually 31 days); lapses (how soon the policy will expire if you don't pay); non-forfeiture surrender values (the money you would have coming, under a cash surrender policy, for instance, if you decided to give up the policy or if you simply let it lapse by not paying for it); extended term and reduced paid-up options (ways you can use the cash values that have built up in your policy to provide continuing coverage without making any further payments); and settlement options (as already described in this chapter).

3. *The application.* This is the application form you fill out in order to get the policy. It lists your age, health, other life insurance policies you have, your occupation and activities that may or may not be considered dangerous to your life and health, and how you wish to exercise the rights you have under the policy, such as changing the designation of beneficiary at a later date.

What about life insurance for women?

For many generations, life insurance has been sold mostly to cover the male breadwinner. But today, with more than half of married American women working at full-time jobs and with more and more single parents, there are many women who should have life insurance.

Any couple or family that depends on two incomes to maintain its lifestyle ought to have life insurance on both the man and the woman. If there are children, this is even more important. Insurance should be provided so a husband can gain some replacement for the wife's income, and vice versa, and so the burden of taking care of children is covered during their young years. Often a group insurance program where either of the couple works can cover immediate cash requirements, but does not replace income.

Any single person who has been married and is responsible for supporting children simply *must* have life insurance that will provide coverage until the children are no longer dependent.

How about the spouse—woman or man—who has given up a job to be the homemaker? She—or he—provides services that would cost dollars and cents, and plenty of them, if household help had to be hired for cooking, cleaning, child care, gardening, decorating, chauffeuring. In addition to calculating the value of all those services, you might figure in the expenses of a major illness and, needless to say, of a funeral when you contemplate life insurance on a helpmate.

To find out how much insurance is needed to replace a homemaker, look at both immediate and future needs. Immediate involves the costs of settling the estate and paying for the funeral. Future includes housekeeping and child care for a number of years. To arrive at a sensible figure, work out the monthly cost in dollars, multiply by 12 months and then by the number of years before the children will be on their own.

Insurance on business partners

If one of you is an entrepreneur or has a small business with one or two partners, life insurance is a must. Probably the business is the largest asset you have. It needs protecting so it will continue if a partner or major shareholder dies.

Life insurance can provide the funds for the surviving members of the business to purchase the share owned by the partner who died, thus saving the widow or widower from the nightmare of trying to take up where the deceased spouse left off, and saving the partners from the difficulty of coping with the surviving spouse's coming into the business—and from the embarrassment of not having enough money to buy this person out.

How much insurance is needed? Enough to equal the partner's or shareholder's interest in the business. The arrangement should be formalized in a buy-sell agreement among the partners.

If you are a single owner of a business, life insurance can give your widow or widower the money to live on while the business is being liquidated—again, avoiding the complications of taking over a business that one may not understand or want to be in, but which provides one's livelihood.

Some key points about life insurance

These are important things to remember about life insurance:

1. Buy whole or straight life, or cash value, insurance if you want the premium to stay the same and if you want to build up savings.

2. Buy term insurance if you want maximum protection for the amount you can afford to spend on insurance now and in the immediate future.

3. Shop around. Costs and policy terms vary from company to company.

4. If possible, take advantage of group insurance. It costs less than an individual policy. Check where you work.

5. Remember that your life insurance program should not be carved in stone. Review it regularly—at least once every five years. Recalculate income versus expenses and decide for yourself whether you need to increase or decrease your coverage. Always match coverage to realistic needs.

6. Be aware of the long-term effects of inflation. Insurance you buy based on today's dollars will be worth less and less in purchasing power. So try to think ahead and budget an amount for life insurance that is the best balance you can reach between what you can afford today and what you might need over the next five years.

7. Consider some of the specialized forms of life insurance, such as:

a. *Mortgage life insurance.* Insurance companies and banks sell policies (usually it's a *decreasing term policy*) to cover the portion of a mortgage that would still be owed if the homeowner died at any time. In decreasing term insurance, the premiums remain the same each year but the amount that would be paid in the event of a claim declines each year as the mortgage is paid off. In most cases, the lending institution that holds the mortgage is listed as the beneficiary and is paid directly by the insurance company if there is a claim. My own recommendation: It's better to consider *all* your insurance needs carefully and on balance, and include enough protection to cover your unpaid mortgage. In fact, in many cases it is not even a good idea to pay off the mortgage if its interest rate is a reasonable one. That big a lump of money might be better used for other purposes.

b. *Credit life insurance.* This is like mortgage insurance, but covers such consumer credit as a loan to buy a car. Sometimes the insurance is built into the loan and you get it whether you want it or not. The premium is added to the loan and financed at the same rate, so you end up paying to insure not only the loan principal but also the insurance premium and all the finance charges. In effect—and in actuality—you are insuring the insurance. Incidentally, it is usually legal for a creditor to require you to have insurance as security for the debt. State laws generally make it illegal, however, for creditors to require you to buy it from them. Chances are it will be much cheaper to buy it elsewhere, and you may also be able to pledge a policy you already have. If you cannot meet the health requirements for other insurance coverage, credit life could be a reasonable way to get some protection. Generally, it is better to include coverage for outstanding credit in your total insurance needs. Credit is a liability, remember. You should figure on having a way to cover it in your insurance.

NOW THAT THEY HAVE BOUGHT A HOUSE . . .

. . . the McQuarters have decided they should take on extra life insurance. For their annual family living costs, they added extra financial responsibilities of home ownership. (See Chapter 12, pp. 115–116, 118–120 and 122–127.) If something happened to either of them, the insurance would cover the mortgage—or could be used as an investment, producing income to help the survivor meet the mortgage payments. Looking into it, they learned it would not be necessary to pay off the bank unless they bought actual mortgage insurance that makes the bank the beneficiary. At their ages, they feel they can get the most for their money by buying term insurance. "When we start a family," says Cathy, "we'll review the whole picture and probably make a lot of changes in our insurance." Meantime, she adds, they are considering disability insurance, which their employers do not provide, as well.

Health insurance

Let's face it: A major illness can dump staggering bills on you. Medical costs have not just gone sky-high in recent years—they've reached outer space. So it is essential for you to understand the various types of health insurance you can get, and how to file claims and get the coverage you are entitled to. If at all possible, you should be covered by a group plan, to cut down costs.

It is equally important to keep up to date on the subject. Review your medical insurance regularly every couple of years, and more often as circumstances change: children are born, grown children leave home, you move or are relocated by your company or change jobs.

If you are covered under a group plan where you work, the personnel office there should be able to help you understand exactly what coverage you are getting. If not, you will have to depend on an insurance broker (who handles policies from many companies and knows the advantages and disadvantages of each) or an insurance agent (who represents only a single company) to explain the facts. Listen carefully. Don't hesitate to ask questions, even if you think you're going to sound dumb or naive. If you find there are gaps in your coverage, ask how to close them, how much it will cost, whether or not it is worth it.

Read any policy carefully. Be sure you understand all the small print. You may hear an agent explain that a particular policy will pay up to $25,000 on your surgical bills. In the small print, however, you may discover that $25,000 is the most the insurance company will pay in your entire lifetime. Quite a difference.

1. *Basic hospitalization.* This is provided by private insurance companies and the various Blue Cross policies nationwide. The policy usually pays all or part of a person's hospital bills, including a semi-private room, food, X rays, laboratory tests, operating room fees, and drugs. Usually there is a limit on the number of days the patient may spend in the hospital during any one illness, with a waiting period (usually 90 days) between stays. The better the coverage, the more it costs.

2. *Basic surgical and medical expense.* Again, private companies provide these policies, although the nationwide Blue Shield (usually associated with Blue Cross) is best known. Fees for surgeons or other physicians are paid separately from hospital fees. Usually the insurance company sets a "schedule" of certain fees which it is willing to pay for certain operations. If your surgeon charges more than that fee, you must pay the difference yourself. Obviously, again, the better the coverage the more it costs.

Note: Often, basic hospitalization is combined with basic medical-surgical coverage, as in the

**Worksheet IX: Example One
Pat McQuarter
HOW MUCH LIFE INSURANCE?**

A. ANNUAL FAMILY LIVING COSTS (from Budget form) *(ASSUMING* $27,180
   HOME ownership)

B. SOURCES OF INCOME AVAILABLE

   • Spouse's Income ___$15,000___

   • Social Security Benefits ___0___

   • Income from Income-Producing
     Assets (from Budget form) ___0___

   • Income from Proceeds of Existing Life Insurance Policies
     (use an assumed rate of interest)

     6%—multiply amount of insurance by .06
     10%—multiply amount of insurance by .10
     12%—multiply amount of insurance by .12

     ___$30,000___ × .10 = ___$3,000___

   • Other Sources of Income ___0___

   TOTAL SOURCES OF INCOME   ___$18,000___

C. ADDITIONAL INCOME NEEDED (subtract B from A)   ___$9,180___

D. AMOUNT OF MONEY TO MAKE UP SHORTAGE
   (at an assumed rate of interest)

   6%—multiply by 6
   10%—multiply by 10
   12%—multiply by 12

   ___$9,180___ × 10   ___$91,800___

E. ADDITIONAL CASH REQUIREMENTS

   Final Expenses _____
   Education for Children _____
   Liabilities (including Mortgage) ___$45,000___   ___$45,000___

F. INSURANCE NEEDS (D plus E)   ___$136,800___

Worksheet IX: Example Two
Cathy McQuarter
HOW MUCH LIFE INSURANCE?

A. ANNUAL FAMILY LIVING COSTS (from Budget form) $27,180

B. SOURCES OF INCOME AVAILABLE

- Spouse's Income $20,000
- Social Security Benefits   0
- Income from Income-Producing Assets (from Budget form)   0
- Income from Proceeds of Existing Life Insurance Policies (use an assumed rate of interest)

  6%—multiply amount of insurance by .06
  10%—multiply amount of insurance by .10
  12%—multiply amount of insurance by .12

  $15,000 × .10 = $1,500

- Other Sources of Income _____

TOTAL SOURCES OF INCOME $21,500

C. ADDITIONAL INCOME NEEDED (subtract B from A) $5,680

D. AMOUNT OF MONEY TO MAKE UP SHORTAGE (at an assumed rate of interest)

  6%—multiply by 6
  10%—multiply by 10
  12%—multiply by 12

  $5,680 × 10 $56,800

E. ADDITIONAL CASH REQUIREMENTS

  Final Expenses _____
  Education for Children _____
  Liabilities (including Mortgage) $45,000 $45,000

F. INSURANCE NEEDS (D plus E) $101,800

INSURANCE: HOW MUCH DO YOU NEED? WHAT KIND SHOULD YOU GET?

Blue Cross/Blue Shield plans. Everyone should have at least this basic coverage.

3. *Major Medical.* This type of policy starts where basic hospitalization and basic medical/surgical insurance leave off. It covers the big expenses that are above the maximums of those policies. Usually a Major Medical policy covers extensive hospitalization, surgery, other doctors' fees, private-duty nursing, home medical care, diagnostic work, therapies, medical devices, and rehabilitation. Major Medical policies contain a deductible feature, so you pay a certain amount (usually from $100 to $1,000) before the insurance company pays anything. (Often, the deductible is annual: With each new year, you pay the first $100 or so of claims yourself before the insurance company pays anything.) Once you have gone beyond the deductible amount, most Major Medical policies pay 80 percent or 85 percent of each claim you file. This is called "co-insurance." Usually if you are paying 15 or 20 percent in co-insurance, it goes up to a point—called the "stop-loss limit" and usually set at $2,000 or so—at which the company takes over and pays 100 percent of all legitimate claims. Even this, however, may have a top lifetime limit or maximum. It can be anywhere from $250,000 to $500,000—or entirely limitless. So read the policy carefully and know where you stand.

Tips: If you are shopping for a Major Medical policy (that is, if you have a choice, rather than having to accept whatever your company's personnel department has set up), consider:

1. How much is the deductible? Is it per person covered or per family? (Some policies have a $100 deductible on you, and another $100 deductible on your spouse.)
2. Is the deductible per year—or per claim?
3. What expenses can be applied toward the deductible?
4. What is the maximum the insurance company will pay after you have met the deductible requirements?
5. How much is your co-insurance requirement then?
6. What is the stop-loss limit?
7. What is the absolute maximum the insurance company will pay?
8. Is the policy guaranteed to be renewable (i.e., does the company guarantee that you can keep on renewing it no matter what your state of health)? How long? To what age?
9. Just what limitations does the policy have?

If you are both working, you can each—theoretically—be cited as a dependent on the other's policy. But something called "coordination of benefits" enters into the situation. It usually prevents you both from collecting claims on both policies. One insurance company will make its policy the "primary carrier" on you, with the other insurance company the secondary carrier. Check with each of your personnel departments. Discuss coordination of benefits, and make sure you understand where you stand (you want to avoid getting into a situation like two outfielders, who each think the other is about to catch the ball). Many employers, recognizing the situation of couples who are both employed and are offered similar benefits, will permit one of you to drop the Major Medical coverage and pick up something else instead—maybe a dental plan that you couldn't otherwise get. This option is called "cafeteria" benefits or a "cafeteria" plan. (See Chapter 9.)

Example: Suppose you have a Major Medical plan with an annual deductible of $100 and a stop-loss limit of $2,000. If you have an illness that brings a $1,800 claim, you will have to pay $340 out of your own pocket:

Total claim	$1,800
Less deductible	− 100
	$1,700
Insurance co. pays 80 percent	− 1,360
You pay	$340

Once your out-of-pocket expenses reach $2,000, the insurance company will pick up 100 percent of the medical bill. Your out-of-pocket expenses are calculated to include the $100 deductible as well as all the 15 to 20 percent co-insurance that you have paid.

Any way you can cut down on the cost of a major-medical policy? Yes.

1. Increase the deductible. This means you assume more of the routine medical costs and the insurance company reduces its share of the risk that you will have really large medical bills.

2. Ask for a higher stop-loss limit.

Either step increases the risk you are willing to take on. What you have to do is decide how much risk you can afford to shoulder. Many people would rather pay a higher premium and not have to worry that the out-of-pocket expenses, if a major illness occurs, will send them to the bank to borrow money.

Some things to look for in health insurance

- Combination plans. Many companies, as well as Blue Cross/Blue Shield, offer plans that combine basic hospitalization and medical and surgical benefits with a major-medical plan. This package deal often has lower deductibles.
- Items that are not covered. Check on coverage for cosmetic surgery, eyeglasses and routine checkups for glasses, regular routine physicals, and psychiatric care (if covered, psychiatric care is usually under some special limitation).
- Guaranteed renewable and non-cancellable policies. Some companies reserve the right to cancel at any time. This could be disastrous if they cancelled some day after you had become uninsurable, or when you have an illness that existed before they cancelled. A non-cancellable policy cannot be cancelled during the period it is stated to run. Nor can premiums be increased during this period. Usually, when the stated period has ended (and it can be as short as one year), the company must renew the policy if the policyholder chooses to have it renewed. The company may, however, increase the premium.
- Shop around and consider the alternatives. Everyone should have Major Medical insurance. A major illness or accident can cause severe economic chaos. If you are eligible for any group medical insurance plan, take advantage of it. If not, compare the cost of Blue Cross/Blue Shield with other plans. Note the various features of each. Consider taking a larger deductible, so you'll have a smaller premium to pay.

Valerie and James Nichols have no job benefits . . .

. . . because they are self-employed. So they have had to shop carefully for insurance. They discovered that they could join a professional organization for musicians that provides group medical coverage for its members. This gives them enough coverage at a price they can afford—much lower than if they bought individual policies. Many professional groups and other associations, as well as trade unions, provide group insurance for their members.

Disability insurance

What happens if either of you is disabled by an accident or an illness? The odds that you will be disabled for an extended period before you reach 65 are greater than the odds that you will die before then. If you are disabled, chances are highly likely for your income to drop and your medical bills to climb—simultaneously. That would be disastrous. So whether you are male or female, if your ability to produce income is vital to your situation, you must have insurance that will replace that income if a period of disability stops it.

Social Security provides disability insurance for those who become severely disabled before they reach 65. It considers you to be disabled if you have a physical or mental condition so severe it prevents you from working and is expected to last (or has already lasted) for at least 12 months, or if it is expected to result in death. You have to wait five months after your disability begins before Social Security starts to pay. It pays the same amount as you would start to get upon your retirement at age 65. To be eligible, you must be fully insured under the Social Security regulations (that is, you must have worked for 40 quarter-years or 10 full years).

Disability insurance as a fringe benefit

Most employers these days provide some sort of disability insurance. Probably either or both of you are covered by one of these two types of plan:

1. *Short-term.* This provides modest benefits for a short period. It usually pays weekly, based on your earnings, but with a maximum that can be as low as $150 a week. The waiting period before it starts to pay is from seven to 21 days (i.e., you must be disabled that long before you can start to collect). Some plans pay only for as few as 13 weeks. Others pay for as long as 52 weeks.

2. *Long-term.* This plan is designed to take care of more serious disabilities. Most plans provide a certain percentage of earnings (probably 50 or 60 percent of your base salary). The maximum monthly payment may be $1,500 or $2,000, or more; the waiting period may be anywhere from three to six months; and the payments may continue (if you continue to be disabled) any number of years (5, 10, or 20), or until you reach 65. The fact is, there is a wide variety of benefits and conditions, because there are almost as many different disability policies as there are employers. Check what your company or both your companies are offering and participate in the one that gives you the best plan.

Why does everything seem to stop at age 65? Because that's when Social Security and Medicare take over. Since these two government programs are so universal, and since most people have traditionally retired at 65, the insurance companies just don't bother to work out actuarial tables or develop premium rates for employee group insurance after 65. However, any number of insurance companies do offer individual policies. Many advertise that they pay a certain flat amount daily, unrelated to any medical bills or hospital costs, "from the first day of hospitalization." Such policies are carried by many people who are over 65. They are, in effect, simple disability policies.

Importance of individual policy

Since Social Security and group plans do not usually pay as much as you really need if you become disabled, it could be important for you to have an individual disability policy. If you buy one, the insurance company will base your premium on your age, condition of health, occupation, and income. Policies vary widely, so be sure you know what you are buying.

Features that affect your coverage include:

- Maximum benefit period. The length of time during which the company will pay. Usually expressed in weeks, months, or years. Some policies run for a lifetime as long as you pay the premiums.
- Perils insured against. Either accident only or accident and illness. Be sure you get coverage for both. Some policies that shout their bargain rates in advertising are accident-only, and will not pay you one cent if you are disabled as a result of illness.
- Elimination period. The time that must elapse, after your disability begins, before the company starts to pay. Usually 30, 60, 90, or 120 days. In some policies, even longer.
- Definition of disability. The conditions under which you will be considered disabled for the purpose of collecting benefits.

In buying any disability policy, make sure:

1. The insurance company cannot cancel, increase the premium, or alter the benefits during the life of the policy.
2. The policy is guaranteed renewable.
3. The period covered makes sense. It may be as short as one year or as long as until you reach 65, or your entire lifetime. The longer the coverage, the higher the premium you'll pay.
4. When benefits start. The longer the elimination period before payments begin, the lower your premium. Policies that pay out early (soon after you are disabled) usually charge disproportionately high premiums.

How much disability insurance do you need—and can you afford?

Go back to your worksheets—especially **Budget Net Worth Statement.** Use Worksheet X to calculate what it costs you to live and what sources of income you would continue to have if you become

> **Worksheet X: Yours**
> **HOW MUCH DISABILITY INSURANCE?**
>
> **A.** ANNUAL FAMILY EXPENSES (Budget form) _____
>
> **B.** SOURCES OF INCOME
> - Spouse's Income _____
> - Social Security Benefits _____
> - Disability Benefits from Work _____
>
>   Income from Income-Producing Assets
>   (Assets Evaluation form) _____
> - Other Income _____
>
>   TOTAL SOURCES OF INCOME _____
>
> **C.** ADDITIONAL INCOME NEEDED
> (Subtract B from A) _____
>
> **D.** AMOUNT OF MONEY TO MAKE UP SHORTAGE
> (at an assumed rate of interest)
>
>   6% multiply line C by 6
>   10% multiply line C by 10
>   12% multiply line C by 12 _____

disabled. Look over your current expenses—and then remember that you can be sure expenses will *rise* if you are disabled. If you should have the bad luck to need special medical provisions and special care, expenses will go up like a rocket.

When Patrick McQuarter calculated how much disability insurance he might require, he got a pleasant surprise. Thanks to the McQuarters' home ownership, Cathy's salary, and Social Security benefits, Pat didn't require any disability insurance.

Property and casualty insurance

What is the biggest investment you have? Probably your home—whether you own or rent. If you had a severe fire in your home, or a hurricane or flood roared through your town, or thieves broke in and took your TV and stereo and silver, could you make repairs and buy replacements out of your financial assets? Few of us could. That's why it's imperative that you cover your home with property and casualty insurance.

Most people understand the basic idea of this coverage: If a fire, theft, damage from wind or flood occur, we will be reimbursed for the loss. But few really understand what will be covered by the insurance company and what they must take care of themselves.

This kind of policy is called a "homeowner's" policy, but you don't have to be a homeowner to get it. Usually it covers:

1. Fire insurance on the house (i.e., the building itself).

Worksheet X: Example
Patrick McQuarter
HOW MUCH DISABILITY INSURANCE?

A. ANNUAL FAMILY EXPENSES (Budget form) (ASSUMING HOME OWNERSHIP) ___$27,180___

B. SOURCES OF INCOME
- Spouse's Income ___$15,000___
- Social Security Benefits ___$12,000 (approximate)___
- Disability Benefits from Work ___0___
- Income from Income-Producing Assets (~~Assets Evaluation form~~) ___$400___
- Other Income _____
  TOTAL SOURCES OF INCOME ___$27,400___

C. ADDITIONAL INCOME NEEDED
(Subtract B from A) ___None___

D. AMOUNT OF MONEY TO MAKE UP SHORTAGE
(at an assumed rate of interest)

   6% multiply line C by 6
   10% multiply line C by 10
   12% multiply line C by 12   _____

---

2. Extended coverage for damage to the house (i.e., the building) by such things as wind, hail, falling objects, smoke, motor vehicles.

3. Allowance for additional living expenses if you have to live elsewhere while repairs are made.

4. Personal property lost because of fire, theft, other damage, or mysterious disappearance (this covers such items as clothing, books, cameras, stereos, all household furnishings).

5. Liability. This covers claims based on any injuries suffered by others on and caused by your property. Classic example: the mailman is bitten by your dog or slips on the ice on your sidewalk. The insurance coverage includes payments for medical expenses.

See Exhibit 9 for the six major types of homeowner policy, each identified by the name used by the insurance company.

Tips: Some things you should know about homeowner's insurance.

- The policy provides protection at a specified address, and usually *only* at that address. Most policies, however, will cover losses that occur when you are traveling or if possessions are in storage or, for instance, at the cleaner's. They won't cover losses suffered by a family member who is, in effect, living elsewhere—say, in a college dorm during the majority of the

Exhibit 9
GUIDE TO HOMEOWNERS POLICIES

These are the principal features of *standard* homeowners policies. Some will differ in a few respects from the standard ones. Policy conditions may also vary according to state requirements.

	HO-1 (basic form)	HO-2 (broad form)	HO-3 (special form)	HO-4 (renters' contents broad form)	HO-5 (comprehensive form)	HO-6 (for condominium owners)
PERILS COVERED (see key below)	perils 1–10	perils 1–17	perils 1–17 on personal property except glass breakage; all risks, except those specifically excluded, on buildings	perils 1–17	all risks except those specifically excluded	perils 1–17
STANDARD AMOUNT OF INSURANCE ON house and attached structures	based on property value, minimum $15,000	based on property value, minimum $15,000	based on property value, minimum $20,000	10% of personal insurance on additions and alterations to unit	based on property value, minimum $30,000	$1,000 on owner's additions and alterations to unit
detached structures	10% of amount of insurance on house	10% of amount of insurance on house	10% of amount of insurance on house	no coverage	10% of amount of insurance on house	no coverage
trees, shrubs, plants	5% of amount of insurance on house. $500 maximum per item	5% of amount of insurance on house. $500 maximum per item	5% of amount of insurance on house. $500 maximum per item	10% of personal property insurance, $500 maximum per item	5% of amount of insurance on house. $500 maximum per item	10% of personal property insurance, $500 maximum per item
personal property	50% of insurance on house; 10% for property normally kept at another residence, minimum $1,000	50% of insurance on house; 10% for property normally kept at another residence, minimum $1,000	50% of insurance on house; 10% for property normally kept at another residence, minimum $1,000	based on value of property, minimum $6,000; 10% for property normally kept at another residence, minimum $1,000	50% of insurance on house; 10% for property normally kept at another residence, minimum $1,000	based on value of property, minimum $6,000; 10% for property normally kept at another residence, minimum $1,000
loss of use, additional living expense; loss of rent if rental unit uninhabitable	10% of insurance on house	20% of insurance on house	20% of insurance on house	20% of personal property insurance	20% of insurance on house	40% of personal property insurance
SPECIAL LIMITS OF LIABILITY		Money, bank notes, bullion, gold other than goldware, silver other than silverware, platinum, coins, and medals—$100. Securities, accounts, deeds, manuscripts, passports, tickets, stamps, etc.—$500. Watercraft, including their trailers, furnishings, equipment, and outboard motors—$500. Trailers not used with watercraft—$500. Grave markers—$500. Theft of jewelry, watches, furs, precious and semiprecious stones—$500. Theft of silverware, silver-plated ware, goldware, gold-plated ware, and pewterware—$1,000. Theft of guns—$1,000.				
CREDIT CARD, FORGERY, COUNTERFEIT MONEY	$500	$500	$500	$500	$500	$500
COMPREHENSIVE PERSONAL LIABILITY	$25,000	$25,000	$25,000	$25,000	$25,000	$25,000
DAMAGE TO PROPERTY OF OTHERS	$250	$250	$250	$250	$250	$250
MEDICAL PAYMENTS	$500 per person	$500 per person	$500 per person	$500 per person	$500 per person	$500 per person

Key to perils covered
1. fire, lightning
2. windstorm, hail
3. explosion
4. riots
5. damage by aircraft
6. damage by vehicles not owned or operated by people covered by policy
7. damage from smoke
8. vandalism, malicious mischief
9. theft
10. glass breakage
11. falling objects
12. weight of ice, snow, sleet
13. collapse of building or any part of building
14. leakage or overflow of water or steam from a plumbing, heating or air-conditioning system
15. bursting, cracking, burning, or bulging of a steam or hot-water heating system, or of appliances for heating water
16. freezing of plumbing, heating, and air-conditioning systems and domestic appliances
17. injury to electrical appliances, devices, fixtures, and wiring (excluding tubes, transistors, and similar electronic components) from short circuits or other accidentally generated currents

INSURANCE: HOW MUCH DO YOU NEED? WHAT KIND SHOULD YOU GET?

year. That's why my parents got so upset when I expected their insurance to cover my stolen stereo.

- Most policies limit the amount they will pay to the actual current cash value of the stolen or destroyed property. The insurance companies take the age of the article into account; they depreciate it for each year you have owned it. Since the actual cash value may be a lot lower than what you will have to pay to replace the item—especially the way property has appreciated in recent years—this practice by the insurance companies can be costly to you. You can, however, ask the insurance company to add a "replacement endorsement" (for payment at replacement value) to your policy for a modest increase in the premium. It will be worth having if a major loss occurs.

- As Exhibit 9 shows, the typical standard homeowner's policy limits the amount the company will pay for a loss of personal property. Usually, the limit is 50 percent of the total amount the building is insured for. The loss is also limited to fire, windstorm, and other specific perils (carefully listed in the policy). If you have some special things that are valuable—antique furniture, an art collection, jewelry, silver, or books—ask for a "personal property floater schedule." This will give you extra coverage. It can be expensive, however. The insurance company will want to have appraisals made, giving a cash value to everything you put on the schedule. If you take out this kind of coverage, be sure to reevaluate these items at least every couple of years, as their value will rise with inflation and may change depending on the market for them. Also, update the list regularly to delete any items you no longer possess, and add any new ones. Usually, to help keep the premium cost down, this kind of coverage has a deductible amount. **Note:** If you are carrying a personal property floater on your homeowner's policy, your own record keeping—including an inventory of items, receipts for purchases, and photographs of items—will be vital.

Homeowners are not the only ones who need coverage. If you are renting, you need personal property and liability coverage just as much as if you are the owner. A person who slips on your rented sidewalk, for instance, can sue you as well as the landlord. So talk to an insurance agent or broker about a tenant's policy. It could provide repayment for theft of your newly acquired wedding gifts or your spanking new appliances or other purchases. It could pay for smoke damage from a fire in the apartment next door to you.

If you're a condominium owner, ask about a special insurance form. You're really kind of halfway between being a tenant and a homeowner. Make sure the condo association is carrying insurance on the common elements: the building itself and the recreational areas, hallways, driveways, and parking spaces you share with your neighbors. But make sure you are covered, as owners of your condo, for everything within your own unit: the interior walls, bathroom and kitchen fixtures, appliances and cabinets, all your household goods, and personal property. And don't forget liability insurance. The association must, of course, carry liability, but if someone should be seriously injured, for instance, in the commonly owned pool, each of you who are unit owners could be assessed to cover any damages above and beyond the association's insurance. The insurance people call this a Loss Assessment Endorsement. You may have to ask specifically for it to be added to your policy, so check the association's policy and have your broker or agent make sure your own policy picks up where the association's leaves off.

How much insurance should you carry on your home? It depends on the replacement value of what you're insuring—the building and its contents. What's important, again, is regular review. You cannot just let your homeowner's policy sit there while you renew it year after year, because inflation as well as the general appreciation of real estate are both adding up all the time to greater replacement cost. Most insurance companies and their agents add an increment every year for that upward spiral, and simply bill you for the increase.

Ask yourselves these questions:

- Are we buying collectibles that call for special insurance?
- Should we get appraisals of certain valuables—antiques, heirlooms—so we can take out a personal property floater?

- Since the floater is relatively expensive, do we want to insure only those items that would be really difficult to replace, such as heirlooms?
- Are we keeping smaller items in a safe-deposit box at the bank—a less expensive way to handle the risk?

Put up an umbrella, too

An "umbrella liability policy" could be valuable insurance on a rainy day. It provides coverage that your homeowner's or your automobile insurance policies do not provide: coverage of special situations. Say your dog inflicts really terrible damage on the mailman—more than your homeowner's liability covers—or you knock over a pile of antique china in a china shop and are sued for damages. (For this, for example, homeowner's will pay you a maximum of $500 despite the fact that you managed to destroy $1,200 worth of china). An umbrella policy can cover the difference. Cost? For an annual premium of about $100, you can get about $1 million in coverage.

Lawsuits are no fun

You should be aware that while liability insurance protects you against lawsuits by the person bitten by your dog or injured on your icy sidewalk, it does *not* cover you in a situation where a repairperson, housekeeper, gardener, or painter is injured while working in your home. They should be covered by worker's compensation. Never assume that a repairperson or housepainter or other contractor has his or her own insurance. Ask to see proof.

How much liability insurance is enough? The range carried by most people runs from $25,000 to $300,000. Knowing how many liability claims there are these days and the size of some of the settlements you read about in the papers, you can well imagine that coverage for as much as $1 million is not a bad idea if you have a fairly substantial combined income and assets. Lawyers who are suing for injured parties usually try for as much as they can, and they dig the well where the water is.

Automobile insurance

In most states, the law requires auto insurance. If you live where it is not required, and if you drive without it, you are asking for trouble. A single accident could put you into financial disaster.

You should be informed on five aspects of auto insurance:

1. *Liability coverage.* This protects you, the owner of the car, from claims that may result from the injury or death of another person or from damage to property. The other person may be a pedestrian or passenger or driver of another vehicle. The situation itself may be almost anything; the newspapers regularly report crazy vehicular accidents that no one could have anticipated. The property? It could be another vehicle or a tree, fence, building, or any other stationary object.

When you look at an automobile insurance policy, you see figures like this: $100,000/$300,000–$25,000. What do they mean? The first two figures indicate that the insurance company will pay up to $100,000 for bodily injuries to any one person, and up to $300,000 for injuries to two or more persons in any one accident. The $25,000 means they will pay that maximum for property damage.

2. *Collision.* This pays for damage to your car caused by a collision with some other vehicle or with any other object, whether stationary or moving. Usually, to cut down on the premium cost, it carries a deductible of $100 to $300, so you will pay for minor repairs yourself. This saves the insurance company from having to handle small claims for minor damage, which would greatly increase their overhead costs and thus raise everyone's costs. Usually the insurance company pays for the cost of all repairs higher than the deductible amount. If the car is totaled, the company pays the actual cash value of the car, less your deductible amount. How much collision coverage you get thus depends on the type, make, and age of the car. The company is never obligated to pay more for repairs than the car was worth before the accident, less the salvage value of the car. Most insurance companies will let you choose how much deductible you want to risk; the higher your risk, the lower your premium cost.

3. *Comprehensive.* Many factors, in addition to driving accidents caused by you or by someone else, are capable of damaging your car: fire, theft, wind,

hail, falling objects, to name a few. So you need comprehensive insurance to cover them. Again, a deductibility clause may reduce your premium.

4. *Medical payments*. This section of your policy covers any passengers who may be injured while riding in your car. It usually also covers any members of your family who are injured while riding in any other vehicle.

5. *No-fault insurance*. The basic principle of liability insurance is that one person must be to blame for an accident in order for another person to qualify for compensation. But proving whose fault it was is not always possible, and it nearly always takes time and may involve a lawsuit. As a result, in order to eliminate the need for liability suits, many states have adopted no-fault insurance laws. Their objective is to make your insurance company pay for your losses, while the other person's pays for his or hers. Under no-fault law, unless the expenses covered by no-fault exceed a certain dollar limit, you may not take action against the other party.

What is the basis for insurance rates? It's a highly complex procedure. Each insurance company periodically computes its income from premiums in each state in which it is entitled to write insurance. Obviously, no company is in business to lose money; each must take in enough to cover what it pays out to settle claims as well as cover its overhead costs and maintain a profit margin. The total amount of premiums in the state is divided among various territories within the state. In each such area, the company establishes a set of base premiums for the individual coverages (liability, collision, comprehensive, medical) that make up an auto insurance policy. These base rates are considered to pertain to a stereotype: an adult male (usually over the age of 25) driving a standard car only for pleasure, not business. Using that as a base, everyone who buys a policy pays more or less than a standard rate, depending on how the company sees him or her as a risk in relation to this stereotypical person.

In effect, you are assigned to a group according to characteristics that the company (or "underwriters") believe predict the group's chances of creating insurance losses. Out of this comes the typical situation in which a policyholder in a large urban area pays more for "the same insurance" than one in a small town or suburban area.

What are some of those characteristics or criteria that determine where you land on the scale? Age, sex, and marital status; record of accidents and previous traffic violations; type of car, number of cars in the family, and mileage traveled in a year; use of the car for pleasure, business, daily commutation, or farming. Each such characteristic is assigned a numerical weight based on its tendency to increase or decrease the probability of an insurance claim or loss. The possible combinations of such rating factors is just about limitless, and it seems to get more complicated every year.

The extreme example of how the total numerical weight of various characteristics could affect *you* is the experience some of you had when you started to drive as an unmarried male under the age of 25. Your parents' auto insurance premium probably doubled—a fact that hit home if they insisted that you pay for the difference. And you have no doubt been aware of this ever since. Now, if you are over 25, or married, or both, you are seeing a decrease in those horrendous premium costs. (Good reminder: If you haven't notified the insurance company of a change in marital status, do so; it could save you some money.)

Tips: If you have an accident, and you've never had one before, remember:

- Your agent should be your best ally. When you are buying auto insurance, find an agent or broker who will assist you in every way and work on your behalf. The policy may not be the lowest-cost one, but the service he or she provides in the event of an accident will be worth its weight in gold.
- When you are filing a claim, you cannot avoid running around to get the estimates the insurance company requires. Certain things must be done, and they take time.
- Always keep your cool in car insurance matters. Do not get rattled. If the insurance company sends an adjuster to estimate damage, don't let this person get to you. Stay calm. Be firm. And try not to talk too much. If you feel you are not satisfied, ask to speak to the adjuster's superior.

When you are buying auto insurance or reviewing what you have, keep these points in mind:

1. Nothing stays the same. Policies must be reviewed and updated regularly.

2. Premium rates vary according to where you live and according to the amount of risk you are willing to shoulder yourself by accepting higher deductibility.

3. Liability coverage should be the absolute maximum you can get. If you have substantial assets, you need substantial liability coverage. Anyone who decides to sue you will go for all they can get.

4. Your car's value diminishes as it gets older. Keep an eye on its cash value. If you own the car long enough, the annual premiums for collision coverage will begin to approach the replacement value of the car. When that happens, it's time to stop buying collision coverage.

5. Shop around for auto insurance. It is high-priced stuff, and many companies are competing for your business. Best approach: Work with an independent broker who will get you the best coverage for the lowest premium cost. Talk to several brokers before you decide.

Some insurance you may never need

Flight insurance is sold at airport counters and through automatic machines. Do you need it? Remember that fewer people die in air crashes than in car accidents, poisonings, accidental falls, or from choking on food. If you buy your airline tickets on some charge cards, they automatically cover you with life insurance during your flight.

When you rent a car, you are usually asked if you want coverage—for an additional fee—in case the rental car gets into an accident. This usually covers the deductible, for which the rental company would hold you responsible. Check your own policy—it may cover you while driving a rented car.

Heard about pet insurance? It's been offered since 1982. One such policy costs from $40 to $80 for up to $2,000 of coverage. When "Baby" cashed in one of his nine lives by falling out a fourth-floor window, an operation to save the other eight lives left both front paws in casts—plenty expensive. Next, he was rushed 120 miles round-trip every day for weeks to get special radiation treatments. Pet insurance would have been mighty nice to have.

Summary

Whatever insurance you are considering and reviewing—life, health, disability, property and casualty, or automobile—you should ask yourselves some basic questions:

What if? What if this, what if that? What risks do we take? What things could possibly happen?

Which of these risks must we assume ourselves, and which can we pay an insurance company to take over? That, in turn, will determine what kinds of policies and coverage are needed.

How much will it cost? Shop around. Get several quotes, or bids, from various agents and companies. Make your decisions based on coverage, service, and cost.

Are we carrying enough insurance—or too much—for our situation right now? Updating and reevaluating policies every so often is most important.

A PRIMER ON TAXES 11

Countless volumes have been written on taxes. How-to books proliferate like flies during the spring tax season. There's more information out there than you could ever hope to absorb. So this chapter is not going to try to tell you everything about taxes. It is simply going to try to fill you in on the basics, particularly as they pertain to a newlywed couple.

Certainly you are aware that the federal income tax, collected by the Internal Revenue Service (IRS), has the greatest impact on the average citizen, followed by the various taxes imposed by our state and local governments.

Before you were married you probably filed a simple tax return (the 1040A). Your employer deducted your taxes and, if more had been withheld than you needed to pay, you got a refund—which you promptly spent. Now you are married and, with the changes and choices you now face, there are a lot of details about taxes to learn and understand. Perhaps one of the biggest changes is that you can now take advantage of the deduction for two-earner married couples that the IRS has (at long last) put into effect to redress the long-standing "marriage tax penalty."

Before we get to some of the details, let's look at the federal income tax system. It is highly complex. Since it was begun in 1913, it has been greatly modified and changes constantly. Today its basic taxing policy states that you must file an income tax return if:

1. You are single and have an income of $3,300 or more for the year.

2. You are a surviving spouse with a dependent child and have an income of $4,400 or more.

3. You are a married person entitled to file jointly and your combined income with your spouse is $5,400 or more, provided that

   a. you and your spouse are living together at the end of the year
   b. no other person is entitled to claim you or your spouse as an exemption
   c. your spouse does not file a separate tax return.

4. Your gross income is $1,000 or more and you are married and filing a separate return but you are

not living with your spouse at the end of the tax year, or you can be claimed as a dependent on your parents' return and you have unearned income of $1,000 or more.

5. You have net earnings of $400 or more from self-employment, even if you do not meet any of requirements 1 through 4.

Tip: For tax purposes, a husband and wife may file a joint return for the year even if you were married only on the very last day of that year.

Forms

The IRS has a number of forms that you will become familiar with over the years ahead. Those who are single use Form 1040EZ if they meet certain requirements. Form 1040A is for all whose income is less than $50,000 and whose itemized deductions do not exceed the zero bracket amount. You file Form 1040 if you can't use 1040EZ or 1040A. If you are self-employed, you add Schedule C, Profit (or Loss) from Business or Profession, to Form 1040.

Deductions

When Alice visited Wonderland, she found that when games were played there was a prize for everyone. The IRS is sort of like that: It has deductions for everyone. Whatever income you have, the first thing you do—before you even consider paying taxes on it—is deduct something from it. For example, every taxpayer gets a built-in deduction right at the start. It's called the "zero bracket amount." The exact amount depends on which of the filing statuses, 1 through 4 (see page 00), you are in; the deduction has been built into all tax tables and tax rate schedules. For unmarried individuals, the zero bracket amount is $2,300; for married individuals filing joint returns, $3,400; and for married individuals filing separate returns, $1,700. Any other permissible deductions you want to make must exceed your zero bracket amount or you may not take them off.

You also deduct "personal exemptions" right at the beginning of the tax form. Currently, $1,000 is allowed for each such personal exemption—one for each of you (whether or not you both had income) and one for each child you have.

Other deductions may be taken for: medical expenses that exceed five percent of your adjusted gross income (see p. 00); a variety of taxes you have paid (including personal property, real estate, sales, and state and local income taxes); interest paid on loans (including mortgage and personal loans, and finance charges on credit cards, bank cash reserve accounts, or other charge accounts); charitable contributions; and casualty and property losses. These are often referred to as "itemized deductions." If you are claiming them, you have to use the IRS's Schedule A, Form 1040, rather than its simpler short form.

Marginal tax bracket

You have often heard that someone is "in the 25 percent tax bracket" or "in the 50 percent tax bracket" or whatever. When the term "tax bracket" is used, it refers to the marginal tax bracket. Here's an example of how it works.

Suppose you are filing a joint return on a taxable income that is more than $24,600 but less than $29,900 (after you have deducted all your allowable deductions). Your tax will be $4,037 according to the tax schedule, plus 26 percent of the amount that is more than $24,600. So your marginal tax bracket is 26 percent.

You can find out your marginal tax bracket by checking Schedule X, Y, or Z—whichever is appropriate to your income level.

To decrease your income taxes . . .

What we all want to do—legally—is increase gross income but reduce our "tax liability" (a fancy term meaning how much you owe). The IRS can't help you increase your gross income, but it does help you reduce your *taxable* income by legitimate means: by letting you make the many types of deduction already listed, by not taxing the income you can earn by owning municipal bonds, by taxing you at a lower rate on capital gains income than the rate you pay on "ordinary," or "earned," income.

What is the difference between ordinary income and capital gains income? Take the example already used. For every dollar earned over $24,600 but below $29,900, you would pay a tax of 26 cents. That's

A PRIMER ON TAXES

Exhibit 10

1983 Federal Income Tax Brackets

Single		Joint	
10,800–12,900	19%	16,000–20,200	19%
12,900–15,000	21%	20,200–24,600	23%
15,000–18,200	24%	24,600–29,900	26%
18,200–23,500	28%	29,900–35,200	30%
23,500–28,800	32%	35,200–45,800	35%
28,800–34,100	36%	45,800–60,000	40%
34,100–41,500	40%	60,000–85,600	44%
41,500–55,300	45%	85,600–109,400	48%
55,300+	50%	109,400+	50%

$26 of tax on every $100 of income over $24,600. But if you sell a capital asset (stocks, bonds, your home, for example) that you have held for over a year, you pay a "capital gains tax" on your profit that is much lower. Say you sell stock and make a gain of $1,000 over what you paid for it. If that $1,000 were ordinary income, you would have to pay a tax of $260 on it (26% of $1,000). But the capital gain tax is figured on 40 percent of the gain (at your marginal tax bracket). You figure 40 percent of $1,000 is $400, and 26 percent of that is $104. This means you pay $156 less ($260 minus $104) on the same amount of income. It is important to understand this before you read Chapter 13 on investments.

Gross income, less adjustments

Not only can you make deductions, you can also make "adjustments." Legitimate business expenses are adjustments. So are savings you put into an IRA. So is alimony you have paid. After you have taken off (deducted) the adjustments, you have what is called "adjusted gross income."

If you have compiled deductions that exceed your zero bracket amount, you may fill out Schedule A and deduct, from your adjusted gross income, any excess that the deductions reach that is more than your zero bracket amount. From that figure you also subtract the exemptions to which you are entitled. That brings you to your total tax liability. From it, you may deduct credits, such as child care credit, and any payments already made (such as tax withheld by your employer as shown on your W2 form, or payments you have already made on your estimated tax). After deducting those last two items, you come to the amount you owe or the refund the IRS owes you. It all looks like this (see Form 1040, starting with Line 32 for adjusted gross income):

    Gross income
    − Adjustments
    Adjusted gross income
    − Excess deductions
    − Exemptions
    Tax liability
    − Credits
    − Payments already made
    Amount you owe or IRS owes you

Some things to remember about taxes

- Tax laws are always changing. The changes are likely to affect you and your tax return. So review key provisions of any new tax laws as

reported in newspapers and magazines. Check booklets put out by accounting firms. Don't miss any new provisions that might reduce or change what you owe the IRS.
- Take advantage of legal deductions. They were put into the tax laws to help you, so there's nothing wrong with using any tax-avoidance technique that is legal.
- Buying a home is probably the first tax-advantaged investment you will make. A person who rents can never match the deductions for interest and property taxes that a homeowner gets.
- Tax-saving investments fall into two categories: 1) those that permit your investment income to grow while deferring and in some cases avoiding taxes on such earnings (example: an IRA), and 2) those that actually reduce the taxes you owe on salary and other income (example: a salary reduction plan).
- If you are making a tax-saving investment, be sure it fits your needs and objectives both when you make it and for the near future. A tax-advantaged investment is no advantage if you soon find that you need the money for something else after all and must cash in the investment and suffer a penalty.

IF YOU ARE SELF-EMPLOYED, LIKE THE NICHOLSES...

... look over their tax forms. First take a look at Schedule C, Profit (or Loss) from Business or Profession (Exhibit 12). It shows that Valerie and James took in a gross total of $25,275 in 1983 as musicians. From this, they were allowed to deduct $220 for advertising, $1,000 worth of car expenses (covering mileage and maintenance related to their business), $270 for office supplies and postage (for sending their promotional mailings, invoices to people they worked for, and payments on purchases made), $220 for supplies (including guitar strings, saxophone reeds, staff paper), $150 for utilities (the share of their electricity and telephone service that were used for business), $1,800 for instruments, and $1,000 for a new public address system. All these deductions add up to $4,660. Taken from the $25,275 gross, this leaves them $20,615 to report as profit. It is entered on line 12 of Form 1040 (Exhibit 11).

Form 1040 shows they are reporting $4,500 in interest income (it comes from their savings and Valerie's inheritance). So their total income is $25,115, from which they deduct $1,186 as a married couple both of whom are working.

On page 2, they deduct exemptions of $1,000 each, giving them a taxable income of $21,929 to look up in the Tax Schedule. It shows their tax to be $3,041. But that's not all. They must also pay a self-employment tax (the same as Social Security), which adds $1,928, so their total tax comes to $4,969.

THE McQUARTERS CHANGED THEIR WITHHOLDING...

If you have the discipline to save voluntarily, you might try doing what the McQuarters did—when you buy a house.

After they got their house, they each had their employers *reduce* the amount withheld from their paychecks because they were now going to itemize and deduct the interest and taxes paid on the house. This means that, instead of waiting half way into next year to get the IRS refund they are entitled to, they will have more money each month to put into house payments or into savings, where it can earn some interest.

The IRS pays you no interest on the money it withholds from your pay, no matter how large a refund you get or how long they have held your money.

HOW THE McQUARTERS GAIN FROM THEIR "TWO-EARNER" MARRIAGE...

The IRS now permits any married couple, both of whom are earning income and who file a joint re-

Exhibit 11

Form 1040 — U.S. Individual Income Tax Return 1983

Department of the Treasury—Internal Revenue Service

For the year January 1–December 31, 1983, or other tax year beginning , 1983, ending , 19   OMB No. 1545-0074

Use IRS label. Otherwise, please print or type.

Your first name and initial (if joint return, also give spouse's name and initial): **VALERIE & JAMES**   Last name: **NICHOLS**
Your social security number: **987 65 4320**

Present home address (Number and street, including apartment number, or rural route): **100 BIG SKY DRIVE**
Spouse's social security number: **042 68 1505**

City, town or post office, State, and ZIP code: **ALAMO, TEXAS**
Your occupation: **MUSICIAN**
Spouse's occupation: **MUSICIAN**

Presidential Election Campaign
Do you want $1 to go to this fund? .... Yes ☒ No ☐
If joint return, does your spouse want $1 to go to this fund? Yes ☒ No ☐
Note: Checking "Yes" will not increase your tax or reduce your refund.

For Privacy Act and Paperwork Reduction Act Notice, see Instructions.

Filing Status
Check only one box.
1. ☐ Single
2. ☒ Married filing joint return (even if only one had income)
3. ☐ Married filing separate return. Enter spouse's social security no. above and full name here.
4. ☐ Head of household (with qualifying person). (See page 6 of Instructions.) If the qualifying person is your unmarried child but not your dependent, write child's name here.
5. ☐ Qualifying widow(er) with dependent child (Year spouse died ▶ 19   ). (See page 6 of Instructions.)

Exemptions
Always check the box labeled Yourself. Check other boxes if they apply.

6a ☒ Yourself   ☐ 65 or over   ☐ Blind
b ☒ Spouse   ☐ 65 or over   ☐ Blind
Enter number of boxes checked on 6a and b ▶ **2**

c First names of your dependent children who lived with you _____
Enter number of children listed on 6c ▶

d Other dependents:
(1) Name	(2) Relationship	(3) Number of months lived in your home	(4) Did dependent have income of $1,000 or more?	(5) Did you provide more than one-half of dependent's support?

Enter number of other dependents ▶

e Total number of exemptions claimed   Add numbers entered in boxes above ▶ **2**

Income
Please attach Copy B of your Forms W-2, W-2G, and W-2P here.

If you do not have a W-2, see page 5 of Instructions.

7 Wages, salaries, tips, etc. 7
8 Interest income (also attach Schedule B if over $400 or you have any All-Savers interest) ... 8 **4,500**
9a Dividends (also attach Schedule B if over $400) _____ , 9b Exclusion _____
 c Subtract line 9b from line 9a and enter the result 9c
10 Refunds of State and local income taxes, from worksheet on page 10 of Instructions (do not enter an amount unless you deducted those taxes in an earlier year—see page 10 of Instructions) 10
11 Alimony received 11
12 Business income or (loss) (attach Schedule C) 12 **20,615**
13 Capital gain or (loss) (attach Schedule D) 13
14 40% capital gain distributions not reported on line 13 (See page 10 of Instructions) 14
15 Supplemental gains or (losses) (attach Form 4797) 15
16 Fully taxable pensions, IRA distributions, and annuities not reported on line 17 16
17a Other pensions and annuities, including rollovers. Total received 17a
 b Taxable amount, if any, from worksheet on page 10 of Instructions 17b
18 Rents, royalties, partnerships, estates, trusts, etc. (attach Schedule E) 18
19 Farm income or (loss) (attach Schedule F) 19
20a Unemployment compensation (insurance). Total received   20a
 b Taxable amount, if any, from worksheet on page 11 of Instructions 20b
21 Other income (state nature and source—see page 11 of Instructions) _____   21

Please attach check or money order here.

22 **Total income.** Add amounts in column for lines 7 through 21 ▶ 22 **25,115**

Adjustments to Income
(See Instructions on page 11)

23 Moving expense (attach Form 3903 or 3903F) 23
24 Employee business expenses (attach Form 2106) 24
25a IRA deduction, from the worksheet on page 12 ...... 25a
 b Enter here IRA payments you made in 1984 that are included in line 25a above ▶
26 Payments to a Keogh (H.R. 10) retirement plan 26
27 Penalty on early withdrawal of savings 27
28 Alimony paid 28
29 Deduction for a married couple when both work (attach Schedule W) 29 **1,186**
30 Disability income exclusion (attach Form 2440) 30
31 **Total adjustments.** Add lines 23 through 30 .... ▶ 31 **1,186**

Adjusted Gross Income
32 **Adjusted gross income.** Subtract line 31 from line 22. If this line is less than $10,000, see "Earned Income Credit" (line 59) on page 16 of Instructions. If you want IRS to figure your tax, see page 3 of Instructions 32 **23,929**

FINANCIAL FITNESS FOR NEWLYWEDS

Exhibit 11 (continued)

Form 1040 (1983) — Page 2

Tax Computation (See Instructions on page 13)

Line	Description	Amount
33	Amount from line 32 (adjusted gross income)	23,929
34a	If you itemize, complete Schedule A (Form 1040) and enter the amount from Schedule A, line 28	

Caution: If you have unearned income and can be claimed as a dependent on your parent's return, check here ▶ ☐ and see page 13 of the Instructions. Also see page 13 of the Instructions if:
- You are married filing a separate return and your spouse itemizes deductions, OR
- You file Form 4563, OR
- You are a dual-status alien.

Line	Description	Amount
34b	If you do not itemize deductions on Schedule A (Form 1040), complete the worksheet on page 14. Then enter the allowable part of your charitable contributions here	
35	Subtract line 34a or 34b, whichever applies, from line 33	
36	Multiply $1,000 by the total number of exemptions claimed on Form 1040, line 6e	2,000
37	Taxable Income. Subtract line 36 from line 35	21,929
38	Tax. Enter tax here and check if from ☑ Tax Table, ☐ Tax Rate Schedule X, Y, or Z, or ☐ Schedule G	
39	Additional Taxes. (See page 14 of Instructions.) Enter here and check if from ☐ Form 4970, ☐ Form 4972, ☐ Form 5544, or ☐ section 72 penalty taxes	
40	**Total.** Add lines 38 and 39 ▶	3,042

Credits (See Instructions on page 14)

Line	Description	Amount
41	Credit for the elderly (attach Schedules R&RP)	
42	Foreign tax credit (attach Form 1116)	
43	Investment credit (attach Form 3468)	
44	Partial credit for political contributions	
45	Credit for child and dependent care expenses (attach Form 2441)	
46	Jobs credit (attach Form 5884)	
47	Residential energy credit (attach Form 5695)	
48	**Total credits.** Add lines 41 through 47	
49	**Balance.** Subtract line 48 from line 40 and enter difference (but not less than zero) ▶	3,042

Other Taxes (Including Advance EIC Payments)

Line	Description	Amount
50	Self-employment tax (attach Schedule SE)	1,928
51	Alternative minimum tax (attach Form 6251)	
52	Tax from recapture of investment credit (attach Form 4255)	
53	Social security tax on tip income not reported to employer (attach Form 4137)	
54	Uncollected employee social security tax and RRTA tax on tips (from Form W-2)	
55	Tax on an IRA (attach Form 5329)	
56	**Total tax.** Add lines 49 through 55 ▶	4,970

Payments (Attach Forms W-2, W-2G, and W-2P to front.)

Line	Description	Amount
57	Federal income tax withheld	
58	1983 estimated tax payments and amount applied from 1982 return	4,500
59	Earned income credit. If line 33 is under $10,000, see page 16	
60	Amount paid with Form 4868	
61	Excess social security tax and RRTA tax withheld (two or more employers)	
62	Credit for Federal tax on special fuels and oils (attach Form 4136)	
63	Regulated Investment Company credit (attach Form 2439)	
64	**Total payments.** Add lines 57 through 63 ▶	4,500

Refund or Amount You Owe

Line	Description	Amount
65	If line 64 is larger than line 56, enter amount **OVERPAID**	
66	Amount of line 65 to be **REFUNDED TO YOU** ▶	
67	Amount of line 65 to be applied to your 1984 estimated tax ▶	
68	If line 56 is larger than line 64, enter **AMOUNT YOU OWE**. Attach check or money order for full amount payable to "Internal Revenue Service." Write your social security number and "1983 Form 1040" on it ▶ (Check ▶ ☐ if Form 2210 (2210F) is attached. See page 17 of Instructions.) $	470

Please Sign Here

Under penalties of perjury, I declare that I have examined this return and accompanying schedules and statements, and to the best of my knowledge and belief, they are true, correct, and complete. Declaration of preparer (other than taxpayer) is based on all information of which preparer has any knowledge.

Your signature — Date — Spouse's signature (if filing jointly, BOTH must sign)

Paid Preparer's Use Only

Preparer's signature — Date — Check if self-employed ☐ — Preparer's social security no.

Firm's name (or yours, if self-employed) and address — E.I. No. — ZIP code

A PRIMER ON TAXES

Exhibit 12

SCHEDULE C (Form 1040)
Department of the Treasury
Internal Revenue Service

Profit or (Loss) From Business or Profession
(Sole Proprietorship)
Partnerships, Joint Ventures, etc., Must File Form 1065.
▶ Attach to Form 1040 or Form 1041.   ▶ See Instructions for Schedule C (Form 1040).

OMB No. 1545-0074

1983
09

Name of proprietor: **VALERIE & JAMES NICHOLS**

Social security number of proprietor: **987 65 4320**

A Main business activity (see Instructions) ▶ **MUSICIANS**   ; product ▶

B Business name and address ▶ **100 BIG SKY DRIVE, ALAMO, TEXAS**

C Employer identification number

D Method(s) used to value closing inventory:
(1) ☐ Cost   (2) ☐ Lower of cost or market   (3) ☐ Other (attach explanation)

E Accounting method: (1) ☑ Cash   (2) ☐ Accrual   (3) ☐ Other (specify) ▶ ....

	Yes	No
F Was there any major change in determining quantities, costs, or valuations between opening and closing inventory? If "Yes," attach explanation.		
G Did you deduct expenses for an office in your home?		✓

PART I.—Income

1 a Gross receipts or sales	1a	25,275
b Less: Returns and allowances	1b	
c Subtract line 1b from line 1a and enter the balance here	1c	
2 Cost of goods sold and/or operations (Part III, line 8)	2	
3 Subtract line 2 from line 1c and enter the **gross profit** here	3	
4 a Windfall Profit Tax Credit or Refund received in 1983 (see Instructions)	4a	
b Other income	4b	
5 Add lines 3, 4a, and 4b. This is the **gross income** ▶	5	25,275

PART II.—Deductions

6 Advertising	220		23 Repairs		
7 Bad debts from sales or services (Cash method taxpayers, see Instructions)			24 Supplies (not included in Part III)		220
8 Bank service charges			25 Taxes (Do not include Windfall Profit Tax here. See line 29.)		
9 Car and truck expenses	1,000		26 Travel and entertainment		
10 Commissions			27 Utilities and telephone		150
11 Depletion			28 a Wages		
12 Depreciation and Section 179 deduction from Form 4562 (not included in Part III)			b Jobs credit		
			c Subtract line 28b from 28a		
			29 Windfall Profit Tax withheld in 1983		
13 Dues and publications			30 Other expenses (specify):		
14 Employee benefit programs			a **INSTRUMENTS**		1,800
15 Freight (not included in Part III)			b **PUBLIC ADDRESS SYSTEM**		1,000
16 Insurance			c		
17 Interest on business indebtedness			d		
18 Laundry and cleaning			e		
19 Legal and professional services			f		
20 Office expense	270		g		
21 Pension and profit-sharing plans			h		
22 Rent on business property			i		
31 Add amounts in columns for lines 6 through 30i. These are the **total deductions** ▶				31	4,660
32 Net profit or (loss). Subtract line 31 from line 5 and enter the result. If a profit, enter on Form 1040, line 12, and on Schedule SE, Part I, line 2 (or Form 1041, line 6). If a loss, go on to line 33				32	20,615

33 If you have a loss, you must answer this question: "Do you have amounts for which you are not at risk in this business (see Instructions)?" ☐ Yes ☐ No
If "Yes," you must attach Form 6198. If "No," enter the loss on Form 1040, line 12, and on Schedule SE, Part I, line 2 (or Form 1041, line 6).

PART III.—Cost of Goods Sold and/or Operations (See Schedule C Instructions for Part III)

1 Inventory at beginning of year (if different from last year's closing inventory, attach explanation)	1	
2 Purchases less cost of items withdrawn for personal use	2	
3 Cost of labor (do not include salary paid to yourself)	3	
4 Materials and supplies	4	
5 Other costs	5	
6 Add lines 1 through 5	6	
7 Less: Inventory at end of year	7	
8 Cost of goods sold and/or operations. Subtract line 7 from line 6. Enter here and in Part I, line 2, above.	8	

For Paperwork Reduction Act Notice, see Form 1040 Instructions.   Schedule C (Form 1040) 1983

Exhibit 13

Schedule W (Form 1040) Department of the Treasury Internal Revenue Service	Deduction for a Married Couple When Both Work ▶ For Paperwork Reduction Act Notice, see Form 1040 Instructions. ▶ Attach to Form 1040.	OMB No. 1545-0074 1983 21

Names as shown on Form 1040: **CATHY AND PATRICK McQUARTER** Your social security number

Step 1 — Figure your earned income

		(a) You	(b) Your spouse
1	Wages, salaries, tips, etc., from Form 1040, line 7. (Do not include any amount your spouse paid you.)	20,000	14,250
2	Net profit or (loss) from self-employment (from Schedules C and F (Form 1040), Schedule K-1 (Form 1065), and any other taxable self-employment or earned income)		
3	Add lines 1 and 2. This is your total earned income.	20,000	

Step 2 — Figure your qualified earned income

4	Adjustments from Form 1040, lines 24, 25a, 26, 30, and any repayment of sub-pay included on line 31. (See instructions below.) **IRA CONTRIBUTIONS**	500	500
5	Subtract line 4 from line 3. This is your qualified earned income. (If the amount in column (a) or (b) is zero (-0-) or less, stop here. You may not claim this deduction.)	19,500	13,750

Step 3 — Figure your deduction

6	Compare the amounts on line 5(a) and line 5(b) and write the smaller amount here. (Write either amount if 5(a) and 5(b) are exactly the same.) **Do not write more than $30,000**	6	13,750
7	Percentage used to figure the deduction (10%)	7	x .10
8	Multiply the amount on line 6 by the percentage on line 7. This is the amount of your deduction. Write the answer here and on Form 1040, line 29 ▶	8	1,375

Instructions

Complete this schedule and attach it to your Form 1040 if you take the deduction for a married couple when both work. You may take the deduction if both you and your spouse:

- work and have qualified earned income, and
- file a joint return, and
- do not file **Form 2555** to exclude income or to exclude or deduct certain housing costs, and
- do not file **Form 4563** to exclude income.

There are three steps to follow in figuring the deduction on Schedule W.

Step 1 (lines 1, 2, and 3).—Figure earned income separately for yourself and your spouse.

Step 2 (lines 4 and 5).—Figure qualified earned income separately for yourself and your spouse by subtracting certain adjustments from earned income.

Step 3 (lines 6, 7, and 8).—Figure the deduction based on the **smaller** of:

- the qualified earned income entered on line 5(a) or 5(b) of Schedule W, whichever is less, **OR**
- $30,000.

Earned income.—This is generally income you receive for services you provide. It includes wages, salaries, tips, commissions, disability income, sub-pay, etc. (from Form 1040, line 7). It also includes income earned from self-employment (from Schedules C and F of Form 1040 and Schedule K-1 of Form 1065), and net earnings and gains (other than capital gains) from the disposition, transfer, or licensing of property that you created. Earned income does not include interest, dividends, pensions, annuities, IRA distributions, unemployment compensation, deferred compensation, or nontaxable income.

Caution: Do not consider community property laws in figuring your earned income.

Qualified earned income.—This is the amount on which the deduction is based. Figure it by subtracting certain adjustments from earned income. These adjustments (and the related lines on Form 1040) are:

- Employee business expenses (from line 24).
- Payments to an IRA (from line 25a).
- Payments to a Keogh plan (from line 26).
- Disability income exclusion (from line 30).
- Repayment of supplemental unemployment benefits (sub-pay) included in the total on line 31. See the instructions on repayment of sub-pay on page 13 of the Form 1040 Instructions.

Enter the total of any adjustments that apply to your earned income in the appropriate column on line 4.

Example.—You earned a salary of $20,000 and had $6,000 of employee business expenses (line 24 of Form 1040). Your spouse earned $17,000 and put $2,000 into an IRA (line 25a of Form 1040). Your qualified earned income is $14,000 ($20,000 minus $6,000) and your spouse's is $15,000 ($17,000 minus $2,000). Because your qualified earned income is less than your spouse's, the deduction is figured on your income. Therefore, the deduction is $1,400 ($14,000 x .10).

Schedule W (Form 1040) 1983

A PRIMER ON TAXES

turn, to take a special deduction from their gross combined income. The deduction allowed is either 10 percent of $30,000 or 10 percent of the earned income of the spouse who has the lower income of the two—whichever is less.

In 1983, Patrick's income was $20,000 and Cathy's was $14,250 ($15,000 less her deduction of five percent for a tax-deferred annuity). Her contribution to an IRA ($500) must be subtracted before she can calculate the Earned Income that qualifies for the new special deduction. Cathy may take $1,375 (i.e., 10 percent of $13,750) off their total gross income.

A ROOF OVER YOUR HEAD — 12

Starting a home of your own is a great occasion. We all rejoice in "our first place." It's great fun to unpack the wedding gifts, arrange the new furniture—or the hand-me-downs. Everything is new—even if it is old. A marvelous time!

I'll bet your parents can describe every detail of their first home. Probably it was a small apartment. Then, as today, very few newlyweds could afford to buy a home. For them, and probably for you, a rented apartment was the answer.

Depending on where you live, finding the right apartment may or may not be easy. The location should be convenient for shopping and getting to work. You need enough living space—ideally, as a minimum, a living room, bedroom, kitchen, and bath, and enough closet space to handle both your wardrobes and all the stuff that should be stored out of sight so housekeeping is easy and the place isn't cluttered. The building and grounds should be well maintained and, if it is an apartment house or complex, it should offer such services as laundry rooms, locked mailboxes, resident superintendent, and parking and—last but by no means least—the rent should be the right price.

The first apartment

How much can you afford to pay for this first apartment? You have to look at your budget, then decide. Figure out how much rent you can handle together, and don't go above it. A favorite old rule still applies: Your monthly rent should not be more than one week's gross pay, or one-quarter of your income. In some situations, you may have to break this rule (as many people who want to live in Manhattan in New York City have learned in recent years), but it is an excellent guideline.

When you're looking over an apartment, and before you sign a lease, make sure all the appliances work and the plumbing is functioning properly (without leaky faucets or shower). Knock on some doors in the building and ask tenants how the heat is in the coldest months and whether the landlord responds quickly to complaints (does it take all summer to get a malfunctioning air conditioner fixed or replaced? Some apartment dwellers have learned that it does).

A lease is a firm contract between landlord or landlady and tenant. It gives you certain rights and obligations and it also gives the landlord some. Be sure your lease contains:

1. Names and addresses of all parties signing.
2. Amount of rent to be paid monthly.
3. Amount of advance deposit received, and conditions for its return.
4. Description of the premises, listing all exceptions that you and the landlord are agreeing on. Example of an exception: damage to a wall. If the landlord does not repair it before you move in, make sure the damage is described in writing so you will not be held responsible for it when you move out. You should make a list of all such exceptions, ask which will be repaired, and get a completion date—on paper—for the work. Attach the list to the lease and keep a copy for your records, to protect you against a claim when you move out.
5. Exact period for which the property is leased to you, and any relevant terms.
6. Description of the purpose for which it is leased.
7. Clause permitting the landlord's repossession if the rent is not paid.
8. Responsibilities of both landlord and tenant.
9. Description of services included with the apartment (e.g., laundry facilities, parking space, garbage removal, cleaning and maintenance of entryways and hallways, etc.)
10. Signatures of the parties to the lease (i.e., landlord/landlady and tenant or tenants).

Tips: Be sure you understand all the terms of the lease. Never assume anything. Don't try to guess what your situation is. Don't rely on the promise "I'll fix that when you move in." Don't accept verbal exceptions to something stated in the lease; once you have signed it, what counts is what is printed in the lease, not what somebody "said." If the lease says "no pets" and the landlord says, "Oh well, I don't mind if you have a cat," make sure he crosses out the line in the lease about pets and writes his initials beside the deletion. Otherwise, you may later be looking for a new home for the cat—or yourselves.

As tenants, you will have certain responsibilities:

1. Keeping the apartment clean.
2. Paying rent promptly.
3. Using plumbing, electricity, and heat responsibly and safely.
4. Taking reasonable care of the landlord's property.

The landlord also has responsibilities:

1. Maintaining the building in good condition.
2. Maintaining all common areas (hallways, grounds, swimming pool).
3. Providing adequate heat and hot water (and summer air conditioning, if the building provides it).
4. Providing garbage removal.

Most landlords ask for one or two months' "security"—in effect, the first and last months' rent in advance. They keep this deposit until you move out, then deduct from it any charges for damage to the premises that may have occurred while you were occupying the apartment. If you leave the apartment in as good condition as you found it, you should get your deposit back in full. Read your lease carefully before signing to be sure you know what reservations or conditions affect the return of your deposit.

It is your responsibility as tenants to know your own rights. If a dispute should occur, it will be resolved in accordance with local and state laws governing leases between landlords and tenants.

You have signed the lease. What next? Boxes are packed, clothes are in suitcases and bags, and on hangers by the armful, furniture is loaded in a van. You are ready to set up your first apartment together. In your mad rush, have you forgotten to have your utilities turned on, if they are not provided by the landlord? Better run down a checklist:

1. Telephone. When your phone is installed, expect to pay the phone company a deposit, to be returned when and if you move away. Find out about different charges and services and styles of phone. Today, you can do something that I could not do and your parents could not do: You can buy your phone from a big selection either at the phone company or in a discount department store or specialty store, and hook it up yourselves. If you make a lot

of long distance calls, you may want to sign up with one of the independent services that bounces such calls off a satellite. Once again, it is time to compare services and costs and figure out where the best buys for your budget can be found.

2. Gas and electric. If these utilities don't come with the apartment, you will probably have to put down a deposit for them, too. Be sure to notify the utility companies well ahead of your moving day, so the services will be turned on when you want them.

3. Insurance. Most landlords carry insurance to cover their rental property. It does not, however, cover your personal possessions. So you should buy insurance to protect against damage or loss of your furniture, clothing, books, or whatever, in case of fire, flood, theft, or vandalism. (See also Chapter 10 on insurance.)

One more tip on renting an apartment: Check your lease to see if it gives you the right to sublet. Never sublet your apartment to someone else, or sublet an apartment from a current tenant, unless you know the lease that is in effect allows subletting. Otherwise you are asking for headaches.

What about live-togethers and leases?

Only recently have landlords and landladies accepted the reality that not all couples who want to rent an apartment are married couples. Many apartment owners have begun to issue leases to two people who live together and share equal responsibility. It is becoming rarer for unmarried couples to run into obstacles.

The key thing is not so much the landlord's approval. What is important is how you set up the responsibility between the two of you. Who is going to pay for what? Are you going to split the rent equally and each pay half? What about the utility bills—electricity, gas, phone? And the insurance? You really have to sit down and figure out all the apartment-related costs, just as you have to budget your food expenses, so it all comes out fair and square. (See Chapter 15, Live-Togethers.)

Owning a home

Now we're talking about something that is as American as Mom, apple pie, and the stars and stripes. To own your own home is the culmination of the American dream. It is a symbol of financial security, of having made it. It is also probably the best single investment available to the average American, because the house bought for $20,000 some 25 years ago is now worth (if it has been maintained well) $100,000 or more, depending on location. The only problem is that, for you and many young couples, inflation and high interest rates have made homeownership nearly impossible.

What are the advantages of homeownership? These three are basic:

1. It is your best chance to accumulate tangible capital. It is an investment you can walk around, improve, add to.

2. It is one of the few almost foolproof ways to shield an investment from inflation. (Real estate values are a barometer of economic changes.)

3. It gives you tax advantages. By allowing you to lower your income taxes through itemized deductions of the interest you pay on your mortgage and the taxes you pay on the property, your Uncle Sam provides an indirect subsidy for your house. (See Chapter 11 on taxes.)

HOW THE McQUARTERS MADE THEIR DECISION . . .

Cathy and Patrick did a lot of paperwork before they made a bid on a house. They went to banks and checked on mortgage rates, then got application forms from the bank that seemed most likely to give them the best rate. These forms included blanks to be filled in so the bank could verify their employment and their savings and money market accounts. "Then we really worked over our Net Worth Statement," says Cathy. "We wanted to be good and sure we could afford the house. And we figured out a whole new budget that we'd have to have if we did actually own a home."

More preparation: They asked the bank to figure out the dollar amount of the mortgage and its monthly payments (including the interest and the amount needed to pay both the local real estate taxes and the homeowners' insurance annually, to be placed into what is called an escrow account.) "That wasn't all," adds Patrick. "We made the real estate agent do some extra work, too, figuring out what the heat in the house would cost us, and adding a sensible guesstimate on what we'd be spending for general maintenance. We rebudgeted all our expenses."

They reworked their budget and here's how some of the figures came out: Average monthly total expense of living in their apartment was $1,889 ($22,668 per year). They figured the new house would average $2,265 monthly ($27,180 a year)—or $376 more per month than the McQuarters were paying. On a yearly basis, however, the average would be considerably less, for now on their income tax return they would be able to deduct from their gross income the interest they paid to the bank as well as their real estate taxes. Their total federal tax savings would be some $2,300, and their marginal tax bracket would drop from 30 percent to 26 percent.

THE McQUARTERS FOUND *THE* HOUSE . . .

. . . after several weekends driving around with a real estate agent. Knowing what they had decided (after much figuring) they could pay, they negotiated with the owners until they agreed on a price of $57,000. The owners gave them a binder to sign (a binder is legally an "offer to purchase") and they gave the owners a check for one percent of the purchase price: $570.

Usually the binder states that it is contingent upon the buyer obtaining a mortgage. If the house is not brand-new, the binder also specifies that a building and termite inspection must be performed, and paid for by the buyers, by a certain date. The binder includes notations on items to be included in the deal, such as draperies, wall-to-wall carpeting, refrigerator, and any special conditions (e.g., if the owners plan to remove a hanging lamp that was attached to the wall or ceiling when the buyers came through).

When all conditions had been met, the McQuarters paid the sellers another nine percent, and at the same time signed a more formal contract in anticipation of getting a formal "mortgage commitment" from the bank. They had, in the meantime, filled out their mortgage application and turned it in at the bank. "Since we'd done all the homework beforehand," says Cathy, "it didn't take us any time to get that application in."

Well before the deadline specified in the binder, the bank notified the McQuarters that it would make them a mortgage commitment for a $45,000 fixed-rate mortgage at 13.5 percent. This was the cue for the McQuarters and the sellers to sign a legally binding contract.

Before the bank made the mortgage commitment, an attorney (in some states it would be a title company) did a "title search," to determine whether there were any liens against the property, any unpaid taxes, land conveyances, or boundary rights that might create problems for the McQuarters and, possibly, for the bank. The search also checked into property assessments and property easements (was there, for instance, a house on the property behind this house that had a right to use of the McQuarters' future driveway?).

ON THE DAY OF THE CLOSING . . .

. . . the McQuarters went through the house with the sellers one last time—*before* they went to the closing. "We'd heard so many stories about people who got stuck because something wasn't in the same condition on the day of the closing as it was when they signed the contract," said Patrick. "So we just wanted to be darned sure about everything."

At the closing, the McQuarters went over all the papers very carefully, checking the closing statement, or statement of sale, for adjustments for taxes; points (a "point" is one percent of the sale price; some banks charge a service fee of one or more points for handling the details of the closing); interest from the date of the closing to the first regular mortgage payment date; attorney's fees; and town or county fees for recording the deed of sale in the town or county clerk's office. "All these fees and adjustments were costing us several hundred dollars," says Patrick, "so we made sure we understood every one of them. We made everybody sit there and explain 'em all."

Usually at the closing, your lawyer and the seller's lawyer will work out how much of the tax year the

Worksheet XI: Yours

Your Home as an Investment

A home can be a valuable source of tax savings, inflation protection, and capital growth.

In many cases, the cost of buying a home isn't any higher than renting. Fill in the following information to determine the difference between owning and renting.

Owning (Annual Costs)

Home Expenses:

Real Estate Taxes	$ _____
Mortgage Interest	$ _____
Mortgage Principal	$ _____
Homeowner's Insurance	$ _____
Repairs	$ _____
Utilities	$ _____
Subtotal I	$ _____

Income Tax Deductions:

Real Estate Taxes	$ _____
Mortgage Interest	$ _____
Subtotal II	$ _____

Your Income Tax Bracket:

State	_____%
Federal	_____%
Subtotal III	_____%

- Multiply your income tax deductions (II) by your personal tax rate (III) to discover your total tax savings (IV).

$$ \$ \underline{}_{\text{II}} \times \underline{}_{\text{III}} = \$ \underline{}_{\text{IV}} $$

- Subtract your total tax savings (IV) from your total home expenses (I) to find the cost of owning your home after taxes (this figure does not include the value of appreciation of your home).

$$ \$ \underline{}_{\text{I}} - \$ \underline{}_{\text{IV}} = \$ \underline{}_{\text{V}} \text{Total Cost of Owning Your Home} $$

RENTING (Annual Costs)

Rent	$ _____
Renter's Insurance	$ _____
Utilities	$ _____
	$ _____ **Total Cost of Renting**

- Subtract Total Cost of Renting (VI) From Total Cost of Owning (V).

A ROOF OVER YOUR HEAD

Worksheet XI: Example
The McQuarters

Your Home as an Investment

A home can be a valuable source of tax savings, inflation protection, and capital growth.

In many cases, the cost of buying a home isn't any higher than renting. Fill in the following information to determine the difference between owning and renting.

Owning (Annual Costs)

Home Expenses:		Income Tax Deductions:	
Real Estate Taxes	$ 1,200	Real Estate Taxes	$ 1,200
Mortgage Interest	$ 6,060	Mortgage Interest	$ 6,060
Mortgage Principal	$ 120	Subtotal II	$ 7,260
Homeowner's Insurance	$ 324	Your Income Tax Bracket:	
Repairs	$ 600	State	6 %
Utilities	$ 1,440	Federal	30 %
Subtotal I	$ 9,744	Subtotal III	36 %

- Multiply your income tax deductions (II) by your personal tax rate (III) to discover your total tax savings (IV).

$ __7,260__ × __36__ % = $ __2,614__
    II   III   IV

- Subtract your total tax savings (IV) from your total home expenses (I) to find the cost of owning your home after taxes (this figure does not include the value of appreciation of your home).

$ __9,744__ − $ __2,614__ = $ __7,130__ Total Cost of Owning Your Home
  I   IV   V

RENTING (Annual Costs)

Rent	$ 3,600
Renter's Insurance	$ 166
Utilities	$ 640
	$ 4,406 Total Cost of Renting

- Subtract Total Cost of Renting (VI) From Total Cost of Owning (V).

$7,130 − $4,406 = $2,724 or $227 per month

FINANCIAL FITNESS FOR NEWLYWEDS

Exhibit 14: The McQuarters

BINDER OF SALE (CONTRACT)

_____ , 19 ___

AGREEMENT between _____ ,

residing at _____ , who hereby

agrees to sell, and _____ ,

residing at _____ , who hereby
agrees to purchase, the property known and described as

_____

_____

under the following terms and conditions:

PRICE _____ DEPOSIT _____ receipt of which is hereby acknowledged.

Sale includes: _____

Contract of sale to be signed, and remainder of _____ % deposit to be made, on or before _____ 19 ___

The full price to be paid in cash or certified check upon delivery of the deed or on terms set forth herein.

Mortgage Contingency: This agreement is subject to buyer's obtaining a commitment for a loan, to be secured by a first mortgage on the property, in the amount of $ _____ , amortizable in equal monthly payments over a period of _____ years upon standard or prevailing terms as to interest, rate and prepayment limitations on or before _____ .

This agreement is further subject to termite and building inspection satisfactory to and at the expense of the buyer, to be completed by _____ .

_____

_____

_____

_____

Adjustments: Taxes, water charges, rents, mortgage interest, and interest on assessments, if any, for municipal improvements are to be adjusted as of the date of closing.

Balances of assessments, if any, for municipal improvements are to be assumed by the buyer.

Property to be conveyed by Warranty Deed in accordance with the usual Connecticut practice.

Closing of Title will be at the office of _____
_____ on _____ , 19 ___

THIS AGREEMENT IS TO REMAIN IN FORCE AND EFFECT AND CONSTITUTE A CONTRACT BETWEEN THE PARTIES HERETO UNLESS OR UNTIL SUPERSEDED BY FURTHER CONTRACT BETWEEN PARTIES INCORPORATING DETAILED DESCRIPTION AS HEREINABOVE PROVIDED.

WITNESSES:	BUYER:
_____	_____
_____	SELLER:
_____	_____
Is the Listing Broker in this transaction	Is the Selling Broker in this transaction

A ROOF OVER YOUR HEAD

seller should pay for and how much the buyer must pick up. The lawyers will also calculate how much oil is in the fuel tank in the house you are buying, and it will be sold to you at the closing.

Among the papers drawn up before the closing were deed of trust notes, legally stating who was to own the mortgage on the home, and a grant deed, legally stating that the McQuarters were the new owners. After the closing, the deed was recorded in town records, then returned to the McQuarters. They put it in their safe deposit box for safekeeping.

The final moment of the closing came when the McQuarters were handed the keys to the house. The home was theirs.

HAS THE McQUARTERS' NET WORTH CHANGED?

Yes. It has changed. But in case you are wondering if it went down by $15,000 when they used $12,000 of their savings as a down payment and $3,000 for legal fees, moving costs, and incidentals—the answer is no. Their net worth did not go down by that amount, because the $15,000 was simply transformed into a different reporting column in the net worth statement.

In fact, their net worth is still pretty much the same. It is reduced only by the $3,000 they spent for moving. Meanwhile, they acquired an asset (the house) worth $57,000 and a liability (the mortgage) of $45,000. And they kept an asset of $3,000 in their money market account.

How much house can you afford? That's a complex question. It used to be simple. An old—but now outdated—rule of thumb was that the price of your house should not be more than two and a half times your annual income, and that mortgage payments—like rent, as I mentioned before, and including taxes—should not be more than one-quarter of your income. That was all well and good when interest rates for mortgages were firmly set at six percent.

Today you must ask yourselves a lot of questions and do a lot of figuring before you can determine how much house you can afford. Start with this checklist, and make notes as you go, for you are sure to come up with more questions than these—questions that pertain to your own particular situation.

1. How large a down payment can we make? Obviously, the more you can put down, the lower your monthly payments will be.

2. How long a mortgage term should we sign for? Mortgages can be set up to span 20, 25, or 30 years; the shorter the period, the less you spend on interest but the higher your payments will be.

3. How large a monthly payment can we comfortably make? Your budget determines this. After you have figured out how much you need for non-housing expenses (including savings and an emergency fund), what is left is what you have to work with for housing. But remember: Insurance, utilities, property taxes, and maintenance are part of your monthly housing costs, too. This question also calls for plenty of thoughtful long-term planning. Look not only at what you are both making now but how much more you can reasonably expect if you get raises regularly . . . at what will happen to your joint income if you have a baby and one spouse leaves the work force either temporarily or permanently . . . at what the cost of child care, if necessary, will do to your budget.

4. What does the location of the home we are buying do to our expenses? Will we be adding commuting costs? A major increase in the weekly mileage on one—or two—cars? Where are the stores? Services? Recreational facilities? Will we have to drive five miles to get a loaf of bread?

5. Just how much will utilities add to the monthly housing expense? What about heat? Heat was part of the deal in a rented apartment. Now you'll have to buy it. Better check with the fuel company that has been supplying the house and see how much fuel was used last winter—or the last two or three winters, so you can average it out.

6. How much more will insurance cost? It is bound to be greater than what you have been paying to cover your apartment.

7. How much will the property taxes be? This one can be ticklish. Find out when the last reassessment occurred. If it's been a while, another could

come around soon and hit you with an unexpected hike in taxes after you move in. Check with a resident who is knowledgeable about what the local policy is. Or call the town or city hall.

8. What local services do we get? Are they free? Do our local taxes pay for garbage collection, or will we get a monthly bill from the garbage collector?

9. How are the schools? This could be the most important question on your list. If you are planning to raise a family in this house, take the time and trouble to investigate the schools thoroughly. Stop in at the school superintendent's office, or at any school principal's office, and ask questions. What is the average ratio of pupils to teacher in the classroom? How much does the community spend each year per pupil—and where does it rank among cities and towns in your state? What percentage of the high school graduates move on to higher education? Some basic demographic statistics about the school system can tell you a lot about whether or not you really should be buying this home.

10. Do we have sufficient reserves to pay the cost of moving and to buy those incidentals that we may not realize we need until we actually start to live in the house: *fuel*, insulation, lawn mower, garden hose, gardening tools, rake, snow shovel? How about landscaping? If you are buying a brand-new house, it is likely to come with a minimum of trees and shrubs. And a new house will probably lack screens, storm windows, and storm doors.

A lot to think about? You bet. But the amazing thing is—millions of Americans have survived the entire process.

How much for a down payment?

If you have asked yourselves all these questions and have come up with a firm "yes" on the ultimate one: "Can we afford a house?" you must now produce the down payment.

Let's say you have worked hard to put away $200 every month for five years. Assuming 10 percent interest on your money, compounded quarterly, you should have $15,084.83 salted away. This should give you enough for a healthy down payment of $10,000, with the balance to be used for closing costs, moving, and all the incidentals I've mentioned. You have watched the pot grow—and now you can put it to work! The next question is: What type of housing? House and lot? Condominium? Cooperative apartment? Mobile home? Let's look at each.

House and lot

Any house you look at is going to be either new—or old. If you're looking at a new house, you are pretty much assured that everything will function properly. The builder should stand behind the work. Furnace and appliances will come with guarantees. You may have plenty to do in the area of landscaping and perhaps painting the interior, if it has been left undecorated.

If it is an older house, you will want to be sure it is in acceptable condition. It takes expertise to evaluate an older home; don't hesitate to get it. If you are not an expert yourself, pay a professional to make an inspection. Don't just ask a friend. This will give you a reliable check on plumbing, heating, paint condition, roof, electrical wiring, insulation—a million and one details that could make the difference between frustration and satisfaction for you as buyers. Nothing is worse than having to buy a new roof or a new septic field for a house just after you bought the house itself. If the inspection reveals that something is wrong you can start to renegotiate the price with the seller, taking into account the cost you face in fixing the problem.

Condominium

The condo is rather new on the American home-owning scene. It is usually a structure on the order of an apartment house, in which you are deeded the title to, or ownership of your unit. It becomes your property. You also own a proportionate interest in the common facilities, such as hallways, grounds, elevators, and recreational areas (tennis courts, swimming pool, even a golf course in some condos). Each month, you pay common charges that cover taxes on the property (the tax portion of your common charge is deductible on your income tax return), maintenance, heat, and utilities. Warning: Common charges have a way of increasing, so make sure your budget is elastic enough to accept increases in them. As owners, you will join a condo-

Exhibit 15: The McQuarters

RESIDENTIAL LOAN APPLICATION

MORTGAGE APPLIED FOR	☑ Conventional ☐ FHA ☐ VA	Amount $45,000	Interest Rate ___%	No. of Months	Monthly Payment Principal & Interest $515	Escrow/Impounds (to be collected monthly) ☑ Taxes ☐ Hazard Ins. ☐ Mtg. Ins.

Prepayment Option

SUBJECT PROPERTY

Property Street Address: 40 High Ridge | City: St. Louis | County: | State: MO | Zip: | No. Units: | Year Built:

Legal Description (Attach description if necessary)

Purpose of Loan: ☑ Purchase ☐ Construction-Permanent ☐ Construction ☐ Refinance ☐ Other (Explain)

Complete this line if Construction-Permanent or Construction Loan: Lot Value Data | Year Acquired ☑ | Original Cost $ | Present Value (a) $ | Cost of Imps. (b) $ | Total (a + b) $

Complete this line if a Refinance Loan: Year Acquired / Original Cost $ | Amt. Existing Liens $ | Purpose of Refinance | Describe Improvements [ ] made [ ] to be made — Cost: $

ENTER TOTAL AS PURCHASE PRICE IN DETAILS OF PURCHASE.

Title Will Be Held in What Name(s): Cathy & Patrick McQuarter | Manner In Which Title Will Be Held: Joint tenancy with right of survivorship

Source of Down Payment and Settlement Charges: CASH

This application is designed to be completed by the borrower(s) with the lender's assistance. The Co-Borrower Section and all other Co-Borrower questions must be completed and the appropriate box(es) checked if ☐ another person will be jointly obligated with the Borrower on the loan, or ☐ the Borrower is relying on income from alimony, child support or separate maintenance or on the income or assets of another person as a basis for repayment of the loan, or ☐ the Borrower is married and resides, or the property is located, in a community property state.

BORROWER

Name: Patrick McQuarter | Age: 25 | School Yrs: 17
Present Address: ☐ Own ☑ Rent | No. Years
Street: 1501 Westway
City/State/Zip: St. Louis Mo
Former address if less than 2 years at present address
Street:
City/State/Zip:
Years at former address:
Marital Status: ☑ Married ☐ Separated ☐ Unmarried (incl. single, divorced, widowed) | DEPENDENTS OTHER THAN LISTED BY CO BORROWER: NO ___ AGES ___
Name and Address of Employer: XYZ TV Station | Years employed in this line of work or profession? 8 years | Years on this job 6 | ☐ Self Employed*
Position/Title: Producer | Type of Business: TV | Social Security Number***: | Home Phone: | Business Phone:

CO-BORROWER

Name: Catherine McQuarter | Age: 27 | School Yrs: 16
Present Address: ☐ Own ☑ Rent | No. Years
Street: 1501 Westway
City/State/Zip: St. Louis, MO
Former address if less than 2 years at present address
Street:
City/State/Zip:
Years at former address:
Marital Status: ☑ Married ☐ Separated ☐ Unmarried (incl. single, divorced, widowed) | DEPENDENTS OTHER THAN LISTED BY BORROWER: NO ___ AGES ___
Name and Address of Employer: City of St. Louis | Years employed in this line of work or profession? 6 years | Years on this job 6 | ☐ Self Employed*
Position/Title: | Type of Business: Teaching | Social Security Number***: | Home Phone: | Business Phone:

122   FINANCIAL FITNESS FOR NEWLYWEDS

GROSS MONTHLY INCOME

Item	Borrower	Co-Borrower	Total
Base Empl. Income	$ 1,667	$ 1,250	$ 2,917
Overtime			
Bonuses			
Commissions			
Dividends/Interest			133
Net Rental Income			
Other† (Before completing, see notice under Describe Other Income below.)			
Total	$		$ 3,050

☞ B—Borrower C—Co-Borrower

MONTHLY HOUSING EXPENSE**

	PRESENT	PROPOSED
Rent	$ 300	
First Mortgage (P&I)		$ 515
Other Financing (P&I)		
Hazard Insurance	14	27
Real Estate Taxes		100
Mortgage Insurance		
Homeowner Assn. Dues		
Other		
Total Monthly Pmt.	$ 314	$ 642
Utilities	53	120
Total	$ 367	$ 762

DETAILS OF PURCHASE

a. Purchase Price	$ 57,000
b. Total Closing Costs (Est.)	
c. Prepaid Escrows (Est.)	
d. Total (a + b + c)	$
e. Amount This Mortgage	(45,000)
f. Other Financing	( )
g. Present Equity in Lot	( )
h. Amount of Cash Deposit	(12,000)
i. Closing Costs Paid by Seller	( )
j. Cash Reqd. For Closing (Est.)	$

DESCRIBE OTHER INCOME

NOTICE: † Alimony, child support, or separate maintenance income need not be revealed if the Borrower or Co-Borrower does not choose to have it considered as a basis for repaying this loan.

	Monthly Amount
	$

IF EMPLOYED IN CURRENT POSITION FOR LESS THAN TWO YEARS COMPLETE THE FOLLOWING

B/C	Previous Employer/School	City/State	Type of Business	Position/Title	Dates From/To	Monthly Income
						$

THESE QUESTIONS APPLY TO BOTH BORROWER AND CO-BORROWER

	Borrower Yes or No	Co-Borrower Yes or No	If applicable, explain Other Financing or Other Equity (provide addendum if more space is needed).
If a "yes" answer is given to a question in this column, explain on an attached sheet.			
Have you any outstanding judgments? In the last 14 years, have you been declared bankrupt?	No	No	
Have you had property foreclosed upon or given title or deed in lieu thereof?	No	No	
Are you a co-maker or endorser on a note?	No	No	
Are you a party in a law suit?	No	No	
Are you obligated to pay alimony, child support, or separate maintenance?	No	No	
Is any part of the down payment borrowed?			

*FHLMC/FNMA require business credit report, signed Federal Income Tax returns for last two years, and, if available, audited Profit and Loss Statements plus balance sheet for same period.
**All Present Monthly Housing Expenses of Borrower and Co-Borrower should be listed on a combined basis.
***Neither FHLMC nor FNMA requires this information.

FHLMC 65 Rev. 8/78   10M R.P.

FNMA 1003 Rev. 8/78

A ROOF OVER YOUR HEAD

This Statement and any applicable supporting schedules may be completed jointly by both married and unmarried co-borrowers if their assets and liabilities are sufficiently joined so that the Statement can be meaningfully and fairly presented on a combined basis; otherwise separate Statements and Schedules are required (FHLMC 65A/FNMA 1003A). If the co-borrower section was completed about a spouse, this statement and supporting schedules must be completed about that spouse also.

☐ Completed Jointly   ☐ Not Completed Jointly

STATEMENT OF ASSETS AND LIABILITIES

ASSETS

Indicate by (*) those liabilities or pledged assets which will be satisfied upon sale of real estate owned or upon refinancing of subject property.

Description	Cash or Market Value
Cash Deposit Toward Purchase Held By ABC Bank	$ 12,000
Checking and Savings Accounts (Show Names of Institutions/Acct. Nos.) ABC Bank checking savings money market	7,250
Stocks and Bonds (No./Description)	
Life Insurance Net Cash Value Face Amount ($)	
SUBTOTAL LIQUID ASSETS	$ 19,250
Real Estate Owned (Enter Market Value from Schedule of Real Estate Owned)	
Vested Interest in Retirement Fund	1,000
Net Worth of Business Owned (ATTACH FINANCIAL STATEMENT)	
Automobiles (Make and Year) ✓	5,000
Furniture and Personal Property	5,000
Other Assets (Itemize)	
TOTAL ASSETS	A $ 30,250

LIABILITIES AND PLEDGED ASSETS

Creditors' Name, Address and Account Number	Acct. Name If Not Borrower's	Mo. Pmt. and Mos. left to pay	Unpaid Balance
Installment Debts (include "revolving" charge accts)		$ Pmt./Mos.	$
		/	
		/	
		/	
		/	
Other Debt Including Stock Pledges		/	
Real Estate Loans		/	
Automobile Loan ABC BANK		$95 / 21	
Alimony, Child Support and Separate Maintenance Payments Owed To			
TOTAL MONTHLY PAYMENTS		$ 95	TOTAL LIABILITIES B $
NET WORTH (A minus B) $			

124 FINANCIAL FITNESS FOR NEWLYWEDS

SCHEDULE OF REAL ESTATE OWNED (If Additional Properties Owned Attach Separate Schedule)

Address of Property (Indicate S if Sold, PS if Pending Sale or R if Rental being held for income)	Type of Property	Present Market Value	Amount of Mortgages & Liens	Gross Rental Income	Mortgage Payments	Taxes, Ins. Maintenance and Misc.	Net Rental Income
B—Borrower C—Co-Borrower		$	$	$	$	$	$
		$	$	$	$	$	$
		$	$	$	$	$	$
TOTALS →		$	$		$	$	$

LIST PREVIOUS CREDIT REFERENCES

Creditor's Name and Address	Account Number	Purpose	Highest Balance	Date Paid
			$	

List any additional names under which credit has previously been received _____

AGREEMENT: The undersigned applies for the loan indicated in this application to be secured by a first mortgage or deed of trust on the property described herein, and represents that the property will not be used for any illegal or restricted purpose, and that all statements made in this application are true and are made for the purpose of obtaining the loan. Verification may be obtained from any source named in this application. The undersigned also acknowledges that discrimination because of race, color, age, sex, marital status, religion, national origin or physical handicap in the sale or rental of residential property is illegal under state and federal laws, and that he has not and will not knowingly violate such laws with respect to said premises. Unless otherwise specified, a copy of the commitment letter will be sent to the real estate agent whose name is indicated on this application. The original or a copy of this application will be retained by the lender even if the loan is not granted. **The undersigned ☐ intend or ☐ do not intend to occupy the property as their primary residence.**
I/we fully understand that it is a federal crime punishable by fine or imprisonment, or both, to knowingly make any false statements concerning any of the above facts as applicable under the provisions of Title 18, United States Code, Section 1014.

_____ Date _____   _____ Date _____
Borrower's Signature   Co-Borrower's Signature

INFORMATION FOR GOVERNMENT MONITORING PURPOSES

The following information is requested by the Federal Government if this loan is related to a dwelling, in order to monitor the lender's compliance with equal credit opportunity and fair housing laws. You are not required to furnish this information, but are encouraged to do so. The law provides that a lender may neither discriminate on the basis of this information, nor on whether you choose to furnish it. However, if you choose not to furnish it, under Federal regulations this lender is required to note race and sex on the basis of visual observation or surname. If you do not wish to furnish the above information, please initial below.

BORROWER: ☐ I do not wish to furnish this information (initials)_____   **CO-BORROWER:** ☐ I do not wish to furnish this information (initials)_____

RACE/ NATIONAL ORIGIN ☐ American Indian, Alaskan Native ☐ Asian, Pacific Islander ☐ Black ☐ Hispanic ☐ White ☐ Other (specify)_____ **SEX** ☐ Female ☐ Male

RACE/ NATIONAL ORIGIN ☐ American Indian, Alaskan Native ☐ Asian, Pacific Islander ☐ Black ☐ Hispanic ☐ White ☐ Other (specify)_____ **SEX** ☐ Female ☐ Male

(FNMA REQUIREMENT ONLY) This application was taken by _____, a full time employee of

_____ in a face to face interview with the prospective borrower
(Name of Lender)

Present Title _____ Present Mortgagee _____
Property Occupied by _____ Name _____ Phone _____
Owner's Value _____ (REFINANCE ONLY) Present Mortgage Balance $_____
Closing Attorney _____ Name _____ Address _____ Phone _____ Closing Date _____
Real Estate Agent _____ Name _____ Address _____ Phone _____

FHLMC 65 Rev. 8/78   REVERSE   FNMA 1003 Rev. 8/78

A ROOF OVER YOUR HEAD

Exhibit 16

STATEMENT OF SALE

Dated April 15, 1984

Lewis to McQuarter

No. 40 High Ridge .... Street .... Avenue

City or Town: St. Louis   State: Mo.

Purchase Price	$ 57,000
Insurance Adjustment	$
	$
	$
City Taxes (Adjusted) 4/15/84 – 7/1/84	$
County Taxes (Adjusted)	$
Sewer " " 4/15/84 – 7/1/84	$ 350
School " "	$
Fuel in Oil tank – 176 gallons	$ 200
	$ 195.50
Total Amount Due Seller	$ 57,745.50

Credits to Purchaser:

Amount Paid Down	$ 12,000
First Mortgage A.B.C. Bank .... To	$ 45,000
Interest From	$
Second Mortgage .... To	$
Interest From	$
	$

FINANCIAL FITNESS FOR NEWLYWEDS

City Taxes (Assumed) .... $ ....
County Taxes (Assumed) .... $ ....
Local Assessment (Assumed) .... $ ....
Rents: (Pro-rated) .... $ ....
.... $ .... $57,000.
                                                                    742.50
Balance Due .... $ ....

Expenses of Purchaser:
Recording Deed .... $ 15.00
Recording Mortgage .... $ 10.00
.... $ ....
Mortgage Tax .... $ ....
Stamps on Bond .... $ ....
loan origination fee % .... $ 570.00
.... $ ....
.... $ ....
Services ... legal .... $ 350.00
                                Total $ ... 945.00

Expenses of Seller:
Continuing Search .... $ 5.00
Revenue Stamps, Deeds .... $ 75.00
Survey .... $ 5.00
Recording Discharge of Mortgage ...... $ ....
Recording mortgage—immediate .... $ ....
Recording mortgage—assignment ...... $ ....
Recording—consent to mortgage .... $ ....
Real Estate Commission .... $ 3,420
Title Insurance .... $ 250
Services .... $ ....
                                Total $ ... 3,755

Received payment this ... 15th ... day of ... April ... 19 84.

_____ SELLER   _____ PURCHASER

_____ SELLER   _____ PURCHASER

A ROOF OVER YOUR HEAD

minium association in which each member has one vote when decisions about the condominium must be made (all members will have agreed to abide by the provisions of a condo agreement).

As a condo owner, you have the same advantages as the owner of a house and lot. Your equity builds up as time goes by (generally, condos have appreciated to match inflation, just like houses). The tax benefits that you can itemize on your income tax return are the same. Your responsibility for repairs and maintenance within your individual unit is also the same as in a house. And, generally speaking, you are entitled to sell your unit to anyone you choose.

Tips: Watch the recreational facilities. Don't be fooled into buying into a condo where the swimming pool and tennis courts are "going to be built soon." And turn your back on any place that has a tiny swimming pool or a single tennis court for a hundred condo units.

Cooperatives

In a co-op apartment, a non-profit corporation owns your unit. What you own is stock in the corporation. The amount of stock you own depends on the size and value of the apartment you take. There is one common mortgage on the building (unless the corporation has bought the building outright or already paid off the mortgage) and all the owners make monthly payments, varying in size according to the value of the individual units, to the corporation. These payments cover, in effect, taxes, interest payment, and maintenance. As a shareholder, you are entitled to list as deductions on your income tax return your share of the property taxes and the interest on the mortgage. When you want to "sell the apartment," you are really selling your shares in the corporation. *Note:* Some co-ops stipulate that any prospective owner must be approved by the other shareholders. The corporation may exercise the option of buying back the shares if the prospective owner isn't approved.

Some questions to ask before you buy into a co-op or purchase a condo:

- What are the rules and regulations? Do you want to agree to abide by them?
- Are those now living there pleased with the living conditions? Is the place noisy? Too hot? Too cold?
- Is it clean and well maintained, indoors and out? Trees and shrubs healthy? Lawn green and manicured?
- Are the recreational facilities adequate? Well maintained?
- How's the parking? Plenty of room?
- What about lighting? Parking areas well lighted? Paths and entryways clear and bright?
- Who pays for utilities? How are the costs apportioned?
- Are you permitted to rent your unit?
- What are the costs of settlement?
- Are there any lawsuits pending against the developer or officers of the association?
- Are most owners living on the premises—or have they rented out their units?

Mobile homes

This is probably the cheapest form of homeownership. It can be your first way—maybe for now your only way—to own low-cost housing.

Here's how it works. Either (1) you rent a small piece of property in an "open" park, then have your manufactured house installed on that property at your own expense, or (2) you buy a home from the management of a "closed" park. This is what many retired people do. In fact, many closed mobile-home parks are designed mainly for retired people.

In some parks, the mobile-home owners may buy their land instead of renting it. This has a certain advantage: If your mobile home is set up on your own land, some banks will offer you a regular real estate mortgage. Otherwise, they want you to finance the purchase of your mobile home like an auto loan, with a low down payment, short repayment period of three to five years at best, and high monthly payments. Recently, the U.S. government has begun insuring mobile-home loans through the Federal Housing Administration (FHA) and the Veterans Administration (VA).

A mobile home may well be a viable start for you. Before buying one, check with a number of lenders about the type of financing they offer. It's worth the effort to find the best possible deal.

Financing

You've analyzed the possibilities. You've got the down payment. You've reviewed your budget and tried to answer the nagging questions about the future. You've decided to do it. Now, how do you finance the purchase of the home you want?

Very few can come up with the full purchase price of a home. So they buy with the help of some kind of mortgage financing.

Just what is a "mortgage"? By definition, it is simply a pledge of property to a creditor as security for a loan. As the borrower, you are the mortgagor. You give the mortgage to the lender, or mortgagee, who takes the mortgage and holds it until you have paid the debt.

A mortgage has three elements: the amount the lender provides, the repayment period, and the rate of interest. Until very recently, once a mortgage loan was closed, none of these elements could be changed. You "got a mortgage" for a certain number of years at a certain rate of interest and that was it—period. But lately lenders, finding themselves stuck for years with mortgages that bring them low payments of interest at a time when they have to pay out high interest on savings deposited with them, have been eager to adapt to changing conditions. The result is that today you may choose between the old-fashioned conventional fixed-rate mortgage and a new type, the adjustable-rate mortgage (ARM). Let's look at each.

1. *The conventional fixed-rate mortgage.* With this type you pay a fixed monthly payment, at a fixed rate of interest, for the life of the loan—as long as 25 or 30 years. Many banks still offer the fixed-rate mortgage, but today the cost is likely to be initially higher—maybe 2.5 percent higher—than the cost of an adjustable-rate mortgage. If interest rates do go up over the long haul, you get the advantage and the bank, or lender, finds that it has loaned you money at a lower rate of return, or profit, than it might have gained by some other investment.

2. *The variable- or adjustable-rate, mortgage.* With this type the initial cost is lower, because you start off at the lowest interest rate the bank, in order to meet competition from other lenders, dares offer today. But you agree to abide by regular review and escalation or de-escalation as interest rates are adjusted up or down by the lender to meet the conditions of the money market. Under strict government guidelines, the rates may change every month. The adjustment, however, is usually scheduled every six months or once a year, with the rate permitted to increase no more than a maximum of two percent a year. The rate changes are tied to a number of interest-based indices published by the federal government, and usually there is a "cap," or ceiling, beyond which the rate may not be raised, as well as a downward floor. In theory, however, there is no limit on how high or how low the rate may go over the life of the loan.

While the ARM interest rate is usually lower at first than that on a fixed-rate mortgage, the risk you take is that it will eventually equal it or even exceed it. If, on the other hand, the adjustable rate holds steady or goes down, you may come out ahead.

Under an ARM, the amount you have to pay to the bank could change every month or every six months as the rates change. With most ARM's, you sign up for a fixed monthly payment that will stay the same through a given period before an adjustment is made. If you are hit with an upward adjustment that is more than your budget can stand, see if the bank will keep the payments the same and extend the life of the loan. What the bank does is determine, based on the current interest rate, how much of your payment to apply to the principal that you borrowed and how much to pay interest at the current rate. If the interest rate goes down, the bank puts more of your payment toward paying back the principal. If the interest rate rises, on the other hand, the bank applies more and more of your payment to interest charges and less and less to paying off the principal. Conceivably, this could increase your debt: If the interest charge becomes higher than the total payment you are sending in each month, you get into what is called "negative amortization," actually increasing rather than "paying down" your loan. Let's look at an example.

> Suppose you obtain an adjustable-rate mortgage for $45,000 for 30 years at 11.5 percent with annual adjustment. Your monthly payment will be $445.64. In the second year, however, the interest rate rises to 12.5 percent. Now your payment *should* be $480.27—but you elect (and the bank allows you) to keep the payment the same. Thus, when each monthly check comes in from you, the bank first takes its payment of interest, at 12.5

percent, then applies anything left over to reducing your principal. As long as the rate of interest stays at 12.5 percent (or goes even higher) you will be falling further and further behind in the amount that is being applied toward your principal. For instance, with a payment of $445.64 at 11.5 percent, let's assume that $400 is for interest payment and the balance goes toward the principal. If you make the same payment at 12.5 percent, the payment going toward the interest will increase, let's say to $410, and thus less will go toward paying the principal. If, on the other hand, the interest rate should fall to 10.5 percent, which would call for a monthly payment of $411.64, and you continue to send in your fixed payment of $445.65, the bank will apply less of your payment to interest and more to reducing your principal balance—and you will be paying down your loan at a faster rate.

Tip: Some ARM's have no cap on the interest rate they may charge you. They can just go up and up. *Avoid them.*

The moral of all this is to try to find a bank that offers an ARM with infrequent adjustments and with a cap on increases in the interest rate or in monthly payments.

Some variations on the ARM that you should know about:

- *Graduated payment mortgage.* With this type of mortgage the monthly payments are relatively low in the first few years. Then they rise until they are higher than conventional monthly mortgage payments would be. The idea is that payments are scheduled to increase at fixed intervals and by fixed amounts, with the extra money used to pay off the principal earlier. The problem is that the payments in the early years might not be covering the interest, so you are not building any equity in your home unless property values are increasing generally.
- *Renegotiable-rate mortgage.* With this type, the interest rate comes up for renegotiation after a set period, usually one to five years, rather than when market factors, such as a change in the prime rate, force it to change.

The new rate is determined, as is the adjustable rate, by the Federal Home Loan Bank Board.
- *Roll-over mortgage.* This is similar to the renegotiable-rate mortgage. The rate is set for from three to five years. Then it is totally renegotiated, or "rolled over." In effect, the roll-over involves a series of short-term loans, with the entire loan coming due at the end of each period and then being replaced by another short-term loan. This goes on for a total of 25 or 30 years, as in conventional mortgages.
- *Balloon mortgage.* For the first few years, this one is similar to the variable, or adjustable-rate, mortgage, and you are paying it off like the conventional loan of 30 years. But at the end of a specified time, usually three to five years, you get hit with a "balloon" payment of the entire balance, which you pay by obtaining a new loan at the interest rates that then prevail. This type of loan is often used in second mortgages. If on the second time around, when the balloon is due, you can borrow at lower interest rates than you were able to get the first time, you have the advantage. This is not a sure thing, however, and, in addition, you could then be in an economic situation that makes borrowing difficult.
- *The assumable mortgage.* Sometimes you can assume the existing mortgage of the person who is selling the house. But you must come up with the difference between the asking price and the balance that is due on the mortgage. Suppose you are buying an $80,000 home on which the owner still owes $30,000 on the mortgage. If the owner's rate of interest is low, this could be an advantage for you, but now you will have to come up with $50,000. You may already have part of that amount as your planned down payment. To provide the missing difference, you could try to obtain a second mortgage. Or you might try making a deal with the bank that holds the previous owner's low-interest mortgage. They might be willing to make a "composite" loan—a new loan at a lower rate than is now prevailing, in order for them to "retire" the previous owner's loan, which has recently been giving them no profit margin at all.

Tip: Banks do negotiate. Banks do make deals. Banks do bend their own rules, if they see that you have a secure future. They will bend over backwards for a young doctor, or for someone who is going into a successful, closely held family business. When they know you are on a fast track, they anticipate future business—and they will negotiate. They will not, however, bend government rules. Don't expect them to. If you cannot get the loan you want and the amount you need, consider what is known as "creative financing." Many lending institutions will handle second mortgages. Often a seller, especially if he or she is anxious to close the deal, will finance part of the buyer's purchase price (a "take-back" mortgage). Many real estate developers offer special financing on new homes.

Remember: Buying your home will probably be the largest and most important investment you will ever make. It's worth taking the time and trouble to check every aspect of your purchase and make the very best deal you can on the house and on the mortgage terms. Remember, too, that even if the price is high and the bank's interest rates are high, your home can be a valuable source of tax savings, capital growth, and protection against inflation. And if it works out right, owning a home often costs no more, or very little more, than renting.

Tax deductions and other savings

What are some of those tax savings you gain as homeowners? Here are four ways you can take deductions from your income tax:

1. *Mortgage interest.* The interest you pay to a lender on a mortgage loan is tax deductible, whether the mortgage is for a place that is for personal use (a place to live in), business use (a place to operate a business in), or income-producing use (a place you've bought as an investment, to rent to others). The interest you pay is deducted from your adjusted gross income. It may be claimed as an itemized deduction only on Schedule A, Form 1040.

Your monthly mortgage payments cover interest on the principal amount you owe, plus repayment of some of the principal. In addition, some banks pay your real estate taxes and insurance for you and add that to the total, so you are paying one-twelfth of those costs each month. Most lending institutions provide you with a statement at the end of the year specifying how much you have paid during the year for each item.

At the time of the closing on your mortgage, you may have to pay some "points." This is a one-time expense. Each point equals one percent of your mortgage ($450, for example, on a $45,000 mortgage). If points are considered to be prepaid interest, they are usually deductible on your income tax return. If they are considered a service fee, they are not deductible, so this is a question to ask when you are shopping for your mortgage. If the points are deductible, insist on paying for them with a separate check, so you have a record, rather than letting the bank automatically take them out of your loan.

2. *Real property taxes.* These are local taxes imposed on all property owners. They are deductible from your federal income tax. The money they bring in is, in most communities, the main revenue that pays for schools and roads and municipal services such as police and fire departments and refuse collection.

Don't be surprised to find that taxes have a way of increasing as the value of property increases. Your city or town will reassess property every few years and increase taxes based on the new assessments. As mentioned earlier, this could happen soon after you move into your home, so before you buy find out what's going on in the locality where you are buying. Then at least you won't be surprised.

3. *Property damage.* As homeowners, you may deduct a casualty loss, for damage to your property, from your income tax—but only if it is caused by fire, storm, or theft. A deduction is not allowed, however, unless the loss exceeds 10 percent of your adjusted gross income. The amount of the loss is figured as either (a) the fair market value of the property before the loss, minus the fair market value immediately after the loss, or (b) the property's original cost adjusted for many things, such as depreciation, to the day of the loss—whichever amount is less.

If you are claiming a casualty loss, you have to be able to prove it. If it is a loss due to fire, an insurance adjuster will come to the scene to determine the amount of loss. And you will have to declare, on your income tax return, the amount that was repaid by insurance and claim a deduction only for any loss you suffered over that amount. If it is a theft loss, you must be able to prove that the item was stolen and you must prove its value—one more reason why record keeping is important: so you can show how much you paid for any item in your home.

Casualty loss is a gray area—very much so. It is always left up to you to prove the size of your loss.

4. *Energy credit.* This type of tax deduction could be valuable for you if you are buying an older home and putting some money and effort into fixing it up during your first several years in it. As a taxpayer, you are allowed a credit of 15 percent of the first $2,000 you spend each year to install elements to conserve home energy. They must have a life expectancy of at least three years. Included are:

- **a.** insulation for ceilings, walls, floors, water heaters, and pipes
- **b.** thermal or storm windows and doors
- **c.** caulking or weather stripping of windows and exterior doors
- **d.** automatic setback thermostats that save energy
- **e.** replacement burners for furnaces, flue modifications, and ignition systems that replace gas pilot lights
- **f.** meters that display the cost of energy use.

You may also claim credit for energy sources that are solar, wind-powered, or geothermal. The maximum allowed per building is 40 percent of the first $10,000 you spend—or up to $4,000—for each principal residence owned. Note that phrase "principal residence"; second homes aren't eligible. The credit must be computed on IRS Form 5695.

If you own a condominium or are a tenant-stockholder in a cooperative housing corporation, the same deductions and credit also apply.

What form of ownership?

Before you get to the closing on your house, you must decide what form of ownership you want to set up. (See Chapter 5.)

INVESTING 13

"Investing?" you ask. "How can we get into investing? We're trying to buy a couple of sticks of furniture and figure out whether we can afford to eat at the pizza parlor tomorrow night!"

This chapter is not written to frustrate you or to tell you that you should be consulting with a stockbroker once a week. Rather, it is in this book because you should have a total overview of the many important aspects of your financial partnership and because, eventually, investing is quite likely to be one of them.

Certainly you must have a sound financial foundation before you start investing—especially if you were only recently married. This chapter is meant as a general primer. Remember that many things can and probably will change—factors such as the general economy, taxes, the investment climate (a bull or a bear market in Wall Street, for instance)—between the time when you first read this and the time when you are ready to invest.

Read up on investing now and get to know all you can, so you will be ready to make sound investment decisions when the time is right for you. Then, when you are ready to make your first step in investing, be sure you do it together. Talk it all out. Get to know one another's risk factor or comfort level. If one of you is more knowledgeable than the other, educate the other. It is extremely important that both of you participate in investment decisions.

The difference between saving and investing

There are important differences. Saving is accumulating money for a specific purpose or to use in an emergency. It is a way of preserving capital and guaranteeing steady income. It is also a way of maintaining liquidity. You can always get at your money if it is put away in savings.

Investing is different. You take a chance when you invest. You accept risk—on the premise that you will get better returns than the dependable but conservative practice of ordinary saving can give you.

Investing not only involves risk. It involves your

time and effort. You must be willing to devote time to it, to study, listen, compare, and make sometimes difficult choices. Investing is a much more active exercise than saving.

Saving is passive. Investing is active. Not only that, but saving is itself one of the foundation stones for investing. For you must have a solid foundation upon which to build an investment program. Such a foundation consists of several fundamentals, including:

- savings for an emergency
- savings for one or more specific goals
- adequate life insurance
- IRA's
- a home of your own.

And you need one more fundamental: enough income to use for investing. Only when you have enough income to meet living and saving expenses and maintain a positive cash flow, or liquidity, should you consider yourselves ready to take the risks that are involved in investing in stocks and bonds or any of the other possibilities of "the market."

"The market" and its risks

You hear stories about people who have "made a killing in the market." You dream that one of those people could be you. But what you seldom hear is that for every one who has made a killing there is a loser—someone who took the risk that goes with investing and then took a loss. That's why it is vital that you establish the solid financial foundation you need.

The loser who was prepared to lose and took the risk is in one situation. Unhappy, yes, but not in trouble. But the loser who could not afford to lose is in trouble. There are few sadder moments than when you find you need the money you have invested for some other purpose, decide to sell, and discover that you must sell at a loss and get back less than you had before.

So you must understand that investing is risky, and you must figure out what your "risk temperature" is—no two people ever have exactly the same one. One person may feel comfortable investing in blue-chip stocks while another keeps her cool best in tax-sheltered limited partnerships, and a third goes in for municipal bonds. No one should ever be talked into any type of investment that makes him or her feel uncomfortable. Yet you cannot make money without taking some risks, and the faster you hope to make it—and the greater the amount you hope to make—the greater the risks you will have to take. What kinds of risks? Here are some to consider, depending on what type of investing you get into:

- *Macroeconomic risk.* Change in monetary policy. Outbreak of a war. Change in OPEC policy.
- *Market risk.* Shifts in capital flows and psychology, unrelated to economic news, that can cause advances or declines in the market (e.g., changes in interest rates).
- *Industry risk.* Changing circumstances within a particular industry: for example, the changes in the automotive industry brought about by OPEC and by fuel-efficient imports.
- *Business risk.* The competitor of the company whose stock you buy comes out with a better product than your company's.
- *Management risk.* Mergers, reorganizations, results of poor management judgment—even an unforeseen event (a plane crash, a fire).
- *Information risk.* Rumors or information that are misleading or false.
- *Natural disaster risk.* Floods, hurricanes, drought, tornadoes that could affect, for example, a livestock or crop investment.
- *Liquidity risk.* Insufficient demand for your investment when you decide to sell (or when you *must* sell to gain cash).

The liquidity risk is the one that affects most people. If you cannot risk liquidity—if you *must maintain* liquidity—put your savings where they will not only preserve the asset (i.e., the amount you have saved) but will give you a nice steady income or rate of return. Whether you can handle the liquidity risk should be your primary criterion as to whether or not you should get into investing.

Decide on investment objectives

How do you decide what your investment goals are? Ask yourselves these questions:

1. Are we looking for income and high yield: steady income that we can depend on, at a fairly high percentage of the investment?

2. Are we looking for current growth: Do we want to see our investment itself grow steadily—and not be so concerned about its producing income—so it will be worth a lot more when we sell it?

3. Are we looking for *aggressive* growth—do we want to make some quick bucks, then sell and do it again?

4. Are we investing to gain tax advantages (e.g., maybe defer taxes or buy tax-free municipal bonds)?

The answer to questions such as these can help you set some investment objectives. Your goals will also be determined by your ages, your temperaments, your current and future financial needs.

Once you have set your objectives—and it is a good idea to write them down and file them with your investment papers—you must stick to them until the time comes when you know they should be changed. Right now, while your income is moving upward and you do not have children to feed, clothe, and educate, your needs probably run in the direction of investing for growth and for tax advantages. Later on, some years from now, when your children are in the expensive teenage and college years, you'll be looking for income and high yield.

What type of investment?

Assuming that you have looked carefully at your budget and net worth and have decided you have enough income to maintain a positive cash flow and take care of expenses, let's look at the kinds of investing you'll want to consider.

1. *Government securities.* Since the U.S. government borrows $200 billion a year, new issues are readily available. These are safe investments simply because the government can print new dollars to repay old debts. There are three types of government securities:

- Treasury bills. Sold every week, these reach maturity within three, six, or 12 months. The minimum investment is $10,000. You buy them at a discount. For example, if you buy a three-month Treasury bill worth $10,000, it is possible to be purchased for $9,850. Three months later it could be presented for full payment of $10,000, realizing $150 in interest.

- Treasury notes. These are sold every four weeks or so. They mature in anywhere from one to 10 years and usually require a minimum investment of $5,000. You pay the full value of the note you buy, and you get cash interest from the government twice a year during the term of the note.

- Treasury bonds. These are not sold on a regular schedule. You have to watch for them (check with your banker regularly if you are interested). Treasury bonds take anywhere from 10 to 30 years to mature, so they are definitely in the long-range category. Usually you can get them for $1,000 apiece. Like treasury notes, they pay cash interest twice a year and you buy them at full face value.

Where do you buy Treasuries? You can purchase them directly at any Federal Reserve Bank. You can buy them through the mail, but this requires a certified check one week in advance. You can also buy them through a broker or a bank (either will add a sales charge).

Tip: If you buy Treasuries through the mail, you won't know what interest rate you are getting until after you have made the purchase.

Hold on to Treasuries until they mature. You can always borrow against them or sell them in the secondary market, where you will get more or less what you paid for them, depending on whether the interest rates have fallen, risen, or stayed the same since you bought them.

Note: Treasuries are not taxed at the state or local level. If you live in a state that imposes a tax on interest income, Treasuries can thus give you a certain tax advantage.

2. *Government savings bonds.* The government now pays a floating interest rate on savings bonds. Series EE bonds mature in eight years, HH bonds in 10 years. If you cash in EE bonds before they mature, the yield is reduced. If you cash in HH bonds during their first five years, their interest is also reduced. Savings bonds have excellent liquidity—you can cash them in any time, at any bank—and they are extremely safe, but their yield is poor.

Why buy them? One reason is if you can't afford any larger kind of government security. Another reason is to force yourselves to save, by buying them through a payroll deduction plan. *Note:* like other treasuries, savings bonds are not taxed at the state or local level.

3. *Corporate bonds.* When you buy a bond, whether it is a government bond or a corporate bond, you are lending your money to that particular government body or corporation for a specified length of time. At the end of that time, that is, the date of maturity, the issuer of the bond pays you back the full amount, or face value, of the bond. Meanwhile, you receive a fixed rate of interest, paid twice a year in most cases. The rate of interest is imprinted on the bond. A 9 percent rate means that a $1,000 bond will pay you $90 a year. This rate does not change once the bond is issued, whether or not bond prices fluctuate.

What is the risk in bonds? The credit worthiness of the corporation that issued the bond can deteriorate. And, as interest rates rise, the value of the bond drops. Bonds that were issued a number of years ago are likely to have lost their value because interest rates are so much higher than they were when the bonds were issued. Such bonds are called *discount bonds.*

Here's an example of how they work:

Say someone purchased a bond in 1968 for $1,000 with a maturity date in 1988, at an interest rate of 6.25 percent (a perfectly respectable rate, back then). Today you might be able to buy this bond on the open market for $820. You will then receive the $62.50 interest each year (at the 6.25 percent rate) and when the bond matures you will receive the full $1,000. The current yield on such a bond would be 7.62 percent—determined by the $820 price you paid for it, rather than by the face value of the bond. (You divide the $62.50 interest you receive by the $820 cost to arrive at the 7.62 yield.) When the bond matures and you get the $1,000, you will have a gain of $180 ($1,000 less $820) that will be taxed at capital gain rates. Thus 60 percent of your gain will be exempt from federal income tax and you will have to pay income tax on only 40 percent of it. (For details on this process, see Chapter 11, on taxes.) Whoever held the bond before you and sold it for $820 will have suffered a loss of $180.

The opposite of all this is that if interest rates go down, a bond increases in value and can be sold at a premium.

In a word, bonds adjust—they adjust to interest movements by changing price.

4. *Tax-exempt bonds.* States, communities and their agencies issue bonds that are usually called "municipals." Their yields are not taxed by the federal government. These are usually recommended only for people in high income brackets. Tax-exempts make good sense if you are in the 35 percent tax bracket (say, a married couple filing jointly at the $42,000 income level). *Tip:* You avoid not only the federal tax but any state or local taxes when you buy a bond issued by the state you live in.

5. *The stock market.* A stock market investment means that you become a part owner of a corporation. You buy a share in it. There are two obvious reasons for making such an investment.

- You believe the company will succeed and that the price of its stock will rise as a result, and eventually you can sell your share in it for more than you paid for it.
- You believe that while you own a share in it, the company will be so well run that it will make a profit and that the company will divide that profit among its shareholders, including you.

In the stock market, you will find no guarantees. A company may do well, or it may not. Stock prices change daily and if you are the nervous type who could be easily upset by a slight drop in the market price of a stock you own, you probably should not be in the market. You must also be willing to do your homework: You should never buy a stock that you have not studied thoroughly, so you know what kind of company issued it, who runs the company, what its goals are, what its record is. Such study is, of course, the specialty of the *securities analyst,* who works full time at this.

Your best approach to the market is through a good stockbroker. Shop for one as you shopped for your banker: Find a person who will take the time and make the effort to understand you and your particular needs. If a stockbroker fails to ask about your entire financial situation—your savings program, your insurance coverage, your respective incomes, your net worth today—he or she is not worth *your* time or your commission payments. If you really know what you're doing, and can choose your own stocks or bonds without assistance, consider using a discount broker, whose commissions for executing a trade are anywhere from 40 to 70 percent less than those of a regular broker.

Stocks are bought and sold, or traded, on exchanges. The largest in the United States is the New York Stock Exchange. That's where the major stocks—shares in the blue-chip corporations—are traded. The American Stock Exchange (AMEX) generally lists stocks of smaller, less well known companies. In addition there are regional exchanges located in other major cities. Many stocks are "unlisted" or sold "over-the-counter."

Tip: To get an idea of the listings, open the business section of a good daily newspaper and you will find them. The *New York Times* or the *Wall Street Journal* will give you the most comprehensive listings.

To buy or sell stocks, you must go through a stockbroker or any bank. The broker or the bank charges a commission on each transaction—buying or selling. The commission rate will vary, depending on whether it is a full-service or a discount brokerage service.

The risk in the market? That depends. On the economy in general. On the stock you buy. You can lose your shirt. You can make a bundle.

Tips (these are tips on what to do if you're going into investing in the stock market; "tips," or advice based on rumors, in the market are something else, and usually they are worthless):

- If you are looking for income, look for stocks that pay regular dividends.
- If you are looking for growth over a long period, buy stock in companies that show clear signs of growing. Probably they will not be paying out high dividends right now, but instead investing their profits in research and expansion to make the company grow.
- If you are building a portfolio of stocks for the long term, do *not* put all your eggs in one basket. Diversification is a must. Buy stocks of companies in several industries, and make different types of investments.

What about mutual funds?

The mutual fund gives you a way to spread out your risk and, in effect, buy diversification in a single purchase. With an investment of $1,000 in some mutual funds, you become part owner of a variety of stocks. The fund is managed by professionals who devote their full time to studying the market and making investment decisions. Because you are pooling your investment with thousands of others, the mutual fund gives you an ideal way to invest on a moderate scale.

You will find a wide variety of mutual funds available. They have various investment goals which they address by concentrating on different types of securities. Once you have decided on a mutual fund, you will be relieved of the need to study specific stocks and make decisions on them. The professional managers of the fund do that.

The various types of mutual funds are:

- *Income fund.* Designed to return a high level of income, these funds are invested in bonds, preferred stocks, and high-yielding common stocks.
- *Growth fund.* If you are looking for long-range capital gains, keep in mind these funds that are invested in companies that are expected to grow faster than the rate of inflation. Emphasis is on preserving capital, but with an effort to produce dividends.
- *Maximum capital gains fund.* The idea here is to go for big profits, usually by investing in small companies and in developing industries. These funds concentrate on more volatile issues and, as you might expect, the greater the push for high profits, the greater the risk.
- *Specialized fund.* In this category, you might find a fund that buys stocks of many companies in a single field, such as high tech. Usually, specialized funds concentrate on only one or two industries.
- *Tax-free fund.* These are invested in municipal bonds. They appeal to those who are in a high income bracket where tax-free income is desirable.
- *Balanced fund.* The balance is between stocks and bonds, with the idea of providing both income and capital appreciation.
- *Money market fund.* These large funds (many are gigantic) buy a wide variety of interest-yielding securities, including short-term certificates of de-

posit in large denominations, U.S. Treasury bills, and other short-term assets.

Mutual funds are either "load" or "no-load." A load fund is bought through a broker, who charges a commission (the load is the commission, or sales charge). If you buy directly from a specific fund, there is no sales charge; it is no-load.

The success of your mutual fund depends, of course, on market conditions, but the idea of the fund is to spread the risk of owning securities. The return you get depends on the type of fund you decide to get into. An income fund will emphasize dividends, while a growth fund will give you smaller dividends but greater capital gains.

Mutual funds give you a number of advantages:

1. Small minimum investment. A small amount can get you started, and subsequent purchases can be even smaller.

2. Diversification. Each share you buy in a mutual fund gives you an interest in a broad range of stocks, bonds, or any other kind of investment the fund specializes in. Diversification helps soften the blow that can come from wide price fluctuations when you own individual securities.

3. Liquidity. When you want to sell, the mutual fund will always buy back its shares—at a time, you hope, when you will realize a gain and not a loss.

4. Automatic reinvestment. You can ask most funds to reinvest automatically, dividends earned, so your account keeps growing. Capital gains can be reinvested, too.

5. Automatic withdrawal. If you want regular cash income as your fund produces dividends, most will set up an automatic withdrawal plan for you. (This can be particularly valuable in your retirement years—far from now.)

6. Exchange privilege. Since many funds manage a "family" of different kinds of mutual funds, they can let you switch your investment from one type to another as your needs and objectives change or as you want to take advantage of changes in the market, known as "investment timing."

A mutual fund's total net assets (the total of all the stocks and bonds and other investments it has bought) are divided by the number of shares it has outstanding (i.e., all the shares that have been bought by people who have invested in the mutual fund).

This gives the value of one share in the fund—called the *net asset value*. The net asset value rises and falls with the market prices of the fund's holdings. It is figured daily. The number of shares you buy when you invest depends on the amount you are investing divided by the net asset value on the day you make your purchase. For example, in a no-load fund, if you invest $1,000 on a day when the net asset value is $21.21, you will own 47.147 shares of that particular fund.

Before you invest in a mutual fund, look over your needs and objectives carefully—and study up on mutual funds. You will find annual surveys on the performance of mutual funds in many magazines. Compare their performance, noting especially how they do when the market is good and when it is bad.

High-risk investments

If you do not need current income and if you can take some high risks, consider investments in some of the more esoteric forms: precious metals (gold or silver), coins, diamonds and other precious gems, stamp collections, art objects. If you want to become really sophisticated, get together with your stockbroker and find out about puts and calls, buying and selling on options, commodities, futures contracts, oil and gas exploration, real estate. There are countless ways to make—and lose—money through investments. Just be sure you know your situation and your objectives before you put any money into the more aggressive and speculative investments.

Avoiding investment mistakes

Some basic tips:

1. Make sure you have a solid foundation. Is money put away somewhere for a rainy day? For a specific goal? Do you have enough life insurance? A positive cash flow? Do you already have the dream house?

2. Work out an investment plan. Decide on middle- and long-range investment objectives. Do you want to accumulate a down payment for a house, in a hurry? Are you looking for security over the long

term? Are you going into the market on a long-term or short-term basis? Do you want (or expect) to "make a killing"? Are you *willing* to invest for the long term, and do you have the patience to do so?

3. Know where you stand financially. Review your situation regularly. Do a Net Worth Statement and a cash-flow analysis.

4. Understand your risk factor and your risk temperature. Don't invest in anything that keeps you awake at night. Know yourselves—and how much risk you are willing to take.

5. Be informed. Read financial publications. Know what you are buying. Ask educated questions (they won't be educated questions unless you keep yourself informed) of a broker or an investment adviser. Take charge. Formulate your own plan—with advice.

6. Be ready to make changes. Remember—you are not married to any stock. If you have a loser, admit you made a mistake and get out. As your needs and objectives change, reevaluate your investments. *Never* get sentimental about a stock.

7. Don't expect miracles. There aren't any. It is easy to talk about gains. You will have losses, too. Remember—there is a trade-off between risk and return—if you want a high return, you have to take high risk.

8. No one type of investment works best all the time.

9. To avoid reversals, you must diversify. Do not put all your eggs in one basket.

10. Think *liquidity* at all times. Know what you will sell to get cash if you have to.

IRA (individual retirement account)

Anyone who has earned income may contribute to an IRA, building a nest egg and paying less federal income tax at the same time. Here's how it works:

When you put money into an IRA, you may deduct it from your income before taxes (your *gross* income). You are not taxed on that money, nor on the interest it earns, until you take the money out of the IRA in your retirement years—when, presumably, your tax bracket will be lower because you will then be earning less.

How much may you put in each year? Up to $2,000 (or up to 100 percent of your *taxable* income—whichever is less). If husband and wife are both wage earners, they may contribute up to $4,000. If one spouse is not working, the other may contribute to an account in the name of the non-working spouse, up to a total of $2,250 in both accounts (or up to 100 percent of the compensation of the working spouse, whichever is less). If you are doing this, you may divide the contributions between your two accounts as you choose, but no more than $2,000 may be contributed to the account of either one in any single year.

You do not *have* to put in $2,000 every year. You may put in as much as you feel comfortable with. But it is important to avoid, if possible, taking money out of an IRA before you reach the age of 59½, because you will have to pay a penalty of 10 percent on the amount you withdraw. So if you take out, say, $2,000, you will not only have to pay a tax on that amount (the tax you were sheltered from when you put the money into the IRA in the first place), but you will also have to pay a $200 penalty.

As a matter of fact, you shouldn't let the penalty deter you from saving for retirement or starting an IRA. There will come a break-even point—the point at which the penalty paid for early withdrawal will even out against other forms of investment that are not tax-sheltered.

By the way, while you are thinking ahead, let me make it clear that you do not *have* to take out your IRA savings when you reach 59½. But you must begin to withdraw the money by the time you are 70½ or face some stiff penalties. (But that's a long way off, of course, and the penalties could change by then—look how bank deregulation in 1983 reduced the "stiff penalties" on cashing in certificates of deposit).

How is the money paid out to you? You get three choices:

1. You may take the entire sum in one lump payment (presumably you would then invest it elsewhere—or would you simply enjoy a six-month trip around the world?).

2. You may decide to receive it in regular installments over a fixed period. The period is limited to your life expectancy or the averaged combined life expectancy of you and your spouse.

3. You may choose an annuity that will make regular payments for as long as you or your spouse live.

What about taxes on the money you put in the IRA? When you start making withdrawals, the money you take out is taxed as ordinary income. If you take it all out in one lump sum, you will be taxed in that year on the total amount. However, there is a way to take the lump sum, using a 10-year income-averaging formula to ease the tax burden.

What happens to the money if you die? The balance in your account is not subject to federal estate taxes *if* payment to a beneficiary is spread over his or her lifetime or over a period of at least 36 months. If the beneficiary takes it as a lump sum immediately, it is included as part of the estate and is taxable.

Must you always keep the money in the same IRA account? No. You may move it to another bank, if you wish, or to a different kind of account—either by direct transfer or by rollover. In a direct transfer, you never gain possession of the money during the transfer. It goes directly from one trustee to another. For example, you may ask your bank to transfer the funds directly to a mutual fund. In a rollover, on the other hand, you actually get a check or cash from the bank. You must then deposit it in another IRA account within 60 days or pay tax on it as ordinary income and pay the 10 percent penalty.

Note: After any rollover, you must wait at least 12 months before you may do it again; direct transfers, however, are not limited to any waiting period.

Does it make any difference when you make your contributions to your IRA? You bet. The earlier in the year, the better. If you deposit money in January, that money and the interest it immediately starts to earn are tax deferred—protected from any tax—for that entire year. And your money has that much more time to grow, because the interest starts from day one. If, on the other hand, you put the money into a regular savings account or money market fund, waiting until before the April 15 deadline the following year to move it into an IRA, the interest it earns will be taxable.

The difference an IRA can make

If you put the maximum of $2,000 into an IRA every year for 10 years and it earns 10 percent, you will have about $35,062 in the account at the end of 10 years. If you put the same amount, at the same interest, in an account where you pay taxes on the interest, assuming that you are in the 25 percent tax bracket, you will have about $23,000 in 10 years. The higher your tax bracket, the less you will have. If you are in the 50 percent bracket, you will have only about $13,207.

Does it make any difference *where* you invest the funds?

Yes. IRA funds can go into almost any type of account. Banks, insurance companies, brokerage firms, and mutual funds are all clamoring for your money. So you need to look at all aspects of your situation and make a decision. How long do you plan to make contributions? What type of risk are you willing to take? At your age you can probably afford to take some risks, knowing that if there are losses you will have time to make up the difference. How much can you contribute each year? Some IRA's allow you to make small or frequent contributions, while others do not. While you do not have to contribute every year, it's a good habit to get into.

Here are some of the ways you can set up an IRA. Before deciding on any one, you should get specific information from the institution you are considering.

1. *Banks.* Most offer a variety of options patterned on those offered by the conventional certificate of deposit. The options involve the kind of interest, the amount of interest, and the length of the certificate. Some offer variable or floating interest; others do not, so you should compare interest rates offered by different institutions. Most banks will let you open an IRA with as little as $100.

2. *Credit unions.* Most credit unions design their IRA's to fit the size and nature of the union. The rate of interest is set by the board of directors. Your initial deposit may be quite low, and deposits may be deducted directly from your paycheck if your employer is willing to extend such a benefit—a real convenience for you.

3. *Insurance companies.* An IRA set up with an insurance company is an annuity. A minimum rate of interest will be fixed through the years, possibly high in the early years, then lower as time goes on. You may have to pay an annual fee and sales costs, with a sizeable penalty if you withdraw the money

prematurely (probably even higher if you withdraw in the very early years of the policy).

4. *Mutual funds*. In this form of IRA you buy shares in a pool of money that is invested in securities chosen by professional money managers. In some mutual funds, your IRA is in a money market fund, where the investment is in short-term securities and the rate of return varies daily. In others, the investment is in stocks and bonds, some in blue-chip companies, others in more risky, emerging companies. As you get older and your investment objectives change, you may move your IRA from one mutual fund to another. In order to do this, many people choose a company that operates several funds. Most funds require a minimum deposit—some as low as $100. Usually a yearly maintenance fee of $2 to $10 is charged.

5. *Investment brokers*. Here is where you will find the widest range of IRA's. You can build your own portfolio, using a "self-directed" plan: You make the decisions on investing in stocks, bonds, mutual funds, or any other type of investment. Each time you buy or sell, you pay commissions. You will also have to pay some administrative fees. Most brokers expect you to invest the entire allowable $2,000 at one time, and it is really best to accumulate from $10,000 to $15,000 before you start to self-direct. Investing in securities, remember, means you risk loss. It is, however, the most flexible IRA route you can choose.

Think of the IRA as one of the foundation stones of financial fitness. It is never too soon to start an IRA. It means you are making a long-term commitment, but it is well worth it—especially in view of the current widespread concern over the future of Social Security.

And, incidentally, don't think you *have* to start with the $2,000 maximum the law allows. Little IRA's grow up big. If you put in only $100 a year, you'll have $1,753 in 10 years, $6,300 in 20 years, $18,094 in 30 years. Or, $500 a year will produce $8,766 in 10 years, $31,501 in 20 years, and $90,472 in 30 years. Not bad, especially if inflation is kept under reasonable control.

Tips on IRA's:

- Shop around. Financial institutions are in competition for your money.
- Check for payroll deduction plans. Your employer can make it easy to build your IRA. Weigh the relative safety of various plans.
- Compare minimum amounts needed to open IRA accounts.
- Understand the kind of interest or other return that is offered. It makes a difference in the dollars coming to you later. Interest on $1,000 contributed every year at nine percent will give you about $55,000 in 20 years. At 13 percent, you will get $91,000.
- Compare interest rates. They vary from locality to locality and from institution to institution. And they can change during the life of your IRA, so keep an eye on them over the years in case it becomes wise to make a direct transfer or a rollover.
- Keep an eye on the marketplace, too. Continue to study the options available so you can make informed decisions on transfers or rollovers.

Join—or form—an investment club

A great way to get yourselves educated about investments, with little risk, is to hook up with an investment club. Maybe talk with several other couples about forming a club if you don't already know of one. A stockbroker in your area will be glad to help you get started.

This is a way to get your feet wet even if you have only a small amount to invest. No one couple in your group would probably have enough money to make significant investments or attract the attention of a broker, but when you pool your resources your investment club will have enough. And you can make the meetings a social as well as educational event.

WHAT PRICE CHILDREN? 14

There is no question but that one of the greatest joys in life is to raise a family.

There is also no question but that you must face some financial realities connected with having children.

Figures on what it costs to raise a child vary widely. The experts say that the cost of bringing up a child from birth to age 18 may range anywhere from $150,000 to $160,000. Add to that the cost of four years in a private residential college and it will take another $75,000 for a child born in 1980 and graduating from college in 2001, at the age of 22.

You could spend more. You could spend less. It all depends on your family, lifestyle, taste, and goals. One consolation: A second or third child does not mean you must double or triple the costs, as the expenses seem to slide upward. Two do not cost a great deal more than one, except for such basics as getting born.

A birth is expensive. It can currently run about $2,300. Presumably you will have Blue Cross and Blue Shield or other medical insurance to cover it. But make good and sure, *before* pregnancy occurs, that your insurance covers pregnancy, because once it is under way there is no way in the world you can delay the course of nature or backdate your insurance policy. Blue Cross, for example, has an 11-month waiting period, from the start of your coverage, before you can claim maternity benefits.

A BABY DOESN'T KNOW WHAT SCHEDULE YOU HAVE IN MIND

I know one couple who hadn't planned on the wife becoming pregnant. But when she did, the dates looked OK. Under their insurance, she would be covered after April 1, and the baby wasn't due until the middle of May. But Michael decided to arrive prematurely on March 28—four days before the insurance went into effect. Because he was premature, he was kept in the hospital for several weeks. In the four days before the insurance became effective, he cost his parents $4,000. After April 1 the insurance company picked up another $3,000 for his hospital costs.

You'll have other "first child" costs, too: nursery furniture, baby clothes, car seat, carriage, stroller, bottles and special dishes, toys, and a million and one other things.

After the initial costs in the first few months, you can get lulled into a false sense of security. Costs don't generally rise much until your child starts school at the age of five. If Mom worked before the birth and is now staying home, however, your budget will be down by the amount of her former income. And when she goes back to work, you will have child-care costs to worry about.

Rising expenses from age five

By the time your first child enters nursery school or kindergarten, you will be patching jeans and buying new shoes every few months. But after the first day of school, you will realize that old clothes are in. You may want your daughter to look neat and sparkling clean, but you are likely to find clay in pockets, sand in shoes, and a creative finger paint design all over an only-this-morning-all-white T-shirt.

With first grade come countless activities outside the house. Soon there are guitar lessons, Little League, special art classes, ballet, swimming at the Y, and—when there is a spare moment—just plain going to Jane's or Fred's house after school. All this may mean miles of very short local auto trips—and up goes the budget for gasoline. The lessons add to the budget, too, and entail buying equipment (ballet slippers, musical instruments, art supplies).

Tip: If music lessons are begun, always check the possibilities of renting the musical instrument, at least for the first few months, until you are sure there is really a strong interest in continuing to play it. But find a way to rent without throwing cold water on the idea of playing and without casting doubts on your child's ability, talent, or interest.

Through the elementary school years, appetites grow, and so do arms and legs and feet. Clothes are outgrown faster than you can wash them. Video games are a must. Day camp first, and then a regular summer camp that makes heavy demands ($3,000 per summer, on average). You can spend weeks sewing name tags on a thousand T-shirts, shorts, socks, towels, sheets, sweaters, and you-name-it, and lay out big bucks for boots, sleeping bag, canteen, camera, tennis racket, baseball glove, or whatever—only to find, four to six weeks later, that half the wardrobe went home in someone else's trunk and the other half is so worn and dirty that the clothes must simply be junked. And where is the tennis racket? The camera? The baseball glove?

Now comes the orthodontist. With more and more companies providing some insurance that covers costs of braces for employees' youngsters, you may luck out on this one. For many families, it has always been a big expense in the subteen and early teenage years. Since you have 10 or 12 years before this cost can hit you, you have time to (1) check insurance plans and maybe even lobby for this kind of coverage where you work if you are not getting it, (2) include it in your savings goals, and (3) hope the two of you have brought together the right genes so there will be no overbite or other such problem.

Even without big dental bills, the teenage years can be a financial disaster area. Clothes? They are expensive. And for some reason or other, the teenager is convinced that a lot of them are needed. If a spot doesn't *come* out, the shirt *goes* out. Hair is washed at least once a day and blow-dried, so electric bills soar (if your child isn't using the hair drier, a friend is). Suddenly there are no *off* switches on the TV or stereo or lights. I can remember coming home to see the entire house ablaze with lights and shaking with sound, and, on entering, screaming, "Turn off the damn stereo and TV," only to find there was no one at home.

Your food budget is likely to zoom, too. There is no such thing as a leftover after hordes of teenagers descend on your refrigerator. The bag of Oreos, the pounds of cold cuts, the six-packs of Coke that were meant to last a week—all are gone in an afternoon.

Out of sheer desperation, you may decide to install a "children's phone," with its own number and listing in the phone book. This can help relieve you of having to listen to giggling on the phone for hours on end, not to mention the fact that no one is able to get through to you.

Who is paying for all this? Probably you are. But you can get some help from—of all people—your kids. Many a teenager pays or helps pay for the children's phone with income from baby-sitting, and many help out with their clothes budgets. It's a good chance, too, for you to lay the groundwork for their own thinking about financial planning and handling money. In fact, you should be sure to start such thinking the first time you reach into your pocket to hand out allowance money—probably late in kindergarten year, when the values of coins will have become established, and certainly some time in first grade. (The value of money is pretty vague to children five years old or less. Kindergartners often think a dollar is good pay for a day's work, or that $100 is a fair price for a sack of potatoes. When they play store, they *always* insist on giving you change—because their concept of money is manipulative rather than numerical. Over the kindergarten year, their concept changes.)

The biggie of the teenage years is the driver's license. If your child happens to be male, along with the license comes an auto insurance bill that is probably double what it was before. And the teenager no longer has legs—he or she has wheels. You decide to go out one evening, only to run out of gas. But you know you filled the tank last night and you haven't driven the car since then.

"But Mom, I put in gas."

"How much?"

"A dollar's worth."

And your kid may be ready to raise the hood and apply what's been learned from an article in *Popular Mechanics* to servicing your car. Then there are the minor dents that the insurance doesn't cover. And the possibility of a major accident that the insurance *will* pay for. (Billy, my neighbor's son, totaled his mother's car the day he got his license. Luckily, he knew what seat belts were for.)

New technology and changes in our culture will introduce new wants and needs that neither I nor anyone else can predict. My own children got through the teenage years before the computer and the video game arrived in the family room. While you can remember when such hardware came in and how you made it commonplace, your children will think the world always had computers for everybody—and their teenage demands for the latest thing will reach even further.

Don't underestimate the cost of a college education

College is expensive. But it will be a fundamental necessity for your children. If you don't start to save for it early enough you will have a tough time. Start to save from the moment of your first child's birth, if not from the first joyous confirming visit to your obstetrician/gynecologist. Make education one of your long-range goals, and stick to it. One nice advantage of such long-range saving is that the investment you make will grow along with the children. Incidentally, you may still be paying off your own college loans and think it's crazy to be saving for your children's education at the same time—but you'll be crazy like a fox if you do it. And with this kind of planning comes the advantage of being able to choose investment options that give you maximum growth. (See Chapter 13 on investments.)

Tip: You might well consider setting up a tax-sheltered trust fund for your child's education. This often requires a lawyer, but your local bank's trust department can give you valuable advice or set up a trust account with minimum start-up expense. Don't think such funds are just for millionaires! They often offer substantial tax savings even for middle-income families.

It is really very difficult to give you any specific figures—anything beyond the general range of from $150,000 to $160,000 to age 18 that I cited at the start of this chapter—on the cost of having children. There are just too many ifs, ands, and buts. If one parent stays home to raise the children . . . if you both work through their childhoods but have the costs of child care, more taxes, commuting, two business wardrobes rather than one, and laundry services or a cleaning person . . . if you have two kids . . . if you have three. . . .

The important thing is not to let dollar signs get in the way. True, raising a family will cost a small fortune. But how often did that ever stop anybody from raising a family? Children are priceless. Their cost is meaningless. You will know that—and you'll remember it—the first time your child gives you a hug and says, "Thank you." And that can happen many, many times over.

The childrearing years pass like a summer storm. I know. Let me be blunt about it by sharing with you a letter I wrote to my daughter soon after she was married. I said:

> You children have been the biggest pain in the ass—yet you've been the greatest source of satisfaction—in my life. My greatest accomplishment has been being a mother. Everything else has been secondary.

NOW THAT THE McQUARTERS ARE IN THEIR HOUSE . . .

. . . they are thinking about starting a family. They are going to look into the cost of child care if Cathy should go back to work. They are a little cautious—maybe methodical is the word—just as they were when they were saving for their home. They have also talked about Cathy, as a former teacher, going into providing a tutoring service right there at home. The main thing is that they realize that the arrival of a child can mean the loss of one wage earner's income, and they are planning on how to cope with that change.

THE LIVE-TOGETHERS 15

The world is no longer shocked when it hears that a couple are living together without a marriage license—without, as they used to say, "benefit of clergy." The decade of the seventies confirmed what the sexual revolution of the sixties predicted; that many couples can and do live together by preference without any legal binding to hold them together. Yet, despite the tremendous increase in the number of such couples, the laws of our land that pertain to them remain extremely unclear.

Money is one of the biggest problems that live-togethers have. Day-to-day finances can be a real hassle. What expenses are shared? Who owns the personal property you buy together—furniture, stereo, kitchen equipment?

No divorce laws apply

When married people get divorced, various divorce laws protect the rights of each party. Property is divided according to state codes or statutes, which vary greatly from state to state and which have been improved by recently enacted equitable distribution divorce laws.

But when live-togethers split, no laws protect either of them. They have to decide, on their own, who gets what. In fact, in some states, they can't even *try* to get help from the courts or other officials because those states consider cohabitation a criminal offense—even though the law is rarely enforced.

Important: a written agreement

It may not seem romantic to sit down with pencil and paper and work out a written agreement that lists the important items of property each of you is bringing to the relationship, and spelling out how property acquired during the relationship will be divided if you decide to split up—but that is exactly what you have to do. And the time to do it is before you start to live together—before either of you moves into the other's house or apartment or you find a new place together.

The written agreement can be simple or complex,

depending on the amount of money and property involved. It may be as simple as a statement that each of you waives all financial claims on the other's property and each will keep what is his or her own. Or it may be highly detailed.

Put into the agreement a clear statement of who will get what if you part, especially the property acquired jointly after you begin living together. Do you split the stereo into its components? Who gets the hide-a-bed? Maybe your best gauge is to divide items of more or less equal monetary value: If one of you paid $750 for the stereo and the other $795 for the hide-a-bed, that's pretty close; you simply have to decide who is to have which.

Tip: Don't get yourselves in a bind trying to put intangible responsibilities, such as who cooks dinner or does the dishes, into your agreement. If you're hassling over those things, maybe you shouldn't be living together.

A written agreement is a contract. Unless it violates some state law, it is likely to be recognized by the courts. If what you are agreeing to can be stated simply, you can draw it up yourselves. Use a fill-in-the-blanks legal form. If it involves many assets and quite a bit of money, (more, say, than just your regular incomes from your jobs), you should see an attorney. However you do it, you must both sign in the presence of two witnesses who watch you sign, and you must have the signatures notarized. Make the agreement in triplicate, so you each have a copy and your attorney or one of your relatives has the third.

Handling day-to-day finances

Avoid joint checking or savings accounts. Remember (see Chapter 7 on banking) that either partner can clean out such an account. You could set up a joint account so that both of you are required to sign each check and even each savings withdrawal, but banks do not particularly like this arrangement. If the two signatures are required one of the two can refuse to sign and thus tie up everything until that person changes his or her mind.

Joint credit cards or charge accounts are also not advisable. Don't get a second card on your existing account for your live-in partner. What if things go sour and your partner starts charging like crazy on a card that he or she is not responsible for?

Separate ownership is the route to go. It gives each of you the best protection and helps avoid a bitter fight over money in case of a breakup. Acquire assets separately—car, stereo, sofa, dining table, food processor, whatever—and keep a detailed list of who bought what. Also keep all receipts, marked with the name of the one who put up the money for the item. These records will protect each of you, even years from now, if there is a split.

Use Worksheet XII on budgeting for live-togethers to help decide who is responsible for household and other flexible expenses. The easiest way, of course, is to split all expenses right down the middle. To do that, put all receipts and cash register tapes on a spindle after marking them with the initials of the one who paid. Go through them at the end of the month or every two weeks (payday is a good time, especially if you are both paid on the same day) and see who has paid the least and thus owes the difference to the other one.

Another way is to mark the budget sheets clearly with initials showing who is to be responsible for each item of expense. Obviously, this is the way to do it if, for instance, one of you earns considerably more than the other and is agreeing to pay a larger share of expenses. Some couples calculate what percentage of the pair's total income is earned by each, and assign that same percentage to paying for expenses, so the one who earns 60 percent of the income, say, is the one who pays 60 percent of the expenses. (This means recalculating when either party gets a raise.)

There is no right way or wrong way. You just have to work out what is fair and agreeable in your own situation. That's why the written agreement is important.

Who signs the lease/buys the house?

When it comes to living arrangements, you should both sign the lease. Then you will both be responsible for its financial obligations. The landlord has to know what is happening. In fact, in 1983 the New York State Court of Appeals ruled that landlords have the right to evict people who are unrelated and who share an apartment without the landlord's approval. (Subsequent appeals could go on for

Worksheet XII: Yours
LIVE-TOGETHER BUDGETING

	MONTHLY INCOME			
1	Salary			
2	Bonus			
3	Gifts			
4	Dividends			
5	Interest			
6	Commissions			
7	Pension			
8	Social Security			
9	Alimony/Child Support			
10				
11	Other			
12	GROSS INCOME			
13	INCOME DEDUCTIONS			
14	Social Security			
15	Income Taxes			
16	Federal			
17	State			
18	Local			
19	Benefits			
20	Other			
21	NET INCOME			
	FIXED EXPENSES	Joint		
1	Rent/Mortgage			
2	Fuel			
3	Electricity			
4	Telephone			
5	Water			
6	Homeowner's Insurance			
7	Disability Insurance			
8	Automobile Insurance			
9	Medical Insurance			
10	Life Insurance			
11	Real Estate Taxes			
12	Income Taxes			
13	Personal Property Taxes			
14	Automobile Loans			
15	Loans Repayments			
16	Other			
17	TOTAL FIXED EXPENSES			
	FLEXIBLE EXPENSES			
1	Food & Beverage			
2	Clothing			

		Joint		
3	Laundry & Cleaning			
4	Home Office Supplies			
5	Animals			
6	Personal Care/Toiletries			
7	Periodicals			
8	Recreation (hobbies, sports)			
9	Entertainment (movies, meals out, plays, etc)			
10	Travel/Vacations			
11	Gifts			
12	Household Maintenance			
13	Lawn & Snow Removal			
14	Maid			
15	Garbage			
16	Repairs (plumber, T.V., carpenter)			
17	Home Furnishings/Decorating			
18	Major Appliance Purchases			
19	Transportation			
20	Gas/oil			
21	Repairs			
22	Licenses and registration			
23	Commutation, Parking, Tolls			
24	Children's Expenses			
25	Allowances			
26	Lessons			
27	Camp			
28	Recreation/sports			
29	Babysitting			
30	Education			
31	Tuition			
32	Room/Board			
33	Books & Supplies			
34	Travel			
35	Medical Expenses			
36	Doctor			
37	Dentist			
38	Drug			
39	Contributions			
40	Church/Synagogue			
41	Other Charity			
42	Savings			
	TOTAL FLEXIBLE EXPENSES			
	TOTAL FIXED EXPENSES			
	TOTAL EXPENSES			
	TOTAL INCOME			
	TOTAL EXPENSES			

THE LIVE-TOGETHERS

many years.) Many leases limit occupancy to the person who signed and the members of his or her immediate family.

If one of you already has an apartment and the other is moving in, it is important to inform the landlord. If possible, have the new arrival sign the lease, even if it is already in effect.

What about buying a house or condo? The best way to work this is for each of you to put up half of the down payment and then split all household expenses fifty-fifty. If and when the house is sold, you will then split the equity in equal parts. Meantime, you would own the place as joint tenants in common.

Another way is for one of you to own the house and pay all property expenses (mortgage, taxes, utilities, insurance) while the other picks up such unrelated expenses as entertainment and vacations. Or one can own the house and the other pay "rent" to the owner.

However you decide, a contract between you that describes the homeownership is imperative. It will spell out who pays expenses, who gets income tax credit for tax deductions or interest paid on the mortgage, how the increased equity is to be shared when the house is sold. Better to spell it out now than battle it out later.

Insurance for Live-togethers

Insurance companies are conservative. They don't change their ways very quickly. So you have to face the fact that they have not raced to the forefront in adapting their policies to the changing world that includes live-togethers. You should think about several areas:

1. *Health insurance.* Group health insurance's "family" coverage just about never extends to an unmarried live-in. So while a married spouse is covered by a working mate's group policy, live-togethers must each have their own protection.

> *Tip:* A not bad idea is to be sure that each of you has the other's medical power of attorney. This means that in an emergency one can authorize surgery or other treatment for the other, just as a husband or wife can in a marriage. This is especially important if the next-of-kin is a parent who is thousands of miles away.

2. *Homeowner's and automobile insurance.* Whether you rent your place or own it, be sure the insurance policy carries both your names so that both of you are covered. If one of you owns the house, the other should get a renter's policy to cover his or her personal possessions. Automobile insurance should be written on the owner of the car (and be sure to avoid joint ownership of a car).

3. *Life insurance.* Often one live-together wants to make the other the beneficiary of a life insurance policy. Insurance companies usually balk at this idea. People have sometimes got around this by simply making someone else the beneficiary—parents or a sibling, say—and then, after waiting a while, notifying the insurance company of a change in beneficiary. Since the policy will then be established, the change will be routine and they won't make a fuss. Leaving life insurance to a live-together can help pay funeral expenses or enable your friend to buy your share of a jointly owned house.

4. *Pensions and profit sharing.* If you are vested (or are going to be vested) in a pension or profit-sharing fund, you can make arrangements to have your live-together named as beneficiary of such a plan if you die before collecting the proceeds. Once you begin to collect on a pension, however, there are no benefits for any survivors. Only a widow or a widower qualifies as a survivor. So you should consider planning that you will take lump sum distribution from a pension plan or purchase an annuity that has a survivor benefit. It is important to remember that starting in 1984 death benefits from a pension to a non-spouse survivor are to be paid either in a lump sum or in a five-year period following a worker's death. (The same applies to an IRA.)

What about wills?

An important subject. Wills are imperative, for each of you. If either of you dies intestate (i.e., without a will), his or her estate—including all money and possessions—will be distributed according to the laws of the state you live in. This means it is possible for children from a former marriage, or for parents, or cousins, or siblings to get assets that you want the live-together to receive. Relatives come out of the woodwork when a person dies intestate—more relatives than you ever thought existed. It is entirely possible that they could end up with assets that your live-together helped contribute to your estate. So make wills. (See Chapter 16 on records, wills, and advisers.)

To sum up, before you start to live together, have some very frank and open discussions about financial matters. It will be important to keep proper records of who owned what before coming into the relationship, as well as of who purchased what after you moved in together. Spelling out things beforehand, and understanding them, can actually give you legal and financial benefits. And if your relationship should fall apart, the contracts, agreements, and other documentation will make it easier for you to go your separate ways without a battle.

The courts may some day extend protection to live-togethers, as they have over many years and many cases extended it to both partners of a marriage. But until that day comes (and it is still plenty far off) you will have to take charge of such matters yourself.

TWO LIVE-TOGETHER COUPLES

Sue and Bob lived together for over a year. They had no written agreement. Each maintained a checking account for personal expenditures. They set up a joint checking account to handle household expenses—rent, utilities, food. This account was supposed to be funded equally by each of them. But look how it worked out:

"I was paid monthly and Sue was paid weekly," says Bob. "This created a problem. She was putting in $100 a week. Then I came along on the 15th, when I got paid, and put in anywhere from $600 to $800. The big bills got paid then. Before the 15th rolled around again, I would have to put in more, to cover food and other household expenses, because her $100 a week wasn't covering those things."

The problem was that, since Bob's money went for paying the major bills in one check-writing session, Sue felt that what she was putting in was "her" money and not "theirs." She held on to what she felt was "hers."

In addition, Bob was letting Sue use his charge cards, with the understanding that she would pay for what she charged for herself. But when the bill arrived, he paid for his charges out of his personal checking account, while Sue paid for her charges out of their joint account.

The inevitable split left Bob to pay Sue's charges that were on his charge card. He had given her a ring and they had expected to be married. He got the ring back, sold it, and paid off the debts.

Looking back, Sue says the fact that Bob got paid only once a month made her uneasy. "His paycheck depended on commissions, so it varied a lot," she recalls. "This drove me nuts. I guess I needed the certainty of knowing there would be a definite amount each week. I couldn't live with the ups and downs."

On the other hand, take Ruth and Simon. They lived together for 10 years before they were married. Even though Ruth is an attorney, they never discussed money. "We went into the living arrangement with a tacit understanding about what each would take care of," says Simon. "I guess we were lucky. It was all very easy and we never had a problem."

Ruth owned a house. Simon moved in. She paid the mortgage, taxes, insurance, utilities, major repairs and maintenance. Simon bought the food and paid for his own telephone and for any household help they hired. When they went out to dinner, the theater, or movies, Simon paid. He also took care of all vacation expenses. Each kept a separate checking account. They never mingled funds. All their investments were made separately.

"Since all the property was individually owned," says Ruth, "we didn't seem to need any contract. If we had split up, what was there to argue about? What was mine was mine and what was his was his."

Worksheet XII: Example
Bob and Sue's
Live-Together Budgeting

	MONTHLY INCOME		Bob	Sue
1	Salary		$2,416	$2,000
2	Bonus			
3	Gifts			
4	Dividends			
5	Interest		50	25
6	Commissions			
7	Pension			
8	Social Security			
9	Alimony/Child Support			
10				
11	Other			
12	GROSS INCOME		2,466	2,025
13	INCOME DEDUCTIONS			
14	Social Security		169	140
15	Income Taxes			
16	Federal		525	383
17	State		80	62
18	Local			
19	Benefits			
20	Other			
21	NET INCOME		1,692	1,440
	FIXED EXPENSES	Joint	Bob	Sue
1	Rent/Mortgage	$475		
2	Fuel	50		
3	Electricity	30		
4	Telephone	35		
5	Water			
6	Homeowner's Insurance	10		
7	Disability Insurance			
8	Automobile Insurance		60	35
9	Medical Insurance		45	
10	Life Insurance			
11	Real Estate Taxes			
12	Income Taxes			
13	Personal Property Taxes			
14	Automobile Loans		115	150
15	Loans Repayments			
16	Other			
17	TOTAL FIXED EXPENSES	600	220	185
	FLEXIBLE EXPENSES			
1	Food & Beverage	350		
2	Clothing		150	250

FINANCIAL FITNESS FOR NEWLYWEDS

		Joint	Bob	Sue
3	Laundry & Cleaning	$25		
4	Home Office Supplies			
5	Animals	15		
6	Personal Care/Toiletries		$20	$30
7	Periodicals	20		
8	Recreation (hobbies, sports)		50	20
9	Entertainment (movies, meals out, plays, etc)	50	100	25
10	Travel/Vacations			
11	Gifts		25	15
12	Household Maintenance			
13	Lawn & Snow Removal			
14	Maid			
15	Garbage			
16	Repairs (plumber, T.V., carpenter)	10		
17	Home Furnishings/Decorating	40	75	
18	Major Appliance Purchases			
19	Transportation			
20	Gas/oil		200	125
21	Repairs		50	25
22	Licenses and registration			
23	Commutation, Parking, Tolls		45	
24	Children's Expenses			
25	Allowances			
26	Lessons			
27	Camp			
28	Recreation/sports			
29	Babysitting			
30	Education			
31	Tuition			
32	Room/Board			
33	Books & Supplies			
34	Travel			
35	Medical Expenses			
36	Doctor		50	100
37	Dentist		200	150
38	Drug			
39	Contributions			
40	Church/Synagogue			
41	Other Charity			
42	Savings			
	TOTAL FLEXIBLE EXPENSES	510	965	740
	TOTAL FIXED EXPENSES	600	220	185
	TOTAL EXPENSES	1110	1185	925
	TOTAL INCOME	3132		
	TOTAL EXPENSES	3220		
		(88)		

THE LIVE-TOGETHERS

RECORD KEEPING, WILLS, AND ADVISERS — 16

From reading all these chapters, you know that managing your money involves being able to prove what you spent, where you spent it, what you spent it for, how it improved or failed to improve your financial situation.

What you need for all this money management is *records*—not a mountain of paper, but a practical system for keeping track of financial matters and important papers related to them over a long period of time.

You should begin keeping records from the time of your first job on through your retirement years. The record keeping itself can be a simple file system of various papers, some items being permanent, some semipermanent, others temporary. For instance, obviously you keep a life insurance policy as long as it is in force. You keep automobile papers as long as you own the car. You keep home improvement records until you sell the house and want to prove how much extra capital you have put into it over the years. You keep ordinary sales receipts and other income tax records for three years, until the statute of limitations runs out: An audit by the IRS may go back no more than three years. However, you should keep your final IRS tax return for each year in a permanent file. It makes an excellent financial history.

A costly failing

Not having a good system of record keeping can be not only embarrassing but costly. The newly widowed woman who cannot find her husband's life insurance policies suffers embarrassment as well as grief. And you don't have to be newly widowed to lose money in another way. Banks regularly take out local newspaper advertisements to list the names and last known addresses of thousands of customers who have left accounts inactive for a specified period. If a bank fails to locate an owner of an account after placing such an advertisement, the unclaimed money goes to the state. Billions of dollars from bank accounts are held in state treasuries simply because no one can trace the assets to their rightful owners. If you move from state to state, as many couples do as a result of corporate relocations or when job opportunities open, you run the risk of forgetting to transfer an inactive savings account with you if you don't have a good system of record keeping.

By the same token, if you own a piece of property, move away, forget to tell the tax assessor where you have gone, and then fail to pay the taxes (people can and do forget such things—it happens in surprising numbers every year), the town may auction that parcel of land to the highest bidder—and keep the proceeds.

Some states exact a personal property tax on cars and boats. In our computer age, any state motor vehicle department can make a quick check on whether the tax has been paid on an automobile and will refuse to renew a car's registration if it has not. I had a client who sold his boat but did not keep the bill of sale. Months later the state demanded tax due on his boat. To prove he no longer owned the boat and therefore owed no tax, he had to trace the boat to a dealer in Florida and get another receipt.

Some people have had to reconstruct the history of an illness a year or more after they got well—because they didn't make medical records promptly and hang onto them. Since most doctors' offices ask for payment at the time of your visit and leave it up to you to handle major-medical and other insurance claims, it is important to make a habit of getting a photocopy of all receipts and claim forms, and of filing all claims promptly.

IMPORTANT: If your doctor (or hospital or diagnostic lab) is not paid at the time of your visit and you are then reimbursed by an insurance company (this is likely to happen with a group major-medical program where you work), be sure you pay the bill immediately when you get the money from the insurance company. If you spend that money on something else, saying "Oh, I'll take care of the doctor [or hospital or lab] later," you are giving yourself a habit that can only lead to problems.

You can replace many records. But it takes time, effort, and postage. Stock certificates are a good example. If you own more than one or two, make an accurate list: by name, number of shares, purchase price, and date of purchase. If you should have to compile such a list after your certificates have been lost, stolen, or destroyed in a fire, it can be horrendous—and the result may not be complete. Before any company will issue a replacement certificate, you will have to sign an affidavit that the certificate was destroyed, then put up a surety bond—which can cost as much as three percent of the current market price.

What goes to the bank, what stays home?

Where should you keep important papers and records? Some belong in a safe-deposit box in a bank. Others can be at home in a sensible file—in a safe place.

Papers that are difficult to replace should be in the safe-deposit box. These include:

Birth certificates
Stock certificates
Marriage certificate
Citizenship papers
Bonds
Certificate of title for an automobile
Real estate deeds
Copy of will (but not the original)
Divorce decree
Death certificates
Passports
Discharge from military service
Veterans Administration papers
Adoption papers
Contracts
Household inventory (including photographs for appraisal purposes).

What about life insurance policies—and why not put the original copy of your will in the safe-deposit box? Because in most states when the owner, or joint owner, of a safe-deposit box dies, the bank seals the box until all tax and legal matters are taken care of. Access is granted only when the bank receives legal permission, and then in the presence of an authorized person. A life insurance company will not pay a claim until the policy is surrendered. The probation of a will cannot begin until the last will is presented to the probate court. Thus, everything is held up if legal permission to open a safe deposit box has to be obtained.

The best place to keep your life insurance policies is at home. The best place to keep the original copy of your will is in the files of the attorney who drew it up.

Fill out the worksheets at the end of this chapter: XIII, **Personal Information**; XIV **Personal Contacts**; XV, **Record Keeping**; and XVI, **Location of Other Important Papers**.

Tip: It is better to jot down too much than too little. Don't be afraid to put in details. Some details may seem obvious. But remember that they will not be obvious to anyone who must track down all this information if you're not on hand to supply it. And lawyers can tell you how much they are paid to take care of "nuisance" details that could easily have been ready in a file.

When you have filled out these sheets, make duplicates. Give a set to someone else to keep for you—someone who will understand the method of your madness.

File—and throw out

What counts is not what your filing system looks like. What counts is how well you have organized it. For some, it may be a collection of shoe boxes. For others, it may be file cabinets with suspension drawers on ball bearings. The key is to get into the habit of filing those papers that are important and *throwing out* those that are not.

Your permanent home file should include:

Annuities
Automobile insurance
Bankbooks and statements
Children's records
Credit histories
Disability insurance policy
Educational records (for each member of the family)
Employment history
Federal income tax returns
Gift tax returns
Gifts
Health insurance coverage and policies
Health records
Home improvements
Homeowner's insurance
Household inventory (with receipts and appraisals)
Inheritances
Insurance policies (if not filed under subject headings, such as auto, medical, and so on)
IRA (individual retirement account)
Keogh plan
Life insurance policies
List of important advisers
Loan applications
Loans
Medical insurance
Medicare policy
Money market funds
Mutual funds
Paid bills
Pension and profit-sharing plans
Property-tax bills and receipts
Real estate investments
Social Security earnings records
Social Security numbers
State income tax returns
Stock options
Stock and bond record book
Warranties and guarantees
Wills (file signed original with attorney)

Records of stocks, bonds, and home improvements

With these items, it is important to know—maybe years from now—what you paid. This is strictly a matter of keeping good records for tax purposes.

If you are into stocks and bonds enough to keep a record book on them, use a different colored pen for each year in which you have stock transactions. If you are using blue ink for this year, for instance, you will know that all blue ink items that are sold must be included in this year's tax return.

It is important to have a record of when you bought a particular stock, and at what price. When you sell it, it will be necessary to figure out the gain or loss on the sale. Even if many years have passed between the purchase and the sale, you will have to pay a tax on any profit.

The same is true of your house or condominium. When you sell, you must pay a tax on the profit (that is, the difference between the original purchase price and the sale price). But the cost of every permanent improvement made over the years may be added to the original purchase price: landscaping, for instance, or converting a garage to a playroom; installing insulation and other energy-saving devices; the addition of a building, swimming pool, deck, or patio; or doing anything else that added value to the house. An accurate record of bills paid and canceled checks will be invaluable when the house is sold.

Tip: Before you move out, take pictures in and around the house. When you prepare your tax return they will jog your memory. You'll be surprised how many improvements you will see in those photos.

Files for income tax returns

A continuing file related to your annual income tax returns is vitally important. If the IRS decides to audit your return any year, the burden of proof will be on you. An accordion file of canceled checks, organized by categories, will help you with tax returns—as well as with budget planning. Filing categories include such items as:

- Automobile expenses
- Bills from specific stores
- Children's expenses
- Clothing
- Contributions
- Education
- Entertainment and recreation
- Household expenses (maintenance)
- Household purchases (major)
- Insurance premiums
- Medical and dental expenses
- Mortgage payments
- Taxes (real estate and personal property)
- Utilities

With this file at your fingertips, you can tackle a new year's budgeting and your end-of-year tax return with confidence in your accuracy. And you can throw out many bills. Do just that. Keep only what you need as evidence for tax purposes.

Make yourself do this kind of housekeeping at least annually.

Tip: One good system is to keep two sets of files: one for tax-deductible items, the other for major personal financial items—some of which may be tax-related. Tax-deductible items would include expenses for business entertainment (if they were not reimbursed by your employer) or subscriptions to professional publications. This file would also include income from free-lance or moonlighting jobs as well as from your regular job, and expenses for major home improvements. The other file would contain your records on insurance, investments, and job benefits where you work.

If the IRS audits you

The IRS does not understand the words "I can't find it." If you want to prove you made an expenditure, you must bring in the proof.

In fact, the IRS considers you guilty until you prove yourself innocent. It is permitted by law to audit you any time up to three years from the date you filed a return. In addition, if it thinks there is reason to charge you with fraud or gross negligence, it may audit you at a later date.

Once the three years have passed, you should *throw out* most of your canceled checks and documentation, keeping only those items that have to do with possible future capital gains tax information, such as home improvements or the purchase of collectibles and stocks and bonds.

What can you do if you are called in for an audit?

Be prepared. Your notice from the IRS will indicate the sections of your tax return that it wants to check on. The letter will tell you to call for an appointment, probably at the nearest IRS office. If your return was prepared by an accountant, contact him or her and see if the accountant will go in your place. (Be sure to find out if there is an additional fee for this service and decide whether to pay it and be represented or, at least for the first meeting, to go by yourself and find out what's on the IRS's mind.) Take with you—or send with the accountant—all the bills and canceled checks relating to the particular items the IRS has said it wants to check on.

Tip: In an IRS meeting, keep your eyes and ears open and your mouth closed as much as possible. Do not volunteer information. Answer only the questions you are asked. Do not chitchat. Control the natural tendency to babble in a nervous situation. Concentrate on counting the holes in the ceiling tiles, if you must, but fight the urge to blurt out something you may regret. You can let out your primal scream when you get out of the office.

Record keeping has its emotional aspects. Being able to put your hands on the right piece of paper at the right time is the greatest relief ever devised for an anxiety attack. If you have been wise enough to let someone else in on the secret of your method of record keeping, you will be in much better shape during an unexpected period of transition or emotional turmoil.

Do we need wills—at our age?

You bet. If you have *anything* to leave behind—a single personal possession or only a few dollars—you want to make certain it will go where you want it to go after you die. And that is what a will is for. In most states, anyone who is at least 18 years old and of sound mind may make a will.

A will is your means of making decisions, putting them on paper, and seeing to it that the paper becomes a legal document that no one can argue about.

If you die without a will, you will be said to have died "intestate." The state in which you lived immediately before death then becomes responsible for deciding who gets your property. Its decisions may or may not fit the ideas you had. The possibilities of inequities are great. For example, suppose you die and leave your spouse with small children. You would probably assume—and desire—that everything you owned would go to your spouse. But the state, under the law, might give your spouse only a little more than one half, with the rest left to your children. The state would also name guardians for any minor children—guardians you might never have wanted.

Your will gives you control not only over who gets what, but over how and when. It conserves and distributes your estate the way you want it done. It names guardians for children—the guardians the two of you have agreed on. (Nothing is worse than a family squabble over who is to take care of children; often a split occurs, with elderly grandparents taking charge and with the children enduring still another change of guardianship when the grandparents die.)

What is an "estate"?

Your estate is everything you own: your money, your house and land, all your worldly possessions. Estate planning is planning for what is to become of it all. It is really nothing more than caring for those who are likely to survive you. From reading this book and filling in its worksheets, you are already well on your way to estate planning, because:

- You have your papers and records in order.
- You know your assets and who owns what.
- You understand income and expenses.
- You know how much life insurance you have—and need.
- You know about your pension.

It will be important to review your will regularly, at least every five years. Here are some of the reasons why you may need to update it:

- the birth of a child
- the death of a beneficiary or of the executor (the person you have chosen to handle the details of the will when you die)
- marriage or divorce
- a move to a different state, where the laws may be different
- a major change in your financial circumstances
- new laws affecting estates.

How is a will made?

A will is a formal document, and making it is a fairly formal procedure. The law will consider it to be an effective document only if it meets certain criteria.

- In most states, a will must be executed in writing.
- It must be signed by the person who is making the will.
- It must be attested by at least two witnesses who sign in the presence of the person making the will. (Your witnesses may be called upon to testify in court that they saw you sign the will.)

How long does a will last—and can it be changed?

A will is in effect until it is revoked. You can revoke your will at any time. If your marital state changes or you have a child (or legally adopt a child), your will is automatically revoked unless a provision is made to cover such an occurrence. Any such change in your circumstances, or any substantial change in your assets, should be your cue to see what changes must be made in your will. It can be changed any time, and as frequently as necessary.

Consult a lawyer

Even if you think you may not have enough worldly goods to justify making a will, look around you. Insurance policies, company benefits, your home, investments, household furnishings—all may add up to more of an estate than you thought you had.

Have an attorney draw up your will. A good lawyer will know the laws of your state, and will avoid problems that you might create by making your own homemade will. You can save your lawyer's time, and your own money, by doing the following:

- Have ready a list of your assets (from your Net Worth Statement).
- Choose an executor, a friend or relative whom you trust. This person will be fully responsible for seeing your will through probate and making sure your estate is disposed of properly. This person should live nearby. If he or she dies, you must revise your will to name another.
- Choose a guardian for your children. Guardians will be expected to provide proper care as well as manage money for the children. Before you name a guardian in your will, be sure you ask the prospective guardian if it is all right with him or her.
- Decide who is to get what from your estate.

Ask your attorney to maintain the original signed copies of your will and your spouse's. Keep duplicate copies in your files at home and, for extra safety, in your safe-deposit box.

Probate—what's that all about?

Your estate is either of two types: *probate* and/or *taxable*. You may have an asset that is jointly owned and that does not go through the probate process. Yet it may be part of your taxable estate. Since federal estate and gift tax laws change frequently, and since there is great variation among state laws, you should ask your lawyer to discuss and explain what happens to a taxable estate where you live.

The function of probate court is to authorize and supervise the payment of funeral expenses, taxes, and debts owed by a person who dies, and to authorize the cost of administering the estate. Usually your executor is paid for handling your estate. The court then sees that any remaining property is distributed to the beneficiaries or to any others who are entitled to it.

The executor works under the supervision and scrutiny of the probate court. If you do not have a will, the court—acting on behalf of the state—will name an administrator.

This is the probate procedure:

1. Probating the will. Application is made for probate of the will, which is filed with the court and declared valid. The court approves the executor named in the will, or names an administrator.

2. Posting of a bond by the executor or administrator (unless your will waives the requirement). The

amount of the bond will depend on the size of the estate.

3. Inventory of all assets that are owned in your name *alone*. This is needed to determine whether your estate is solvent. Assets must be evaluated. Appraisers will be called in to judge the value of real estate and certain collectibles such as coins, jewelry, and so on. An up-to-date Net Worth Statement can be a great aid at this point.

4. Advertising for claims against the estate. This is in case any unknown debts are "out there" somewhere. The notice will specify that all claims must be submitted within a stated period, otherwise they need not be honored. At the same time, all recent and outstanding bills, such as funeral or medical expenses, are paid.

5. Filing of state and federal tax forms, as required by various laws, and payment of the taxes.

6. Final accounting and distribution of the remaining estate to those named in the will.

That is the probate procedure. It involves certain time limits set by state law (the inventory, for example, must be completed within a certain time). The entire procedure can take anywhere from nine months to two or three years, depending on the complexity of the will, size of the estate, and number of beneficiaries.

Note: Once a will has been probated, it is a matter of public record. That's why many people prefer to establish trusts for their beneficiaries; trusts are not made public.

What about jointly held property?

Any property that is jointly held is not included in the probate procedure. Under the Economic Recovery Tax Act of 1981, a spouse may leave the surviving spouse an unlimited amount of property without its being taxed. It will be taxed only when the surviving spouse dies, but, as the taxable amount decreases each year, fewer and fewer people are being affected.

State inheritance tax laws are different from the federal laws. No two states seem to have the same rules. Many have neglected to make changes that coincide with federal law.

Jointly held property has certain advantages, including these:

- It passes immediately to the survivor, staying out of probate.
- It is easy to set up.
- It assures an inheritance for a spouse with no funds of his or her own, because jointly held property cannot be sold without the permission of the other spouse.
- It can eliminate ancillary probate (that is, probate in another state). This is important, for instance, if you own a vacation home in another state. Be sure the place is jointly held, in order to avoid probate fees.
- Creditors may not be able to seize jointly held property, unless the surviving spouse assumed liability. Again, each state has different laws.

You should also be aware of some disadvantages of jointly held property:

- Signatures of both spouses are needed in order to sell property. This can be a problem in a divorce situation or if one spouse is absent and has not given a power of attorney to the other.
- Either spouse can clean out a joint bank account.
- Jointly held property cannot be willed. Neither spouse has any say in how the surviving spouse is to dispose of property.
- It may be subject to gift taxes.
- In a large estate, when one spouse dies, jointly held property added to the surviving spouse's estate may swell it to too large a size, making it tax prone. By careful planning while both spouses are living, wills can be drawn to pass certain property directly to the children or grandchildren.
- Accounts can be frozen by banks, preventing the survivor from using the money.

Wills and estate planning

One more point about wills. As your assets grow and you get into estate planning, your will should be revised in conjunction with such plans. By developing the two together—will and estate plan—you and your lawyer can not only take care of the needs of your spouse and family, you can also take advantage of many ways to reduce or eliminate taxes and other expenses that could otherwise shrink your estate. Your will not only tells people what you want done with your assets, it also helps to preserve them.

How to choose professional advisers

The various aspects of your financial life will call for experts in various fields to give you advice. At one time or another you will need an attorney, an insurance agent, a real estate broker, an accountant, a financial planner, a stockbroker, a banker. But don't forget that within each of these professions there are specialists, just as there are within the medical profession. You wouldn't go to an ear, nose, and throat doctor if you had a broken ankle. By the same token, the lawyer who handles the closing on your home may not be the right one to see when you want to draw your will or incorporate the business firm you are forming. So always seek the appropriate professional. See if he or she has the area of expertise you need. Ask people you know who are in your situation. See who they used, and how satisfied they were.

The most important thing is to feel comfortable with any professional you are using. You're going into a long-term relationship, so take your time, interview, ask questions, really get to know the individual.

It's important, too, to find professionals who understand your needs and objectives. Tell them your goals. Be open and honest. Recognize your own risk factors and let your advisers know what they are. And never be afraid to make a change if you are unhappy, feel you are not getting enough attention, or discover that you have been getting poor advice.

Above all, don't put yourself in the "I don't want to bother him/her with such a silly question" frame of mind. That, I have to tell you, is ridiculous. Your advisers are there to be bothered with any questions you have. In fact, you could pay very dearly for not having sought advice or for taking bad advice. That's why it's important to be sure your adviser is a specialist in the subject you seek help with.

VALERIE AND JAMES NICHOLS KEEP METICULOUS RECORDS . . .

They must. Their income is almost entirely from self-employment. No employer withholds money from their pay to send in to the IRS or to Social Security. They must keep an accurate record of every penny they earn. "I keep a calendar on my desk to mark down income from every gig we play," says Valerie. "On any day that either of us receives a check, I note the amount right on that day on the calendar. I also put it down in a book, so we can double-check. We fell into this sytem when we first started, and now it is habit."

"We pay all expenses for our business either by check on the spot or by charging them and paying by check later," says James. "Then we file the bills according to categories in an accordion file."

The Nicholses can watch their total income and the expenses incurred in earning it and know where they stand at any time. Because no tax money is withheld by those who hire them, the two musicians have to estimate their income taxes four times a year and send payments in to the IRS. Then, when they do their tax return, they file a Schedule C (Profit or Loss from Business or Profession). The profit (or loss) shown on Schedule C is entered on Form 1040's line 12. Because they have no Social Security payments deducted for them, they also fill out Schedule SE, which calculates the Social Security payment based on the profit from their profession.

Worksheet XIII: Example
The McQuarters
Personal Information

Yourself:
1. Name: Patrick McQuarter   Address: 1501 Westway
   City/State: St. Louis, Mo.   Telephone Number: (314) 342-8900
   Place of Birth: St. Louis   Date of Birth: March 15, 1959
   Social Security #: 042-30-5867   Marital Status: Married

2. Spouse's Name: Cathy McQuarter   Address: 1501 Westway
   City/State: St. Louis   Telephone #: (314) 342-8900
   Place of Birth: Des Moines, Iowa   Date of Birth: Feb. 11, 1957
   Social Security #: 045-68-5106

3. Children:

Name	1	2	3	4
Address				
City/State				
Telephone				
Place of Birth				
Date of Birth				
Social Security #				
Marital Status				

4. Parents
   Name: Joan & Jim McQuarter   Address: 4100 Town Ave
   City/State: St. Louis, Mo.   Telephone #: (314) 592-6000
   Place of Birth: St. Louis   Date of Birth: 10/12/35 - Mother
   Mother's maiden name: Smith   7/13/32 - Father

5. Spouse's Parents
   Names: Ellen & John Higgins   Address: 8200 Corn Drive
   City/State: Des Moines, Iowa   Telephone: (515) 243-3480
   Place of Birth: Des Moines   Date of Birth: 8/15/34 - Mother
   Mother's Maiden Name: Hudson   5/3/31 - Father

Next of Kin:
Name: Eric McQuarter   Relationship: brother
Address: 1800 Beacon Boston   Telephone #: (617) 437-9346

Neighbor or Close Friend
Name: Martha & Fred Horn   Address: 1475 Westway
City/State: St. Louis   Telephone: (314) 555-1111

Worksheet XIV: Example
The McQuarters
Personal Contacts

	NAME	ADDRESS	TELEPHONE NUMBER
Attorney	Cathy's Dad John Higgins	Des Moines	(515) 243-3480
Accountant			
Clergyman	Rev. William Ryan	2nd Church	(314) 593-8000
Stockbroker			
Physician	Dr. Michael Brody	University Hospital	(314) 555-6666
Trust Officer			
Banker	Mary Chester	State Bank	(314) 555-1234
Life Insurance Agent	Marjorie Hill	145 Arch St.	(314) 463-0000
Other Insurance Agents			
Homeowner	Don Hill	Tower Insurance	(314) 555-1980
Automobile	Don Hill	Tower Insurance	(314) 555-1980
Medical	at work		
Disability			
Executor of Estate	Eric McQuarter	Boston	(617) 437-9346
Financial Planner			
Others			

RECORD KEEPING, WILLS, AND ADVISERS

Worksheet XV: Example
The McQuarters
RECORD KEEPING

1. CHECKING ACCOUNTS, SAVINGS ACCOUNTS, CREDIT UNION ACCOUNTS, OTHER CASH ACCOUNTS

Name of Institution	Type and # of Account	Interest Rate	Current Balance	Owned By	Location of Checkbook or Passbooks
ABC Bank	Checking 17451	0	$1,500	Joint	desk
ABC Bank	Money Market #7841623	8.5% – 10%	$2,000	Joint	desk

2. MONEY MARKET FUNDS, CERTIFICATES OF DEPOSIT, TREASURY BILLS AND NOTES

Name of Institution	Type and # of Account	Maturity Date	Amount Invested	Interest Rate	Owned by	Location of Passbooks

TOTAL

3. SECURITIES

Stocks & Mutual Funds:

Number of Shares	Company	Date Purchased	Cost	Current Market Value	Owned By	Location of Stock Certificate	Annual Income

TOTAL:

Bonds: Corporate & Municipal

Face Amount	Company	Purchase Date	Maturity Date	Total Cost	Interest Rate	Current Market Value	Owned by	Location of Book	Annual Income

4. REAL ESTATE (RESIDENCE, RECREATIONAL, INCOME PROPERTY)

Location: 1. 40 High Ridge   2. _____   3. _____
Date Purchased 4/15/84
Cost $57,000
Current Market Value $57,000

FINANCIAL FITNESS FOR NEWLYWEDS

5. LIFE INSURANCE

	1.	2.	3.	4.
Insured	Patrick	Patrick	Cathy	
Company	World	Friendship Life	Friendship Life	
Type of Policy	Term	Term	Term	
Number of Policy	45619887	78911412	17432210	
Face Amount	$75,000	$75,000	$100,000	
Owner	Patrick	Patrick	Cathy	
Beneficiary	Cathy	Cathy	Patrick	
Cash Value	—	—	—	
Amount Borrowed Out	—	—	—	
Location of Policy	desk file	desk file	desk file	

6. ANNUITIES, PENSIONS, PROFIT SHARING PLANS, INDIVIDUAL RETIREMENT ACCOUNTS

Description	Participant	Company or Institution	Benefits	Present Value

7. BUSINESS INTERESTS

Company Name	Type of Business	Percentage of Ownership	Value of Your Interest

8. CREDIT OBLIGATIONS

Real Estate (Residence, Recreational, Income Property)

	1. ABC Bank	2.	3.
Mortgage Holder	ABC Bank		
Mortgage Balance	$45,000		
Interest Rate	13½%		
Monthly Payment	$615 (with taxes)		

Other Debt Obligations (automobile loans, education loans, life insurance loans, home improvement loans, etc.)

Lender	Type of Loan	Interest Rate	Balance Due	Monthly Payment	Co-signer
ABC Bank	Auto	15%	1,995	95.00	

Credit Cards:

Name of Card	Number of card	Balance Due
Visa	7143816 21	$50
MasterCard	4381 29876	0

RECORD KEEPING, WILLS, AND ADVISERS

Worksheet XVI: Example
The McQuarters
LOCATION OF OTHER IMPORTANT PAPERS

Homeowner's Insurance _desk file_
Name of Company _Tower Insurance_ Policy Number _0998-82-02_

Automobile Insurance _desk file_
Name of Company _Tower Insurance_ Policy Number _9718-41-3867_

Medical Insurance _at work_
Name of Company _The Blues_ Policy Number _91156899-1_
Type of Policy _Major-Medical_
Location of card _Wallet_ Group Number _____

Disability Insurance _____
Name of Company _____ Policy Number _____

Last Will _with Cathy's Dad_

Codicils _____

Birth Certificates _safe-deposit box_

Mortgage Papers or Lease _safe-deposit box_

Deeds to Real Estate _safe-deposit box_

Titles to Automobiles _with bank till loan paid off_

Military Discharge Papers _____

Citizenship Papers _____

Divorce Decree _____

Social Security Cards _wallet_

Income Tax Returns _desk file_

166 FINANCIAL FITNESS FOR NEWLYWEDS

Worksheet XIII: Yours
Personal Information

Yourself:

1. Name_____ Address_____
   City/State_____ Telephone Number_____
   Place of Birth_____ Date of Birth_____
   Social Security #_____ Marital Status_____

2. Spouse's Name_____ Address_____
   City/State_____ Telephone #_____
   Place of Birth_____ Date of Birth_____
   Social Security #_____

3. Children:

Name	1	2	3	4
Address				
City/State				
Telephone				
Place of Birth				
Date of Birth				
Social Security #				
Marital Status				

4. Parents
   Name_____ Address_____
   City/State_____ Telephone #_____
   Place of Birth_____ Date of Birth_____
   Mother's maiden name_____

5. Spouse's Parents
   Names_____ Address_____
   City/State_____ Telephone_____
   Place of Birth_____ Date of Birth_____
   Mother's Maiden Name_____

   Next of Kin:
   Name_____ Relationship_____
   Address_____ Telephone #_____

   Neighbor or Close Friend
   Name_____ Address_____
   City/State_____ Telephone_____

RECORD KEEPING, WILLS, AND ADVISERS

**Worksheet XIV: Yours
Personal Contacts**

	NAME	ADDRESS	TELEPHONE NUMBER
Attorney			
Accountant			
Clergyman			
Stockbroker			
Physician			
Trust Officer			
Banker			
Life Insurance Agent			
Other Insurance Agents			
Homeowner			
Automobile			
Medical			
Disability			
Executor of Estate			
Financial Planner			
Others			

Worksheet XV: Yours
RECORD KEEPING

1. CHECKING ACCOUNTS, SAVINGS ACCOUNTS, CREDIT UNION ACCOUNTS, OTHER CASH ACCOUNTS

Name of Institution	Type and # of Account	Interest Rate	Current Balance	Owned By	Location of Checkbook or Passbooks

2. MONEY MARKET FUNDS, CERTIFICATES OF DEPOSIT, TREASURY BILLS AND NOTES

Name of Institution	Type and # of Account	Maturity Date	Amount Invested	Interest Rate	Owned by	Location of Passbooks

TOTAL _____

3. SECURITIES

Stocks & Mutual Funds:

Number of Shares	Company	Date Purchased	Cost	Current Market Value	Owned By	Location of Stock Certificate	Annual Income

TOTAL: _____

Bonds: Corporate & Municipal

Face Amount	Company	Purchase Date	Maturity Date	Total Cost	Interest Rate	Current Market Value	Owned by	Location of Book	Annual Income

4. REAL ESTATE (RESIDENCE, RECREATIONAL, INCOME PROPERTY)

Location: 1. _____ 2. _____ 3. _____
Date Purchased _____ _____ _____
Cost _____ _____ _____
Current Market Value _____ _____ _____

5. LIFE INSURANCE

Insured 1. _____ 2. _____ 3. _____ 4. _____
Company _____ _____ _____ _____
Type of Policy _____ _____ _____ _____
Number of Policy _____ _____ _____ _____
Face Amount _____ _____ _____ _____
Owner _____ _____ _____ _____
Beneficiary _____ _____ _____ _____
Cash Value _____ _____ _____ _____
Amount Borrowed Out _____ _____ _____ _____
Location of Policy _____ _____ _____ _____

6. ANNUITIES, PENSIONS, PROFIT SHARING PLANS, INDIVIDUAL RETIREMENT ACCOUNTS

Description	Participant	Company or Institution	Benefits	Present Value

7. BUSINESS INTERESTS

Company Name	Type of Business	Percentage of Ownership	Value of Your Interest

8. CREDIT OBLIGATIONS

Real Estate (Residence, Recreational, Income Property)

                        1. _____   2. _____   3. _____
Mortgage Holder   _____   _____   _____
Mortgage Balance   _____   _____   _____
Interest Rate   _____   _____   _____
Monthly Payment   _____   _____   _____

Other Debt Obligations (automobile loans, education loans, life insurance loans, home improvement loans, etc.)

Lender	Type of Loan	Interest Rate	Balance Due	Monthly Payment	Co-signer

Credit Cards:

Name of Card	Number of card	Balance Due

Worksheet XVI: Yours
LOCATION OF OTHER IMPORTANT PAPERS

Homeowner's Insurance _____
    Name of Company _____ Policy Number _____

Automobile Insurance _____
    Name of Company _____ Policy Number _____

Medical Insurance _____
    Name of Company _____ Policy Number _____
    Type of Policy _____
    Location of card _____ Group Number _____

Disability Insurance _____
    Name of Company _____ Policy Number _____

Last Will _____

Codicils _____

Birth Certificates _____

Mortgage Papers or Lease _____

Deeds to Real Estate _____

Titles to Automobiles _____

Military Discharge Papers _____

Citizenship Papers _____

Divorce Decree _____

Social Security Cards _____

Income Tax Returns _____

RECORD KEEPING, WILLS, AND ADVISERS

YOUR OWN BALANCE SHEET 17

If you have read this far and worked along in the worksheets, I think by now you have gained a strong sense of the financial fitness you can attain in your marriage. I like to think of it, as I have referred to it frequently in these pages, as a financial partnership—a closer partnership than you will ever find in the usual business partnership because it involves all the fun and excitement and rewards of building your lives together . . . sharing in working out goals and solving problems and creating a lifestyle and a family.

At the outset, I said I wrote this book because I was sure that your generation wants to know how to manage money—in a way that earlier generations never knew. Yours is a generation that wants to see things as they are, tackle problems head-on, shoulder responsibility. You want to *manage*. And you want to keep in shape (the recent boom in physical fitness and exercise gear alone should prove that point!).

Let's take just a couple of pages for a summary and review of what's involved in maintaining your balance sheet on your financial partnership.

1. Have you set your goals?

Having sat down and figured out what are the most important short-range and long-range goals for each of you, have you reached agreement on priorities? This is important, remember, as the foundation for all your financial planning and management. Your goals evolve out of your own personal value systems. A frank analysis of your values—of what constitutes ego fulfillment for each of you—can be tremendously helpful in putting your goals in order. And it can help you reach real understanding of one another.

2. Who's managing—and how?

Have you put your heads together and figured out who's going to pay for what . . . how you are going to set up checking and savings accounts . . . which of you seems to be the better money handler, at least for now? This gets you into deciding whether to maintain separate checking accounts and a household account, and takes you right into the realm of your budget—the real key to how to manage your money right down to the last penny you spend for popcorn at the movies.

This is where you set up your disciplines—the regular habits you will follow as you proceed along the road map laid out by your budget. Here I trust that you have thought of—and put down on your worksheets—every item of income (or receivables) and every item of expense (or expenses) that come in and go out for each of you.

Don't forget that you are also setting up your fixed expenses and your flexible expenses so you can control funds held in reserve for each—and be sure your savings include regular monthly amounts needed to reach specific goals.

3. Worked out your net worth?

This is what really gets you down to the nitty-gritty, so I hope you have very conscientiously analyzed the value of your tangible assets and listed every single liability you can think of to give yourselves a true picture of where you stand. If you have done that, you should have a good sense of security—from knowing you have a positive net worth, or from discovering you have a negative net worth and realizing you must do something about it.

4. Banks and bankers, credit and creditors

Banks, bankers, checks, checkbooks—there's so much to get to know. It's worth it, however, for these are the services and methods which enable you to manage so much of your money. Have you set up at least one savings account? Is it one in which your money earns the most it can? Have you established a personal connection with your bank or banks, so at least one bank officer knows you? This will be important when you want to obtain a mortgage or other credit.

Is credit a problem? Have you found it hard to get credit cards—and have you used the tips I've suggested to see if you can get credit. Or—on the contrary—have you found it easy to let credit card charges mount up, until suddenly you're over your heads in debt? If you have worked out your debt ratio and analyzed your situation, you may need to kick the spending habit for a while. Check back on that chapter and make sure things are under control.

If you are repaying a student loan, are you taking advantage of your Sallie Mae OPTIONS?

5. What about insurance, and job benefits?

Have you checked your personnel office at work on retirement benefits? On insurance coverage and possible choices from a "cafeteria" plan so that you and your spouse don't get duplicate coverage but do get coverage from one of your employers that you can't get from the other? Are you into two IRAs—one for each of you if you are both working, or a full IRA and a spousal IRA if one is not working?

How about insurance? Are you covered in all risk areas—life insurance, homeowner's, disability, major-medical, hospital/surgical/medical, automobile, umbrella liability? If you are working on any of these, don't forget to shop around. And don't forget to plan on reevaluating your coverage and needs at least every couple of years—more often if your family grows or your situation changes.

6. The roof, the market, the kids

Chances are, you have been working through this book while living in your first apartment. If you're looking at the possibility of owning a home, have you done the homework to figure out how large a down payment you can afford, how long a mortgage you should sign up for, how large a monthly payment you can handle? Have you reviewed condo versus house and lot versus mobile home? Are you armed for dealing with bank talk about ARM (adjustable-rate mortgage)?

One of the most important considerations is the tax saving you will gain as a homeowner. If details on that are not clear, be sure to go back and review pages 131–132.

As to the stock market, remember that investing in the market is not something you enter into lightly. It comes *after* many other things: your solid basic savings, your emergency fund, your careful management of credit cards, your cautious analysis—*together*—of whether you have reached a point where you can assume the risks that come with investing.

Are you ready to face the financial realities of

YOUR OWN BALANCE SHEET

having children? Have you fully grasped the idea (I must admit, it's hard for *me* to grasp!) that if you invite a baby into the world next year it could cost you as much as a quarter of a million dollars to see that child through college at age 22? That calls for plenty of planning by your financial partnership to see that there will be everything from rattles to ballet slippers to summer camp to braces and textbooks. (And all of it worth it for the joy the kids will give you.)

7. Got the records under control?

If you have set up a good records system from the start of your marriage, you are way ahead. Good record keeping proves its worth over and over. Records are vital for budgeting, for seeing where you must shift the weight a little; change emphasis, cut expenses or increase them. You cannot create your budget road map without good records.

I hope you will use this book not only as a workbook but as a ready reference. Reread it now and then and redo the worksheets maybe once a year or every couple of years. It will help you to keep control—to *manage*, as I said at the outset, to take charge and keep charge of your finances. The more you work over your figures and understand them, the more comfortable you will be and the more your financial partnership will prosper. It will be financially fit.

A couple couldn't ask for more than that.

INDEX

Advisers 163
American Express 7, 47, 62, 64
American Stock Exchange 137
Annuities 88
Apartments 113. See also Tenant
Assets: Appreciation of 44. Depreciation of 44. Extra income from 44. Income-producing 44. Liquid 6. Net worth 43-51. Non income-producing 44

Bankruptcy 74-76. "Chapter 7" 77. "Chapter 13" 76, 77. Reform Act of 1978 76
Banks 52-61. Automatic teller machine (ATM) 54, 56. "Cash reserve" funds 7, 53. Checking accounts 15, 53. Credit 66. Electronic fund transfer (EFT) 54, 56. Fixed-expenses account 17, 19. Getting to know bankers 52. IRA's 142. Liquid assets funds 6. Money market accounts 6. Mortgages 129-130. NOW account 53. Personal identification number (PIN) 54.
Safe deposit box 155. Savings accounts 57-59. Three-account system 21. Tips on negotiating with 131. Statements 54
Blue Cross 80, 81, 82, 91, 95, 142
Blue Shield 91, 95, 142
Bonds 135-136. Records of 156. Tax exempt 136.
Budget 16-38. "Envelope system" 21. Flexible expenses 21. Income and outgo 17. Questions 14. As road map 16, 20. Saving on food 15

Certificate of deposit (CD) 58
"Chapter 7", "Chapter 13" 76-77
Charge accounts. See Credit
Checking accounts 15. Three-account system 21
Children 1, 2, 142-145. Cost of 142. Education 144
Community property 39, 40. States with 40. Wills 40
Co-signer 12
Credit 61-79. "Almost free" money 77. Annual percentage rate (APR) 63. Banks 62. Bureau 67, 68.
Cards, applying for 63. Cost of 63, 77. Debt ratio 72. Equal Credit Opportunity Act 71. Fair Credit Billing Act 68. Installment loan 62. At life insurance companies 62. Open-ended 62. "Over-extended" 72. Record 65. Report 68. Revolving 62. Secured versus unsecured loans 63. Small loan companies 62. Tips 63, 64, 77. Unions 62

Debts 61-79
Diner's Club 62, 64
Disability. See Insurance, Disability

Economic Recovery Tax Act of 1981 41, 160
Electronic fund transfer (EFT) 54, 56
Emergencies, money 7, 19
Employment changes 82. Fringe benefits 82-84
Equal Credit Opportunity Act 71
Estate planning 160, 162
Expenses, fixed 17, 19. Flexible 17

175

Fair Credit Billing Act 68, 71
Federal Housing Administration (FHA) 128
Federal Reserve Bank 135
Federal Trade Commission 63
Federally Insured Student Loans (FISL) 80
Files. See Record keeping
Finance charges 79
Financial planning and goals 7, 8, 11

General Motors Acceptance Corporation 62
Goals and priorities 7, 8, 11
Guaranteed Student Loan Program (GSL) 78

Homeownership 115-132. Condominium 123. Cooperative 128. Financing 129-132. Home improvements 156. House and lot 123. Insurance 97-101. Live-togethers 147, 150. Mobile home 128. Mortgage 115-122, 129-132

Individual Retirement Account (IRA) 40, 82, 106, 107, 112, 134, 139-141, 150
Inflation 6
Insurance 44, 83-103. Automobile 101-102. Blue Cross 80, 81. "Cafeteria" plan 94. Cash values 84. Credit life 90. Dental 81. Disability 81, 95-97. Fire 97-101. Flight 103. Group policy 81. Health 81, 91-95; basic hospitalization 91; basic surgical and medical 91; major medical 94. Homeowner's 97-101. IRA's 140. Liability 97-101. Life 80, 81, 83-91. Live-togethers 150. Pet 103. Policy loan 84. Property and casualty 97-101. Rented cars 103. Settlement options 88. Theft 97-101
Interest rates in savings accounts 57
Internal Revenue Service (IRS) 106-114, 156, 159
Investments 135-143

IRA. See Individual Retirement Account

Joint property 16

Law: Community property 39, 40. Fair Credit Billing Act 68. In marriage 39. Property rights 39. Tax 41. Who owns what? 39-42
Leases 114, 115
Liabilities 47
Live-togethers 148-155. Day-to-day finances 147-148. Landlords 147-148. Leases 115. Written agreement 146-147
Loans. See Credit and Student Loans 78

Marriage and the law 39. Community property 39, 40. Financial partnership 6, 7. Ownership 40, 160. Premarital agreement 41
Married Women's Property Acts 39
MasterCard 7, 47, 52, 62, 63, 64, 78
Medicare 98
Money market funds 6
Mortgage financing 129-132
Mutual funds 129-138. IRA's 140

Net worth 43-51
New York Stock Exchange 137
New York Times 137
NOW account 53

Ownership, types of 40. Joint 40, 160

Pensions 81-82
Personal identification number (PIN) 54
Premarital financial agreement 41
Probate 159
Property. See Homeownership; Law; and Ownership, types of
Property and casualty insurance 97-101

Record keeping 15, 21, 154-166
Retirement benefits 81-82

Safe deposit box 155
Sallie Mae OPTIONS 78
Savings 6, 56-59. Bonds 135-136. Certificates 7. Certificates of deposit (CD's) 58. Effective yield 58. Fixed expense 19. 401k plan 81. Habits 20. Interest rates 58. Life insurance 84. Money market 57-58. Passbook 57. Payroll 81. Salary reduction plan 81. Three-account system 21. Time deposits 58
Savings and loan associations 62
Securities 134-141
Shopping lists 19
Singer, Isaac 62
Social Security 85, 95, 96, 107, 141, 161
Spending habits 19, 20, 21, 74
Stocks and stock market 134, 136, 156
Student Loan Marketing Association (SLMA, or Sallie Mae) 78, 79
Student loans 78. See also specific types

Tax Sheltered Annuity Plan (TSA) 82
Taxes 106-114. Estate 40. Exempt bonds 136. IRA's 140
Tenant: By entirety 40. In common 40. Joint 40
Time deposits 58
Trans Union Credit Information Company 63
Treasury bills, bonds and notes 135
Truth in Lending Law 63

Vesting 82
Veterans Administration (VA) 128
VISA 7, 47, 52, 62, 63, 64, 78

Wall Street Journal 137
Wills 154-166. Community property 40. Live-togethers 150-151
Wives, working 8
Women: Life insurance 89. Property rights 39